KIDNAPPED

PRAISE FOR *KIDNAPPED*

"The exploitation of children by growing numbers of American and global corporations is far more widespread and deeply entrenched than recognized, and more insidious than was the travesty of child labor. I heartily endorse Drs. Acuff and Reiher's work in Kidnapped *and will do all I can to promote it."*
Joseph Chilton Pearce
Lecturer, Author of *Magical Child*

"Everyone who cares about kids should read Kidnapped. *Drs. Acuff and Reiher take their combined 50 years experience working with the world's largest companies to show exactly how some marketers and media moguls exploit our kids. But they don't just explain the problem. They provide the solutions for both parents and professional marketers."*
David Walsh, Ph.D.
Founder and President, National Institute on Media and the Family

"This is a very important book for parents, teachers, and public policy professionals who are concerned about the influences of media on children. Senators Sam Brownback, Joseph Lieberman, John McCain, and Hillary Clinton represent the thoughtful voices in Congress who have expressed concern, even outrage, about the ways in which violent media exploit our children, and Kidnapped *is the book that will help the public understand these concerns and deal with the issues."*
John P. Murray, Ph.D.
Professor of Developmental Psychology (Distinguished Professor of Euthenics), School of Family Studies and Human Services, College of Human Ecology, Kansas State University

"There is no greater threat to the health and well being of our children than their daily exposure to the excessive and gratuitous violence permeating our culture. From ease of accessibility to guns to excessive violence in film and music, on TV and in videogames, far too many parents and adults of America en loco *parentis continue to put hate and killing within easy reach of our nation's children.* Kidnapped–like no other book before–places responsibility where it belongs and challenges all of us to take the actions necessary to create a more safe and peaceful world for our children and ourselves."*
Pamela Eakes
Founder and President of Mothers Against Violence in America

*"*Kidnapped *is timely and important, providing information and analysis to empower all parents who want to protect their children from predatory outsiders in the media."*
Michael Medved
Nationally Syndicated Radio Talk Show Host

HOW IRRESPONSIBLE MARKETERS ARE
STEALING THE MINDS OF YOUR CHILDREN

KIDNAPPED

DANIEL S. ACUFF, PHD & ROBERT H. REIHER, PHD

Dearborn™
Trade Publishing
A **Kaplan Professional** Company

President, Dearborn Publishing: Roy Lipner
Vice President and Publisher: Cynthia A. Zigmund
Acquisitions Editor: Michael Cunningham
Senior Project Editor: Trey Thoelcke
Interior Design: Lucy Jenkins
Cover Design: Jody Billert, Design Literate, Inc.
Typesetting: Elizabeth Pitts

Library of Congress Cataloging-in-Publication Data

Acuff, Dan S., 1942–
    Kidnapped : how irresponsible marketers are stealing the minds of your children / Daniel S. Acuff, and Robert H. Reiher.
        p.   cm.
    Includes bibliographical references and index.
    ISBN 1-4195-0503-3
    1. Advertising and children 2. Violence in mass media. 3. Child consumers—United States.   I. Reiher, Robert H.   II. Title.
    HF5415.32.A246   2005
    659.1′083—dc22

                                                                          2005003904

*To my mother, Sally Reiher, whose devotion and acceptance
provided me with a solid developmental foundation.
And to my wife, Bobbie Ross Reiher, my pal,
devoted confidant, and lover of life.*
Robert H. Reiher

*To my parents, Guy and Maryanne Acuff.
They were always there for me with love, support,
and encouragement, and provided me with
great models for my own life and parenting.
May every child everywhere be blessed with that gift.*
Daniel S. Acuff

Above all others, we acknowledge those tireless, committed souls at work every day in the cause to better protect and nurture our world's greatest resource—its children. Often against daunting odds, they are the founders and staff members of non-profit organizations, government agencies, and schools. They are local, state, and national leaders who are standing up for our young and standing tall against those forces that would undermine their healthiest development and happiness. They are manufacturers and marketers who care as much about the impact their products and programs have on children as they do about the bottom line.

And in the daily "trenches" of homes everywhere, we acknowledge those moms, dads and other caretakers who are purposefully and intelligently designing a healthy and enriching environment for their children to grow up in. We appreciate their courage to say "no" to the negative influences of materialism, irresponsible marketing, and inherently dangerous products and programs. We applaud their commitment to say "yes" to all that will enrich and empower their children and families. We are all the beneficiaries of their vision, dedication, and courage.

We'd also very much like to acknowledge Michael Cunningham of Dearborn Trade Publishing for his foresight and dedication to making *Kidnapped* a reality, and a special acknowledgement to our editor, Lorna Gentry, for her guidance and brilliant ability to add to, delete from, and enhance the final result.

Parents, your children today are in greater physical, psychological, emotional, and ethical danger than during any other era of modern civilization.

If you doubt that this dire warning is true, you might be shocked by the sobering realities of these alarming developments.

- *Screen time now dominates your children's waking hours.* The average young person spends more than one-fourth of each day in front of media screens (TVs, computers, video games)—more time than with any other activity except sleeping.
- *The suicide rate among young people has tripled since 1960.* Approximately 5,000 of our young people between the ages of 15 and 24 are killing themselves each year.
- *One million young people in the United States now take antidepressants and are twice as likely to become suicidal as those who don't take them.* While illicit drug use remains problematic, a marked increase in the use (and abuse) of prescription pharmaceuticals has occurred. Pain-reliever usage in the ten years from 1992 to 2002 increased from 6.8 percent to 22.1 percent. The most striking increase is a 15 percent rise in prescription drug abuse by people between the ages of 18 and 25. Research indicates that more young people are trying prescription pain relievers for nonmedical reasons, including a 5 percent increase in the recreational use of these drugs by children 12 years and older.
- *Obesity has tripled.* Three factors have contributed to tripling the obesity of young people ages 6 to 19 over the past 30 years: (1) increases in unhealthy food consumption, (2) increased inactivity, which is linked to spending so much screen time, and (3) excessive cortisol, a stress hormone linked to obesity that is released because of increased levels of stress and anxiety. Some researchers

now believe excessive cortisol release is caused in great part by the threatening and violent nature of much of TV, film, and video-game content.

- Type 2 childhood diabetes rose more than 300 percent between 1990 and 2004.
- *Your children's exposure to age-inappropriate sexuality and violence in the media has increased dramatically.* Amid a growing concern about desensitization to violence, more than 80 percent of video games contain violence—some shockingly brutal and dehumanizing. About 70 percent of TV programming contains sexual content in one form or another.
- *Overall, an exponential rise in materialism, consumerism, and entitlement among young people has occurred.* In the new age of excess, too many parents today find themselves raising insatiable kid consumers, with more than 50 percent of their kids saying that if they buy certain products they feel better about themselves. Kids who have been overindulged and given too much too easily are growing up to be irresponsible adults without the necessary skills for creating personal independence, effective relationships, good financial management, and job success.
- *Children and teens are prime targets for advertisers, with spending for and by this group totaling more than $600 billion.* Estimates are that the average child will view as many as 40,000 commercials each year.

TARGET MARKETING AND CHILDREN AS "SITTING DUCKS"

Kids today have become "sitting ducks" in the high-powered, adult-manipulated world of commercialization and dollar-driven products and programs. For example, present-day marketers are experimenting with magnetic resonance imaging (MRI) to "read" and track children's brain functions while they are being shown products, programs, and advertisements. Marketers then can use the data they gather to develop even more powerful "triggers" for the lucrative youth market. The development of *neuromarketing techniques* signals a future in which unethical marketers will possess unprecedented abilities to manipulate your child's desires and behavior. Those who would take advantage of the sitting-duck vulnerability of children for profit demonstrate a complete disregard for the latest research on brain-based learning and the core developmental milestones and needs of children.

These alarming trends represent a real and growing danger to the healthy growth and development—and the happiness and success—of your children, and young people throughout the world.

Children are vulnerable during the relatively long period of time over which they develop the abilities to reason and distinguish between reality and fantasy, truth and fiction. As children age, their developmental vulnerabilities change. We call these vulnerabilities *blind spots*, because they are psychological and biologically based conditions beyond awareness or understanding that can limit a child's developmental potential. In *Kidnapped*, we have identified 15 of the most important blind spots demonstrated by children throughout the course of their physical and emotional development. These blind spots, and their associated vulnerability to manipulation and outside influence, form a key part of the case we build in *Kidnapped* against irresponsible marketing to youth. Throughout this book, we discuss key findings from current brain and child developmental research that reveal just what factors make children particularly vulnerable at each stage of their development and, therefore, easy prey for potentially harmful or manipulative forms of media, products, and advertising.

As parents, making the right choices and providing solid guidance for the well being and positive growth of your children can be challenging and perplexing. Armed with key information about specific vulnerabilities and dangers, you and other youth caretakers can more knowledgeably provide the nurturance and protection your young people need.

HOW *KIDNAPPED* CAN HELP

With an eye to the future, *Kidnapped* outlines and explores a variety of disturbing new social trends in depth while analyzing how the irresponsibility of certain youth marketers contributes to these dangers. Currently, we hear little public discussion about unethical youth-marketing practices, and few sources provide clear-cut guidelines for identifying such practices. One of our primary goals in writing *Kidnapped* is to fill this gap; we have devised a simple yet comprehensive system of categorization that anyone can use to determine what products, programs, and marketing practices they want their children to be exposed to, at any developmental stage.

Based on more than a quarter of a century of work in the trenches with youth-marketing companies, in addition to substantial secondary research, we have determined that youth-targeted products and programs *can* be categorized as being typically positive, neutral, or inherently dangerous in their impact on young people. *Kidnapped* provides an easy-to-understand framework for applying these categorizations, along with many practical strategies for parents, other youth caretakers, and youth marketers for carrying out their commitment to protect and nurture children.

The primary goal of *Kidnapped* is to provide parents and caretakers with important strategies for combating the debilitating effects of irresponsible marketing while promoting products, programs, and experiences that enrich children's lives. We call these strategies Youth Enrichment Strategies (YES!) and they include:

- Concrete ways to protect your children from overexposure to technology and the media
- Eye-opening guides to determining manipulative advertising approaches and techniques for making your children more ad and media savvy
- Keys to understanding product and program "messages," based on the latest child-developmental research
- Specific strategies to ensure child safety on the Internet
- Information to assist in gauging the level and potential impact of violence in toys, games, TV, and film, and for determining what to allow and what to avoid
- Insights into the behavior-linked causes of childhood obesity and important strategies for helping your children make healthier food and beverage choices
- Concrete guidelines to minimize the very real threats of alcohol, tobacco, and drugs
- Effective techniques for lobbying against harmful products and programs
- Empowering, enriching product and program alternatives

Chapters 4 through 8 of *Kidnapped* deal with specific ages and stages of child development, outlining the developmental capabilities for children during these age ranges and detailing their key vulnerabilities. You will want to read each of these chapters to understand how children's developmental capabilities and vulnerabilities evolve as they age, and how these factors shape any child's interactions with media, products, and marketing. As we explain the dangers and vulnerabilities your children face at every stage of their development, we suggest using YES! to help you guide your children to make sound product, program, and activity choices. You will find YES recommendations specifically located throughout Chapters 4 through 8 and summarized at the end of each of those chapters. These strategies are designed to be key antidotes to the age/stage-related vulnerabilities we've identified within the text.

THE CRISIS POINT

The deterioration of culture doesn't happen overnight, so it's difficult to pinpoint a real crisis point. Instead, cultures decay through a slow meltdown of values and behavior that undermines the societal fabric. When we define with certainty what we believe to be good and bad influences on our young people and resolve firmly to surround our children with healthy alternatives and limit the exposure and impact of unhealthy and dangerous product and marketing influences, we can declare that *now is the crisis point. Now* is the time for parents and all who care for and about children to make meaningful changes to protect their future.

It's time to stand firm and make decisions to protect our children from those who continue to disregard their safety and well being. It's time to speak out against manufacturers, producers, marketers, and retailers who are populating our stores and our airways with harmful products and programs. It's time to stand up for those who commit to the development of positive, healthy, nurturing products and programs. By our choices and actions, we can promote the development of healthy products for our children, and we can effectively manage our children's media consumption.

Kidnapped isn't intended as a manifesto against all youth marketers. *Many* advertisers and product developers are ethical and responsible in their youth-marketing efforts. Many others, however, fail to demonstrate any understanding of exactly what constitutes good or bad youth-marketing practices, and the potential dangers of the latter. We can, through our purchasing decisions and effective lobbying techniques, help to educate these manufacturers and marketers and encourage them to focus on producing positive, enriching products and programs for our children.

As professionals who have spent the past decades working with youth-marketing groups, we're very disturbed by marketing practices and techniques that are in any way manipulative or unethical. We've seen firsthand the continued disregard for the damaging impact on our children of violence, age-inappropriate sexuality, alcohol, and tobacco. We have become increasingly concerned about the promotion of unhealthy food and beverages and their resulting negative effects on our young people's physical and mental health. For these reasons, we have written *Kidnapped* as an educational tool for parents, educators, child caretakers, *and* marketers.

WORKING TOGETHER TO RAISE HEALTHY CHILDREN

Raising healthy children truly "takes a village," with everyone playing their part. The final responsibility for controlling our children's consumption of harmful media and products quite clearly rests with all of these group.

- *Parents.* Most parents are stretched for time, and far too few of them give adequate attention to the very real threats to their children's well-being that are posed by excessive and unethical marketing. Even fewer parents stand up and take action to protect their children from these threats and guide their media-consumption habits. *Kidnapped* gives parents the inspiration, information, and practical tools they need to understand what makes their kids sitting ducks in this new and powerful world of overindulgence and commercialization and what to do about it.
- *Child caretakers.* Educators, grandparents, and other caretakers also bear responsibility for protecting children from negative influences. *Kidnapped* gives these caretakers information to help them identify potentially harmful products and programs, along with

practical advice and proven techniques for imposing policies and restrictions necessary to protect the children placed in their care.

- *Youth marketers. Kidnapped* provides those who market and develop products and programs for children with a clear, factual, and research-based guide to sound and responsible marketing techniques. Manufacturers, producers, marketing personnel, distributors, and retailers can use *Kidnapped*'s precise guidelines and strategies to adopt positive, child-healthy approaches to marketing.

The responsibility for bringing about meaningful changes in the product marketing and media-consumption habits of our culture rests with each of us as individuals and all adults as a committed team. Through our decisions, policies, and guidance as parents, caretakers, and youth marketers, we determine whether our society's children and, indeed, our future will be nurtured or damaged by the day-to-day realities of our modern consumer-driven culture. We've also written this book to help manufacturers, producers, marketers, and retailers in their efforts to develop and market products and programs that are age-appropriate and healthy.

Childhood should be a celebration of positive growth and learning, of discovery and the excitement of being alive. The invitation and challenge is for each of us to become as knowledgeable as possible about the potential dangers and pitfalls along our young people's paths toward healthy adulthood so we can guide them away from harm and toward maximum positive development and happiness.

1

THE STATE OF THE STATE
OF BEING A KID

Life is no brief candle to me. It is a sort of splendid torch, which I have got a hold of for the moment, and I want to make it burn as brightly as possible before handing it on to future generations.

George Bernard Shaw

In so many ways we appear to be leading our children—and the future of planet Earth—in the wrong direction: away from the best ideas, values, and behavior of which humanity is capable and toward the worst. Irresponsible, manipulative, and deceitful marketing efforts push products and programs that harm children physically, emotionally, socially, mentally, morally, and even spiritually. Children today face increased exposure to sex, drugs, alcohol, tobacco, guns, foul language, bullying, violence, and fattening foods. And many of us are simply standing by as increased materialism and commercialism undermine our culture's basic values. What's at the source of these problems? How dangerous are they? What and who is to blame? Most important, what can and should we do to stop this decline in values?

As we stated in the introduction, this is no industry-wide indictment aimed at those who develop and sell to the youth market. Many manufacturers and advertisers work hard to create responsible products and programs, and the results of their work actually contribute positively to the quality of your children's lives. This book *is,* however, an indictment of those who violate your children's minds and betray their innocence and trust. These marketers are stealing the minds of your children by exposing them to physically and emotionally damaging products and programs. They are manipulating your children and exploiting their inability to discriminate between good and bad, fact and fiction, reality and fantasy.

SITTING-DUCK PSYCHOLOGY

Young people have what we refer to as a *sitting-duck psychology* that makes them more vulnerable than adults to their environment. A sitting duck in hunting terms is a duck that, unconscious to imminent danger, merely sits as he is lined up in the hunter's cross-hairs. We call children sitting ducks because, by the natural evolution of their developmental capabilities, they can be defenseless against the influence of advertising and programming.

As we have stated, part of the dynamic that makes children so vulnerable to advertising messages and other external influences is the existence of developmental "blind spots." A *blind spot,* as we are defining it, is a developmental condition, either biological or psychological, beyond awareness that can prevent children from making accurate, sound, and discriminating choices. These blind spots can place children's responses to their environment "on automatic" and can leave the children vulnerable and in harm's way.

DANGEROUS TIMES

Some individuals claim that we are in the "best of times" for kids. Our kids are brighter, more motivated, family-oriented, and happier than at any time in history, they proclaim. Recently, at a conference dedicated to marketing children's products, the keynote speaker addressed several hundred marketers, giving them the good news that there is essentially little to worry about! Our kids are in great shape. The message was loud and clear: Keep doing what you're doing. It's having no ill effect on our kids.

This could not be further from the truth.

Just what is the reality of the well being of your children in a marketplace crowded with products and programming that can only be labeled "the good, the bad, and the ugly"? How are your children faring? What's different and more dangerous about growing up today, as compared to growing up two or three decades ago?

To set the scene, let's compare a week in the life of a typical, suburban 15-year-old in 1975 with the life of a 15-year-old of today. We are well aware of the vast differences between the situations of different ethnic groups, rural versus city youth, and young people from such different contexts as growing up poor, blue-collar, white-collar, or rich, but the hypothetical settings and individuals described here can serve as examples of the vast social changes that have occurred over the past few decades.

Johnnie in 1975

- *Home/family.* Johnnie's parents are still together and doing well enough despite rising divorce rates (from 15 percent per 1,000 married women over the age of 15 in 1970 to 21 percent in 1990 and on the rise). Johnnie typically sits down to a meal with the family at dinnertime. Discussions revolve around such topics as each person's day, sports, school, dating, homework, and chores. Parents provide a base of support, modeling attitudes, values, and the wisdom of experience along with setting the tone for responsibility and achievement.
- *School.* Johnnie experiences normal pressures to achieve good grades in school. He's a member of the Spanish Club and the Letterman's Club, and is running for sophomore class vice president in the spring. Johnnie eats prepared lunches in the school cafeteria; the only vending machine on the school's campus is a soft-drink machine located near the gymnasium, for use during ball games.
- *Sports.* Johnnie is on the football and baseball teams at school and plays summer baseball. He also spends time with friends outdoors, especially biking and skateboarding.
- *Television.* Johnnie watches a normal amount of TV, approximately 12 hours a week. His favorite shows are sports and sitcoms.
- *Video games.* A variety of simple video games and some arcade games are available. Atari, Sears, Magnavox, and Coleco are the main video-game companies. Johnnie doesn't have a home system but likes the arcade games, especially Pong and Tank.
- *Computers/the Internet.* Computers and their use in school are essentially nonexistent. The Internet has not yet arrived.

- *Safety.* Globally, the threat of the Cold War looms and is of some concern emotionally for Johnnie. Locally, in his hometown and neighborhood, Johnnie feels quite safe. He walks the mile to high school and often hangs out with his buddies at a local park on the way home.

Johnnie in 2005

- *Home/family.* Johnnie's parents are divorced. He lives with his mom and sees his dad every other weekend. Johnnie arrives home for dinner at a different time than the other members in the family. On a typical day, he either "fends for himself" by rustling up something in the refrigerator or freezer or takes part in a "fast-food fest" (pizza, burgers, etc.) with other family members. Johnnie takes his food into his bedroom to watch TV or play video games while he eats. Other members of the family do similar things.
- *School.* There are still the normal pressures to do well in school. The increased presence of drugs on campus as well as more sexual and drug activity among his age group creates dangerous pitfalls. Post-Columbine, Johnnie has to pass through a metal detector on his way in through a newly erected fence-and-gate system that surrounds the school. Johnnie is also subjected to increased product advertising. His cafeteria offers fast food from outlets such as Pizza Hut and McDonald's, and in class he and his classmates watch Channel One for news and with it comes product advertising—for soft drinks and snack foods among other things.
- *Sports.* Johnnie is on the football and baseball teams at school and plays summer baseball. He's a member of the Letterman's Club.
- *Television.* Johnnie watches approximately 18 hours of television a week. His favorite shows are sports, sitcoms, and reality shows. When he's with his dad on weekends, he stays up late and watches adult-targeted shows on cable that contain violence, nudity, and sexual situations.
- *Video games.* Johnnie spends about ten hours a week playing video games. His favorites are the first-person, shoot-'em-up, blood-and-gore variety. Most games are on his home-game system, and occasionally he plays in arcades.

- *Computers/the Internet.* Johnnie spends about eight hours a week at his computer. Seven of those hours are taken up with computer games, surfing the Web, and e-mailing friends. He sneaks onto porn sites from time to time. About half an hour is used doing school-related work.
- *Safety.* Johnnie's mom picks him up from school in the afternoons. He can roam around his own neighborhood freely, but he's not allowed to hang out at the park with his buddies and can't go to the mall by himself. There is some concern about conflict in the Middle East and about terrorism, but so far most of that seems far enough away.

Thirty years have dramatically changed the child-rearing landscape. The little Johnnies and Janes of the world are growing up in a much more precarious world.

INVISIBLE AND INTANGIBLE INFORMATION OVERLOAD (IIIO)

Exactly what makes your children's world more dangerous? Beyond the obvious pitfalls, such as increased exposure to drugs, alcohol, tobacco, violence, and premature sexuality, technology also poses a little recognized threat. Like a mixed pragmatic blessing and digital curse, the information age—fueled by television, computers, and the Internet—has invaded homes, workspaces, and our minds, becoming more pervasive with each passing decade. The result is something we refer to as IIIO—*Invisible and Intangible Information Overload.*

Digitized and high-speed everything—from TVs with 200 channels to cell phones that are combo walkie-talkie/text messager/camera/mini-TVs—is dominating your children's time and capturing their attention. The result is more stress and a dangerous trade-off of less time spent in physical activity and face-to-face human interaction. The term *high tech, low touch* has never been so appropriate.

We're not against technology. It's impossible to refute or question technology's many advantages. We are advocates, however, of a cautious approach by parents, educators, and other child caretakers as they manage their children's exposure to technology. The dangers of IIIO are great; the solution is caution plus a balanced approach to combining tech time with play and time spent with people.

Melinda Davis, in her book, *The New Culture of Desire,*[1] talks about this information overload and states that it has brought our culture into a new phase of development, which she calls "Human History, Part II." Davis, CEO and founder of The Next Group, initiated the Human Desire Project in 1993 to provide a new resource for people making high-stakes gambles on the future. Her company observes, investigates, and analyzes human behavior in the trenches of their lives and through theoretical models. After nearly seven years of inquiry, Davis has determined that we have entered a phase of human behavioral development in which individuals are being inundated with conceptual information and messages from a deluge of competitive forms of media. These communications, driven by new and often invasive technologies, become part of a child's world, forming an inner, artificial reality. This new artificial form of reality changes the concrete and tangible world we once knew, creating stress, instability, and strategies to compensate for our disequilibrium.

In a culture that has been invaded by IIIO, all of us are being assaulted and "shaped" by myriad forces that are beyond our awareness and understanding, and therefore beyond our control. These forces are extremely powerful and carry the potential to create new and heightened levels of stress, even as they work to shape our values and beliefs. Unfortunately, our children are most vulnerable to these forces, and they suffer the consequences of our unconscious collusion with the perpetrators of stress.

The TV Factor

To fully understand the implications of IIIO, let's focus on just one dimension of information overload—television. The days of three or four network choices are gone, and instead most households have hundreds of television channels available for viewing. Gone, too, are the idyllic days of all-family TV programs such as *The Adventures of Ozzie & Harriet, Father Knows Best, The Cosby Show, Eight Is Enough,* and *The Waltons.* While television still offers a variety of wholesome options for children and families, including shows for the very young child, much racier network shows now have invaded the tube—shows with highly questionable role models for family life, programs with brutal violence, harsh language, and nudity. Sexual content is now in two-thirds of all television programming, according to the February, 2003, Kaiser Foundation Report.[2] It's this staggering amount of nonwholesome television fare that should concern parents, educators, and child welfare specialists.

Far too few parents today take time to really monitor the programs their children watch and to censor unacceptable, nonage-appropriate TV programming. In fact, many parents are unaware of the hidden dangers of excessive TV watching. The mere act of watching television, especially for extended lengths of time, not only decreases the amount of time spent in more thought-engaging activity, but also results in reduced physical activity and increased "couch potatoism." Even more dangerous, perhaps, exposure to violent programming may actually release biochemical elements into the brain that are a direct reaction to stress and overload. Cortisol is one of these elements.

The Physical Effects of Stress, Cortisol, and IIIO on Children

From a brain-based perspective, IIIO enters our senses sending messages that activate various centers of our brain, including our new brain or cortex. The cortex is directly linked with older and more primitive centers of the brain that include the hypothalamus, adrenal medulla, and amygdala. When we experience high levels of stress or threat, there is a release of a stress hormone called cortisol into our system.

Cortisol, from an evolutionary perspective, is critical to flight or fight reactions in the face of threats. In today's world of IIIO and media driven imagery, our brain can release cortisol in response to imagined threats as well as actual or real threats, activating the stress response system. Cortisol is involved in multiple body systems and facilitates other hormones and body functions.

Contemporary research is currently studying the effects of high levels of cortisol, and some researchers believe there are links to depression, cancer, autoimmune deficiency, Alzheimer's disease, and other major health problems. Others are currently investigating cortisol overproduction and its link to obesity, which is related to increased diabetes.

In *A User's Guide to the Brain,* John Ratey explains: "Cortisol, the stress hormone, works by binding to receptor sites in the hippocampus, but when emotion gets too high, too much cortisol binds to each neuron. The onslaught increases the metabolism of the cells so much they essentially overheat and die."[3]

Higher-than-normal levels of stress also can lead to such symptoms as elevated blood pressure, and to the development of diabetes, fatigue, depression, moodiness, and other disorders. The dangers of such reactions are especially high in children, who have few "tools" to filter the increasing levels of incoming stress. This lack of stress-filtering capabilities in children often goes unrecognized, even as parents and marketers inadvertently overload children with more difficult and stress-producing processing tasks, in the name of making children smarter and more "successful."

OTHER DANGERS KIDS FACE TODAY

As can be concluded from our review of Johnnie's life in 1975 compared to Johnnie's life today, far more pitfalls exist in these early years of the 21st century. Your children today face dangers from exposure to violence and age-inappropriate content on television, in feature films, in music, and in video games. They also face a number of societal threats to their physical, emotional, and mental well being.

Media Violence and Age-Inappropriate Content

American children between 2 and 18 years of age spend an average of 6 to 7 hours each day using media (television, commercial or self-recorded video, movies, video games, print, radio, recorded music, computer, and the Internet). When simultaneous use of multiple media is accounted for, that exposure increases to eight hours a day. A large proportion of this media exposure includes acts of violence, witnessed by young people on television and movie screens or "virtually perpetrated" in video games. Some sources estimate that by age 18, the average young person will have viewed 200,000 acts of violence on television alone. In how many of those acts of violence have these children *virtually* committed themselves as the "shooter" in first-person video games?

The American Academy of pediatrics in a 2001 Policy Statement recognized "exposure to violence in media, including television, movies, music, and video games, as a significant risk to the health of children and adolescents. Extensive research evidence indicates media violence can contribute to aggressive behavior, desensitization to violence, nightmares, and fear of being harmed."[4]

Particularly disturbing in light of our exploration of irresponsible marketing to today's young people was the Academy's conclusion that "despite the fact that their own ratings systems found the material appropriate only for adults, these industries practiced pervasive and aggressive marketing of violent movies, music, and electronic games to children."

Here are just a few of the ways media threaten our children today.

- *Feature films.* Today's feature films, compared to those of the 1970s and 1980s, contain far more violent and sexually explicit content overall. Even PG 13–rated movies often push the limits of sexuality and brutality.
- *Electronic games.* Video games are amping up their violence, many featuring raw carnage in which the object is to blast apart the "enemy" (Doom) or shoot people in cars (Grand Theft Auto). How much violence is in video games? Research shows as much as 80 percent of some of the most popular video games (Sega, Nintendo, PlayStation, Xbox) have violent content, and 21 percent model violence toward women! Some of the content of video games is appallingly horrific. Barbara Meltz of the *Boston Globe* writes, regarding Grand Theft Auto Vice City:

  "Among other things, a player gets points for hiring a prostitute, having sex with her, beating her to death, and then taking back his money."[5]

  Following up on the success of Grand Theft Auto, Rockstar has released Manhunt. In *Manhunt,* there are three levels of violence—three levels of how brutally you can kill someone. For level one you might just sneak up behind your victim and clamp a plastic bag over his head. For level two you get to smash him into submission with a baseball bat, and for level three you go in for the bloodiest kill.

Many believe that such violent, reality-based electronic games have influenced teens to behave in similar violent ways.

- *Music.* Gangsta rap and other lyrics with violent, foulmouthed, and misogynistic content are being listened to by increasing numbers of our children and teens today. The musical genre of hip-hop, also with its abundance of sexually explicit, misogynistic, and vile language, has taken its hold on our youth and is a major source of revenue for the music industry. "Officer, I want to see you layin' in a coffin, sir" is the lyric of one gangsta rap "song," for example. In *The Chronic* album, by Dr. Dre and Snoop Doggy Dogg, the singers put a gun in a man's mouth, then ask, "Do you know Lucifer?" When he replies "No," they tell him, "Well you're about to meet him." The songs on this album contain abusive language, violent and sexually explicit lyrics, drug references, and misogyny. Following is from a recent study on the effects of listening to violent music lyrics:

  [These] experiments . . . demonstrated that college students who heard a violent song felt more hostile than those who heard a similar but nonviolent song. Experiments . . . demonstrated a similar increase in aggressive thoughts.[6]

Fighting the "Violence Sells" Mind-Set

The outcries against the promotion of inhumane and raunchy values are on the rise, and include the strong voices of Senators John McCain and Joseph Lieberman. Senator Lieberman has criticized the entertainment industry for selling "debasement," "garbage," and "cultural poison" to children. In particular he has denounced violent videogames, misogynistic gangsta rap music, trash TV, and sexually explicit prime-time TV programming.[7]

Senator Lieberman and others are busy recruiting new warriors for the battle. Taking on Hollywood is, in reality, taking on big money. Billions of dollars are being made selling violence and abuse. This is a problem that is not going away and will not be won with minor skirmishes.

Threats to Physical and Mental Well Being

The conditions that make for more dangerous times for today's young people include a number of threats to their physical, emotional, and mental well-being. Here are some of the most serious.

- *Depression and suicide.* For every two homicides in the United States, there are three suicides. Every hour and 45 minutes another young person commits suicide. The rate of suicide for this age group has nearly tripled since 1960, making suicide the third leading cause of death of adolescents and the second leading cause of death among college-age youth.[8] We must ask ourselves: What societal changes have we instituted, encouraged, or allowed over the past 30 years that would result in this dramatic increase in the suicide rate among young people?

- *Teen pregnancy.* U.S. teens have twice as many pregnancies as do teens in most other developed nations, including France, Great Britain, Canada, and Sweden. A March of Dimes fact sheet reports that almost 1 million teenagers in the United States become pregnant each year, and about 485,000 give birth. Nearly 13 percent of all U.S. births in 1997 were to teens (ages 15 to 19).[9]

- *Child abuse.* Child abuse, including emotional as well as sexual and physical abuse—the most extreme form of which is murder—is common in our society today. Studies show that one in four girls and one in eight boys will be sexually abused before they are 18 years old; and most agree that the majority of abuse incidents never get reported. In 2000, about 879,000 children in our country were victims of maltreatment. Approximately 1,200 children died of abuse or neglect that same year.[10]

> *"Mommy, Mommy, they're raping me!" Then click and a dial tone—a 2:30 AM call to Alma Kidd. Her 14-year-old daughter, Norma "Hope" Robbins, was trapped in a Washington State foster-care home. Kidd immediately reported the incident to police. Police said, "Ms. Kidd, you're in Washington State now. They can chain her 24 hours, 7 days a week, and there is nothing you can do about it."*
> Reported in *Insight* magazine, November 24, 1997

- *Obesity and childhood diabetes.* In 2002, the American Obesity Association reported that more than 15 percent of all American children and adolescents between the ages of 6 and 19 are obese. The dramatic increase in obesity among American youth over the past two decades is the result of a variety of factors, including decreases in physical education programs in schools, unsafe parks and play areas, and increased involvement with media such as TV and computers to the exclusion of free and outdoor active play.[11] Linked to obesity and to diet is childhood type 2 diabetes. Between 1990 to 2000, childhood type 2 diabetes rose from 4 percent to 20 percent. Two groups of children appear to be most susceptible: Children who are overweight, sedentary and have a family history of diabetes, and minority children.

- *Tobacco.* Tobacco use among young people 12 and older is down, thanks to a bright spot in marketing—the successful antitobacco ad campaigns. In addition to national efforts to air these antismoking ads, some tobacco manufacturers have made real efforts (albeit forced) to downshift youth marketing in the United States. Unfortunately, many of these same tobacco companies are redoubling efforts to target youth abroad.

- *Alcohol.* Always a danger to young people, alcohol use remained relatively constant from 1970 to 2002. In a 2002 survey by the U.S. Department of Health and Human Services, an estimated 120 million Americans age 12 or older (51 percent of those surveyed) said they drink alcohol. About 54 million (22.9 percent) participated in binge drinking at least once in the 30 days prior to the survey, and 15.9 million (6.7 percent) were heavy drinkers.[12]

- *Drugs.* About 9.7 percent of youths ages 12 to 17 reported current illicit drug use, meaning they used an illicit drug at least once during the 30 days prior to a survey interview. This compares to a 9.8 percent rate in 1999. Leading indicators of drug use—including rates of use among the youngest age group and the number of new users—suggest possible future declines. Among youths ages 12 and 13, a key target audience of the National Youth Antidrug Media Campaign, the rate of those claiming to have used illicit drugs (including marijuana, cocaine, heroin, hallucinogens, and inhalants) during the past month declined from 3.9 percent in 1999 to 3.0 percent in 2000. The estimated number of new marijuana users has also declined slightly.[13]

Loss of Innocence

Beyond the overt dangers of media violence, the rise in obesity, poorer childhood health, and other threats, there is also a covert danger that threatens children today: loss of innocence. Children regularly are immersed in age-inappropriate information, stimuli, and situations. The result is often confusion and the formation of unhealthy values and behavior. At youth-marketing conferences, the topic of "Kids Getting Older Younger" (KGOY) is recurrent. Indications are that boys and especially girls are developing physically at younger ages for reasons not fully understood. Increased divorce rates result in children who are burdened with more responsibility at younger ages and who receive less parental guidance and support. Free play, outdoor play, and interaction with family members was the norm a few decades ago; now homes are rich in technology but poor in human interactions. Sexual values are under assault, and, as we've discussed, children are faced with increased violence in the media (TV, video games, music) and the regrettably very real threat of violence on the streets and in schools.

The collapse of New York's twin towers in 2001 marked yet another collapse—a major rent in the perceived "safety net" that had surrounded the United States and protected its citizens from fear of physical harm on national soil. In the end, however, external terrorist threat may not compare with the insidious internal threat of loss of innocence as reflected in the societal changes that have occurred over the past several decades.

Many individuals have hoisted red flags over this loss of innocence. Film critic Michael Medved and his wife, clinical psychologist Diane Medved, in their 1998 book, *Saving Childhood: Protecting Our Children from the National Assault on Innocence,*[14] describe life in the America of their childhood as an idyllic "Garden of Eden"—a place where parents enjoyed being home for the kids "and peers came over for basketball in the driveway and homemade lemonade." The Medveds go on to prescribe ways they have protected their own children from influences they believe to be potentially harmful, including not allowing their children to watch television, strictly censoring home videos and books, and screening playmates.

Runaway Commercialism and Entitlement

Materialism and the overcommercialization of our youth is at its peak today, with young people being barraged with product and program advertising on TV, outside the home, and in schools. (Remember, it's estimated that children may view as many as 40,000 commercials each year.) Our children are buying into materialism with our help. There is a disturbing trend toward entitlement among our young and increasing numbers of "spoiled brats" are whining and nagging away in pursuit of "stuff."

If you want to see what children can do, you must stop giving them things.
Norman Douglas

In more than 25 years of consulting to youth-marketing companies, we have conducted a great many focus groups with mothers. In the past two decades, many of these women have expressed an underlying sense of futility as they have felt driven by our consumer society to succumb to their children's pleas for the latest sugary cereals, electronic game systems, cell phones, clothes, skateboards—in other words, the latest everything.

Children will not remember you for the material things you
provided but for the feeling that you cherished them.
Richard L. Evans

Our observations have convinced us that kids today are having far too much handed to them. By meeting their incessant demands for more material objects, we teach our children bad habits of excessive consumerism that will make their lives more difficult and that, in many cases, will eventually translate into reduced workplace productivity. Personal responsibility, initiative, discipline, and hard work are commodities that are difficult to achieve and harder to come by in society today, where we tend to reward the children who demonstrate "spoiled brat syndrome" in pursuit of unchecked consumerism.

Dr. Brian Swimme in his 1996 book, *The Hidden Heart of the Cosmos,* offers his perspective on the rampant consumerism of modern culture suggesting that it's as if we're all part of a consumer cult. Dr. Swimme encourages readers to challenge advertisers by limiting their power to "promulgate a worldview, a minicosmology, that is based upon dissatisfaction and craving":

> The fact that consumerism has become the dominant world faith is largely invisible to us, so it is helpful to understand clearly that to hand our children over to the consumer culture is to place them in the care of the planet's most sophisticated preachers. . . . in American and European and Japanese society, and increasingly everywhere else, we are so blinded by the all-encompassing propaganda we never think to confront the advertisers and demand they cease. On the contrary, as if cult members ourselves, we pay them lucrative salaries and hand over our children in the bargain.[15]

While we share Swimme's concern about overconsumerism, we don't believe the finger should be pointed at all advertisers, and we would never be so naive as to expect that advertisers should cease their work altogether. In a capitalistic, free society, advertisers and marketers have just as much right to exist as do firefighters and letter carriers. But we agree with Swimme that true danger lies in the unconscious way we allow advertisers and marketers unlimited access and influence over our children. In Chapter 2 of our book *What Kids Buy and Why–The Psychology of Marketing to Kids,* we cited Stephen Vincent Benet from his book, *John Brown's Body.* That citation is worth reading again:

> Some men wish evil and accomplish it. But most men, when they work in that machine, just let it happen somewhere in the wheels. The fault is no decisive, villainous knife, but the dull saw that is the routine mind.[16]

Because of our country's economic prominence and the broad reach of our media and other products, the United States has become the largest exporter of values in the world—and materialism and consumerism hold a disturbing prominence at the top of our export list. It's time to wake up to the reality of these threats to our children, to our society, and to people throughout the world.

ACCEPTING RESPONSIBILITY

Who exactly is responsible for the problems of unethical product and program marketing today? If you take the time to analyze the problem carefully, you'll find that some of the individuals and entities that bear responsibilities for these problems include:

- Product manufacturers
- Product/program producers (TV, film, home video, video games, software)
- Product/program marketers, including corporate staff, advertising and promotion agency personnel
- Media organizations such as TV and radio broadcasters, Internet entities, print publishers, and outdoor advertisers
- Product and program retailers, including movie theater chains and video game arcades
- Legislators, policy makers, and child advocates
- Parents and educators
- Young people themselves

On what basis can intelligent decisions be made about what children are allowed to consume and experience? More important, how can we educate and train our children to make healthy choices for themselves? The next chapter explores these topics and provides key information about common sources of harm in our society, along with a user-friendly process for distinguishing between healthy and unhealthy—even dangerous—examples of products and programs to which most of our children have ready access.

> *I dream of a world that can utilize its knowledge and resources for the advancement of mankind not its detriment. I dream of the day when corporations will discontinue—on their own—the production of products that are harmful to humanity and the environment—no matter what the financial loss . . . –There is so much violence in our movies, TV shows, and games. Do you ever ask why? . . . –it is because WE BUY THEM! . . . If the market goes away, then the products will disappear and the industry will create new ideas. WE HAVE THAT POWER! YOU HAVE THAT POWER! CREATE NEW IDEAS!*
> Greg Smith, at age ten

2

CLASSIFYING GOOD, NEUTRAL, AND DANGEROUS PRODUCTS AND PROGRAMS

It is our choices . . . that show what we truly are, far more than our abilities.

J. K. Rowling, *Harry Potter and the Chamber of Secrets*

If we are going to be intelligent and comprehensive in our exploration of the problems we perceive in much of what is marketed to today's youth, we need to narrow down the threat. We can begin this process by establishing some specific product and program categories to classify items parents don't need to concern themselves with, items they need to be cautious with, or items they need to label as potential real dangers. We refer to these categories as "typically positive," "neutral," and "inherently dangerous."

TYPICALLY POSITIVE PRODUCTS AND PROGRAMS

Several categories of products and programs, because of their largely utilitarian nature, are almost always inherently *positive* and good for everyone. These include:

- *Sports equipment.* Roller skates, bicycles, bats, balls
- *School supplies.* Paper, pencils, notebooks
- *Personal hygiene items.* Toothbrushes, combs, lotions, shampoo
- *Traditional board and card games.* Checkers and most kid card games
- *Baby and toddler items and accessories.* Play and learning toys

It's hard to imagine a scenario in which any of these items might be harmful. Parents and the companies who manufacture and market them have essentially nothing to be concerned about when it comes to nurturance and protection of young people.

THE NEUTRAL: PRODUCTS AND PROGRAMS TO MONITOR

The types of products and programs covered in this section fall into what we term a *neutral* category and therefore need to be monitored to ensure they produce no negative effects. Consumed, used, viewed, or listened to appropriately and in moderation, most of the product types highlighted here cause no harm and, in fact, may add to the quality of life. However, each of these product groups includes items that can be potentially harmful for children during certain stages of their development.

- *Apparel.* Obviously, everyone needs clothes and most apparel is both highly practical and innocuous. However, clothing and accessories represent certain values and communicate key "messages" to those around us. For example, eight-year-olds who are allowed to mimic the dress (or "undress") of sexually daring entertainment icons are, in our view, communicating potentially negative messages and values through age-inappropriate behavior.
- *Cosmetics, piercing, tattoos.* Today's young girls and boys are growing up fast enough without the aid of age-inappropriate toy cosmetics. Body piercing, wildly colored hairstyles, and tattoos at too young an age can communicate lifestyles that have questionable values and behavior associated with them.
- *Radio.* For the most part, listening to the radio whether it's a talk show, news, sports, or music is an innocuous-enough activity. But parents and caretakers need to take care to protect their children from the sexually explicit content of certain talk shows, questionable lyrics of some hard rock, hip-hop, and gangsta rap songs, and the negativity inherent in so many political "rant" programs.
- *Telephone/communication devices.* With normal or moderate use of a telephone, a young person talking with friends, for example, is

no problem. Often, however—especially in the tween and teen years—excessive time spent on the phone can take away from other healthy and valuable activities such as reading, time with family, or homework. Mobile phones are also becoming increasingly sophisticated, many functioning as handheld computers with Internet access and the potential for danger this represents.

- *Educational software.* One might be surprised to find that educational software could be suspect in any way. In fact, most content of an educational nature is highly positive and laudable, and with age-appropriate and moderate use, it can genuinely contribute to healthy development. But educational software makes our list of potentially problematic products and programs because of its potential for age-inappropriate or excessive use—especially for children at or under eight years of age. (After age seven or eight, kids tend to self-regulate more when it comes to learning software. If it doesn't fit them, they'll bail out.) Too many parents, in their fervor to give their kids a "head start," place their little ones in front of a computer or computerlike play or learning machine and insist on their performance. Be careful to watch for signs of disinterest or stress as children work with these types of programs and limit the amount of time your very young children are in front of these screens.

Other product groups that fit within this neutral category require even closer scrutiny and monitoring. These groups include:

- Toys, dolls, and action figures
- Food and beverages
- Music and publications
- Room decor
- Technology

Some of these neutral products and programs may have aspects that have proved damaging for children at various stages of their development. Most can threaten the well being of children who engage with them excessively or inappropriately. The following sections talk about each of these neutral product categories in more detail.

Toys, Dolls, and Action Figures

Appropriately utilized, toys are an important part of a child's developmental process. One area in which toys can have a harmful effect on kids, however, is with modeling and its associated behaviors. When considering the potential positive and negative impact of dolls and toys, remember that *everything communicates; everything has associated learning.*

Little girls playing with dolls—"What could be more innocent?" most might ask. But, as much pleasure and fun as fashion dolls provide for young girls, many child welfare specialists have criticized these dolls, blaming them for serving as unrealistic body-type and beauty ideals for young girls. If little Leticia happens to have been born with big bones and a roundish body, her self-esteem may be negatively affected by these unrealistically proportioned dolls. The fashion doll category has moved way beyond Barbie.™ As reported by psychologist Dr. Patricia Farrell, in an Associated Press release, now there's a whole lineup of dolls from the most conservative types such as the collectible American Girls dolls and the wholesome Groovy Girls to the "Bratz, Flavas, and My Scene Barbies with voluptuous bodies and come-hither fashions like leopard-print bustiers and skintight low-rise jeans. Their accessories include black stretch limousines."[1] Dr. Farrell goes on to say that the selection of a doll "will tell you what the little girl's aspirations are, how she is being pushed by her family." Sociologists also stress the important role dolls play in shaping a girl's values.

We aren't suggesting the elimination of "questionable" dolls from toy stores. First of all, anyone would be hard-pressed to prove the superiority of one value over another in the arena of fashion and what's appropriate and what's not. Parents should carefully consider the potential problems associated with these dolls, however. With this evidence in mind, a parent might choose to steer the child toward dolls that offer realistic and positive models, and away from dolls that dress in ways that are associated with hip-hop styles and looser sexual boundaries.

Of much more concern in this category are aggressive toys such as play guns, violence-based action figures, and war games that are all about aggression and violence and acting out bloody behavior. Research shows a definite relationship between fantasy fighting, gunplay, and real-life aggression. Most action figures fall into one of three categories:

1. *Strong men.* Wrestlers or boxers or martial arts guys whose main strength rests in their ability to kick the stuffing out of their adversaries.
2. *Fantasy heroes.* Whether their context is the past (He-Man, Masters of the Universe series, cowboys), the present (Batman, Superman, X-Men), or the future (Star Wars), many of these heroes battle the forces of evil with violent actions and weapons including spears, guns, rockets, missiles, and lasers.
3. *Military.* Action figure–heroes who use every kind of weapon, including flame-throwers, grenades, rockets, and bombs to kill the enemy.

Nothing good ever comes of violence.
Martin Luther

Based in Bethesda, Maryland, the Lion & Lamb Project is a group working to identify and eliminate the marketing of violence to children through public education and advisory functions.[2] Every year before Christmas, this group presents its list of violent and unwholesome toys and games that parents should avoid. They call this list their "Dirty Dozen." Appearing on that list recently was the Army Forward Command Post, made by Ever Sparkle Industrial Toys. This toy is essentially a bullet-riddled dollhouse for boys. It comes with numerous accessories such as a machine gun, rocket launcher, and explosives. As the Lion and the Lamb noted, the Army Forward Command Post playhouse "trivializes the harsh realities of war."

Also on the Lion and the Lamb's Dirty Dozen list was Total Chaos (an entire line of Spawn figures), manufactured by L McFarlane Toys. "Cornboy is just one of six ultra-action figures in this set that have missiles shooting from cybernetic arm guns. One of these action figures, Cornboy, a "hulking mutant monstrosity" with an assortment of cybernetic weapons built into his body, also comes packaged with add-on guns and ammunition."

Retailers Bear Responsibility, Too

To reemphasize the responsibilities of wholesalers and retailers as well as manufacturers in providing youth-empowering products, we point to the fact that the Army Forward Command Post "dollhouse" with minor variations was, at the time of this writing, carried by several major retailers, including KB Toys, JCPenney, and Toys "R" Us stores. Toys "R" Us reportedly pulled this toy from the Amazon.com Web site (the online retailer for Toys "R" Us). JCPenney had also removed this toy from its Web site, but was not returning phone calls regarding whether the toy could still be ordered from its catalog.

Food and Beverages: The Best and Worst Foods for Children

Our children's health and behavior are being affected negatively by the quality and quantity of what they are consuming daily. Children who are raised on junk food and sugary drinks are not only more likely to contract diabetes and become overweight, but are also prone to more physical sickness and depression. Teachers have long reported that children with poor diets lack adequate energy to perform in school. Young bodies are more resilient than older ones, so serious maladies such as heart disease and diabetes often don't show up until adulthood. Research has now shown that the left ventricle of the heart is often oversized in overweight children and this can lead to heart problems.

It's critical that we begin to take seriously this very real dietary threat to our children's physical and mental well being and start to do something about it. For parents and caretakers wishing to help guide children toward better food choices, the solution is threefold: Model healthy food and beverage intake yourself, purchase and prepare healthy meals and snacks at home, and set down food and beverage guidelines and limits for your children when they are away from home.

We could spend volumes on the topic of foods that are bad for our kids when consumed in excess. Let's look a bit more closely at just two: sugars and fats.

Sugar and its impact on your child's health. "Sugar consumption is off the charts," reports Michael F. Jacobson, Executive Director of Center for Science in the Public Interest (CSPI), "Added sugars—found largely in junk food such as soft drinks, cakes, and cookies—squeeze healthier foods out of the diet. Sugar now accounts for 16 percent of the calories consumed by the average American and 20 percent of teenagers' calories." A government study found that back in 1977–1978, added sugars (as opposed to sugars that occur naturally in fruits, vegetables, and grains) provided only 11 percent of the average person's daily intake of calories. "With all the focus on fat, we've forgotten about sugar. It's time to rethink our national infatuation with sweets," concludes Jacobson.[3]

According to the USDA, people consuming 2,000 calories a day should eat no more than about 10 teaspoons of added sugar per day. Surveys show, however, that the average American consumes almost twice that amount. Soft drinks, which contain about 9 teaspoons of sugar per 12-ounce can, are a leading contributor to increased sugar consumption. Since 1942, when the American Medical Association (AMA) expressed concern about sweetened carbonated beverages, candy, and other foods rich in sugar but poor in nutrients, soft-drink consumption has increased about sevenfold (excluding diet soda), and overall sugar consumption has increased by one-third.

Consumers can check the levels of added sugar in any packaged food by reading the Daily Values labeling, required and regulated by the Food and Drug Administration (FDA). Many of the foods children consume on a daily basis provide large quantities of added sugar, and each serving of some of those foods meets or exceeds the USDA's recommended daily sugar limits. For instance, a typical cup of fruit yogurt provides 70 percent of a day's worth of added sugar; a cup of regular ice cream provides 60 percent; a 12-ounce Pepsi provides 103 percent; a Hostess Lemon Fruit Pie provides 115 percent; a serving of Kellogg's Marshmallow Blasted Froot Loops provides 40 percent; and a quarter of a cup of pancake syrup provides 103 percent.

Restaurants are not required to provide nutrition labeling, however, and many of their products exceed recommended added sugar levels by an incredible amount. By some estimates, a Cinnabon cinnamon roll provides 123 percent of the USDA's recommended target; a large McDonald's shake, 120 percent; a large Mr. Misty Slush at Dairy Queen, 280 percent; and Burger King's Cini-minis with icing, 95 percent. One of the biggest problems with high-sugar foods is that they often replace more healthful foods in a person's daily diet. According to USDA data, people who follow diets high in sugar get less calcium, fiber, folic acid, vitamin A, vitamin C, vitamin E, zinc, magnesium, iron, and other nutrients. They also consume fewer fruits and vegetables.

The Role of Fats in Healthy (and Unhealthy) Diets

For all the talk about the dangers of fat in the modern diet, we should remember that fat is essential to a healthy body. The FDA says this about the healthy aspects of fat:

> Fat is a major source of energy for the body and aids in the absorption of vitamins A, D, E, and K, and carotenoids. . . . when eaten in moderation, fat is important for proper growth, development, and maintenance of good health. As a food ingredient, fat provides taste, consistency, and stability and helps us feel full. In addition, parents should be aware that fats are an especially important source of calories and nutrients for infants and toddlers (up to two years of age), who have the highest energy needs per unit of body weight of any age group.

Our bodies cannot manufacture all the fatty acids we need. Alpha-linoleic acid (ALA) and linoleic acid (LA) are essential fatty acids (EFAs) we must obtain from food. Healthy fats include the fats found in olive and canola oil, for example, and in fish—particularly salmon, mackerel, and herring.

So, we know that good fats are necessary for a healthy diet, and if your children's diet included just ordinary animal and vegetable fats, the regulation of their intake of fat would be a much less challenging task than it is today. But the modern diet carries the hidden danger of "trans fats." Trans fats are created when oils are partially hydrogenated—the process that transforms these oils into semisolid fats such as vegetable shortening or stick margarine. In addition to making these oils semisolid, hydrogenation also makes them more stable; hydrogenated oils, therefore, give foods a longer shelf life.[4] Many common snack foods, such as cookies, crackers, and fried foods, carry measurable quantities of trans fats. Bodies don't break down these fats very well, and they contribute to arterial plaque, high LDL cholesterol, and coronary heart disease.

Making Smart Choices

We have ample information available to us about good and bad food choices for children. The United States Department of Agriculture (USDA), for example, offers its "Eat Smart, Play Hard" nutritional program, complete with informational brochures for parents on building healthy eating habits. It also has a Power Panther walk-around costumed character who visits schools to promote healthy consumption. Visit its Web site at http://www.fns.usda.gov/eatsmartplayhard for details.

CSPI, a privately funded consumer advocacy and nutrition information group located in Washington, D.C., also promotes consumption habits that lead to overall health, strong physical development, and weight control. It lists the top ten best and worst foods for children.[5]

Ten of the Best Children's Foods

1. Fresh fruits and vegetables (especially carrot sticks, cantaloupe, oranges, watermelon, strawberries)
2. Chicken breasts and drumsticks without skin or breading
3. Cheerios, Wheaties, or other whole-grain, low-sugar cereals
4. Skim or 1 percent milk
5. Extra-lean ground beef, or vegetarian burgers (Gardenburgers or Green Giant Harvest Burgers)
6. Low-fat hot dogs. (Yves Veggie Cuisine Fat-Free weiners or Light-life Fat-Free Smart Dogs)
7. Nonfat ice cream or frozen yogurt
8. Fat-free corn chips or potato chips
9. Seasoned air-popped popcorn
10. Whole wheat crackers or Small World Animal Crackers

The Link between Diet and Attention Deficit and Hyperactivity Disorder (ADHD)

In a new review of two dozen scientific studies, the nonprofit Center for Science in the Public Interest (CSPI) contends that food dyes and certain foods can adversely affect children's behavior. The CSPI, in a 32-page report titled "Diet, ADHD (Attention Deficit and Hyperactivity Disorder), and Behavior,"[6] charges that federal agencies, professional organizations, and the food industry ignore the growing evidence that diet affects behavior.

ADHD's main symptoms are reduced attentiveness and concentration, and excessive levels of activity, distractibility, and impulsiveness. An estimated 3 percent to 5 percent of school age children have ADHD, though some surveys put the percentage as high as 17 percent. Stimulant drugs, such as Ritalin and amphetamines, are often highly effective in reducing the symptoms of ADHD, and millions of children have been treated with them. One recent study found that 18 percent to 20 percent of fifth-grade white boys in two cities had been diagnosed with ADHD and were being treated with drugs.

These drugs, however, don't offer a risk-free solution to controlling ADHD or other behavioral problems. Ritalin and other drugs sometimes cause side effects, including reduced appetite, stomachaches, and insomnia. A 1995 study conducted by the federal government's National Toxicology Program (NTP) found that Ritalin caused liver tumors in mice. If Ritalin also can contribute to the onset of cancer in humans, shouldn't we be concerned that the millions of children currently taking Ritalin may be especially vulnerable to this threat?

Ten of the Worst Children's Foods

1. Soda pop
2. Hamburgers
3. Hot Dogs
4. Ice Cream
5. Bologna
6. Whole Milk
7. American Cheese

8. French Fries and Tater Tots
9. Pizza loaded with cheese and meat
10. Chocolate Bars

Here is the CSPI's list of the worst artery-clogging offenders.

- Most large-size fast-food french fries
- Most prepared or frozen chicken and fish such as fish sticks, chicken potpies, fast-food fish and chicken sandwiches, chicken nuggets, fried chicken meals, and buttery seafood dinners
- Butter, lard, and many of the most popular margarines
- Baked goods and frostings, especially doughnuts and pastries
- Many popular crackers and snacks

You may also want to visit CSPI's Web site (http://www.cspinet.org) to find a variety of healthy dietary suggestions and resources for young people and families. For example, they have a "Lunchbox Makeover" section where you'll find ten tips for packing a healthy lunchbox. There's also a cool site for kids, (SmartMouth.org), which assists them in making healthier food, snack and beverage selections.

Music and Publications

We continue our look at neutral products and programs by turning to the music and publications groups. Most music is either positive in its impact on the healthy growth and development of our young people or neutral—that is, of no significant consequence or impact. Too often, however, the values of violence, disrespect for authority, age-inappropriate sexuality, and even mistreatment of women are far too often imbedded in some music lyrics and modeled in the antics and gyrations of music icons on stage and screen.

A study by researchers at Emory University's Rollins School of Public Health shows an association between "gangsta" videos, a propensity toward violence, and sexually permissive behavior.[7] Researchers studied 522 unmarried African-American females, ages 14 to 18, from nonurban, lower-socioeconomic neighborhoods. The study found that among black teen girls in the study, those who watched more rap videos were more likely to get in trouble with the law, use drugs, and become infected with sexually transmitted diseases. That same study found that those subjects who watched more than 14 hours of rap videos per week were:

- Three times as likely to hit a teacher
- Two and a half times more likely to be arrested
- Nearly twice as likely to have sex with multiple partners

Some publications can be harmful as well. Magazines with explicit sexual content are just one example of publications that are inappropriate for viewing by children. Also potentially harmful are comic books that glorify violence, negative role modeling, age-inappropriate sexuality, and sexual stereotyping of women.

YES!

For ages seven and above, consider establishing a monthly family meeting to discuss topics related to consumerism, values, and media and advertising influences and how to deal with them.

We believe in appropriate censorship when young people are involved. Given the level of saturation of these types of negative messages in society, even the most watchful and effective parents cannot totally shield their young from harmful books, music, and other published media. Some of the negativity that does get through may, in fact, be a necessary tool for helping our youth learn to deal effectively with the reality of school and street life. Parents and teachers can support children in sorting through this negativity through communication and media education. Today's media-saturated environment demands new approaches to some aspects of parenting, including setting aside time to regularly sit down with your children and talk with them about what they're seeing and hearing in advertising messages and other media. Parents also should become staunch advocates of media education programs in their children's schools.

Room Decor

Parents too often abdicate all responsibility and control over their children's room decor. These parents view the room as their child's sacred space with which the child can do as he or she likes. But parents need to exercise guidance—if not censorship—in controlling the decorations and accessories in their child's room.

The decor of a child's room is the "context" within which the child lives life and expresses himself or herself. If the child is surrounded by images and items that send positive, even loving messages, those values get communicated. On the other hand, if by the time little Maria is in junior high and those precious Winnie the Pooh posters begin to be replaced with dark images and items associated with certain hard rock groups, witchcraft, and black magic, or half-naked poster boy hunks, then—Parent Alert!—it's time to consider some transformational measures. If you feel that your child's room decorations are communicating messages that aren't healthy, positive, or age-appropriate, then you shouldn't hesitate to sit down with your son or daughter for a serious discussion and—if necessary—to insist on certain rules and parameters for room decor.

Technology

Technology designed strictly for use by children, from electronic baby toys to toy robots and computer games, is becoming more common with each passing year. These programs and electronic toys can be very entertaining for children, and they can offer learning opportunities as well. Computers can provide fast and extensive resources for information to support study and schoolwork; using computer technology also can benefit certain skills such as eye-hand coordination and some types of problem solving. Learning software, in particular, can enhance a child's grasp of such things as math and foreign language, and numerous other types of curriculum content.

There can be a flip side to these benefits, however, and that's why we place technology in the neutral category. A child's use of technology requires parent and caretaker monitoring and management to remain a positive influence and experience for the child. Technology can be detrimental in a variety of ways.

- *Technology used purely for amusement can absorb too much of a child's life.* Time spent in front of computer and electronic game screens is time taken away from other—perhaps more healthy—activities such as free play, reading, outdoor play, and social interactions with family and friends.

*Western society has accepted as unquestionable a technological imperative
that is quite as arbitrary as the most primitive taboo: not merely the duty
to foster invention and constantly to create technological novelties,
but equally the duty to surrender to these novelties unconditionally,
just because they are offered, without respect to their human consequences.*
Lewis Mumford

- *Technology can become a physically unhealthy pastime.* Sitting in front of a screen for lengths of time is a physically passive activity and can contribute to obesity and other negative health outcomes. We all need to periodically let go of pent-up emotions and energies by engaging in physical activity. Play and exercise are the greatest ways for your children to meet this need for release and the broad availability of technology pastimes such as watching television, playing computer or video games, or simply surfing the Web have helped place these healthy physical activities on the endangered list.
- *Technology contributes to IIIO.* As we mentioned earlier in this book, IIIO, or Invisible and Intangible Information Overload, can be a negative by-product of the increased quantity of information delivered to young people through technology. Combined with the way young people interact with technological information delivery systems, IIIO adds to the daily stress experienced by everyone, including both children and adults.

If it keeps up, man will atrophy all his limbs but the push-button finger.
Frank Lloyd Wright

You might be surprised to learn that technology may also actually limit children's overall intelligence, when defined in the broadest of terms. The work of Harvard University's Howard Gardner has indicated that intelligence extends beyond the commonly recognized abilities of linguistic and mathematical skills. In his landmark 1983 book, *Frames of Mind,*[8] Gardner proposed seven different kinds of intelligence, which he later extended to include an eighth. Gardner's eight types of intelligence are:

1. Linguistic
2. Logical mathematical
3. Spatial
4. Body kinesthetic
5. Musical
6. Interpersonal
7. Intrapersonal
8. Naturalist

Without question, technology can be used to assist our children with certain aspects of these kinds of intelligence. For example, many people have feared that young people today will be unable to perform simple mathematical functions because they can so easily use a calculator or computer to perform these tasks. The 2003 National Assessment of Education Progress study showed, however, an increase in math ability, from "proficiency" levels of 18 percent for fourth graders in 1992 to 32 percent in 2003. It's possible that technology has, in fact, positively contributed to higher math scores.

At the same time, it isn't difficult to see how the misuse or overuse of technology might actually limit our children's intelligence in an alarming number of ways. Here's a closer look at the potential impact of technology on some of Gardner's designated types of intelligence.

- *Linguistic intelligence.* Watching television in particular is a passive activity. When both the verbal and visual content is provided by outside media, there is no need, or room, for the imagination to come into play. Reading, by comparison, requires the exercise of a child's "imagination muscle" for the child has to visualize (imagine) what he or she is reading. Overall, children are engaged in more passive, technology-based activities these days and less engaged with reading. One alarming result of this shift is a decrease in their ability to think more deeply about what they are experiencing. Educators like Benjamin Bloom would categorize this as a lessening of the higher order, more complex thinking skills, including the abilities to analyze, synthesize, and evaluate information.[9]

- *Body-kinesthetic intelligence.* Small motor movement skills such as those needed for computer keyboards and for electronic games may be increased because of technology. But what about the body-kinesthetic intelligence that comes from more whole-body free play and outdoor play? This kind of intelligence appears to be in decline—not to mention the concomitant reduction in time spent exercising.

- *Interpersonal intelligence.* Interpersonal intelligence is reflected in how well an individual is capable of participating in interactions with others. The more our young people are alone with tech screens, the less time they spend in social interactions. Family dinnertime has changed from time spent around the table together in communication to everybody scattering to separate rooms to turn on TVs, computers, and game systems. An increase in interpersonal intelligence can only come through practice. Although tweens and teens spend a great deal of time interacting through telephones, instant messaging, and chat rooms, we don't believe that those types of interactions replace the quality of face-to-face interaction. Isn't something lost in the machinery?

- *Intrapersonal intelligence.* This refers to how smart one is about oneself. This kind of intelligence is developed through social interaction as well as through self-reflection in one's alone time. Technology consumes so much of our "free" time these days that little time is left for perhaps one of the most important activities: thinking about oneself and one's own thinking or self-reflection. This kind of self-reflection time is key to the development of intrapersonal intelligence in children and critical for creativity, imagination, and problem-solving skills.

- *Natural intelligence.* This type of intelligence is demonstrated by how smart a person is about the natural world. While it's true that television, for example, broadcasts a great many informational shows about nature, allowing children and all of us access to many natural geographical, cultural, and animal wonders, this cannot compare with the knowledge of the natural world we gain through direct contact via hiking, camping, skiing, fishing, or just strolling along the beach. As children spend more time indoors with technology, they spend less time playing outdoors, and become less comfortable with and knowledgeable of nature.

Is Technology Making Our Children Dumber?

Jane Healy in her book, *Failure to Connect: How Computers Affect Our Children's Minds and What We Can Do about It*,[10] explains in technical yet understandable terms how our children's emotional brains and prefrontal cortexes are suffering from underdevelopment, in part because of computers and technology.

In our increasingly electronic world, we witness escalating attention-deficit disorder, antisocial behavior, poor motivation, depression, and ineffectual work habits. All these originate in the brain's emotional centers. As in the thinking brain, the habits and connections in this "feeling" brain are sculpted during childhood. Its most important needs can't be met electronically: Frequent and affectionate human interaction, models of thoughtful behavior, and physical exercise are far more important. . . . many scientists are convinced that too many violent computer (or video) games—coupled with too little human affection—may negatively affect susceptible individuals.

If what Healy and many others are saying is true, then we have a big problem on our hands: how to humanize our children (and all of us) as they and we become more and more technologized. We need highly developed "executive systems" at the helms of our families and cultures, not crippled, underdeveloped, ineffectual cerebral leadership.

Finding Balance through Monitoring Neutral Products and Programs

In summary, the neutral category—from toys to technology—is populated by products and programs that are practical, useful, life-enhancing, and often potentially harmful. Parents and other child caretakers must take care to effectively guide their children at every step along the way to ensure that their interactions with these items and programming result in the healthiest of outcomes. Seek ways to balance tech-related activity with nontech-related activity. Set limits for the amount of time your children spend in front of screens. Turn off the machines and insist on free playtime indoors and outdoors. Encourage activities and hobbies that involve music and art and social interaction. Organize camping trips to bring children close to nature. Insist on spending family dinnertime together. Read to your children when they are very young. Encourage and insist on their reading alone. By limiting the hours your children are involved with machines, you encourage them to expand their experiences—and intellects—by pursuing a wider range of activities. As promised, in Chapters 4 through 8 we will be providing key Youth Enrichment Strategies (YES!) to assist with this guidance.

THE BAD: PRODUCTS AND PROGRAMS THAT ARE INHERENTLY DANGEROUS

Our last category includes *inherently dangerous* products and programs that we believe present the most threats to our young people. This category includes:

- Drugs, alcohol, and tobacco
- Guns
- Violence-centered electronic games
- Violent TV and film content
- Internet violence, age-inappropriate content, and Web marketing

These are the products and programs that require the strongest parental/caretaker vigilance and the strongest limitations and boundaries. Let's take a closer look.

Drugs, Alcohol, and Tobacco

Are drugs, alcohol, and tobacco being actively marketed to young people? The keyword is *actively*. As you'll learn later in this section, the active marketing of alcohol to underage individuals is very real—and a very real concern. In the case of drugs, there may be no active marketing going on—no TV ads, no billboards, no magazine print ads. However, many of our entertainment icons glorify the use of these addictive substances.

Our young people, in their vulnerability and naïveté, unfortunately far too often imitate celebrities. In cable TV programming, music video, and film, writers, producers, and entertainers depict the "rich and famous" frequently modeling the use of drugs, alcohol, and tobacco. Even our sports "heroes" are tarnished by illegal drug use—especially steroids —that not only reflects horribly on the athletes' characters and undermines their athletic accomplishments, but also "sends the wrong message to our young people—that there's a shortcut to accomplishment," according to President George W. Bush.

This type of modeling is a form of "passive marketing," and it's the responsibility of the producers of these entertainment events as well as the entertainers and athletes themselves to not portray alcohol, tobacco, or drug use as positive. It's also the responsibility of the "retailers" of these shows and icons—the TV networks, cable, Dish, and Internet providers—to consider not broadcasting this type of negative modeling content or at least severely limiting it, and to do everything possible to restrict age-inappropriate exposure to these images and icons.

The most outrageous and the lowest form of marketing of all is the active marketing of alcohol and tobacco products to young people under the age of 21. In fact, we believe it is criminal and offenders should suffer legal consequences. We talk more about alcohol and tobacco youth marketing in the chapters on the teen years.

Peddling death: marketing alcohol to young people. Most of us don't require statistical data to convince us of the dangers alcohol represents for young people. Nevertheless, a number of studies and reports have presented compelling evidence on this topic. The Center on Alcohol Marketing and Youth (CAMY) of Georgetown University, for example, spells out the threat that alcohol represents to young people between the ages of 12 and 20:

> The consequences of underage drinking are real and tragic. Alcohol use plays a substantial role in all three leading causes of death among youth—unintentional injuries (including motor vehicle fatalities and drownings), suicides, and homicides. Children who begin drinking before the age of 15 are 4 times more likely to develop alcohol dependence than those who wait until the age of 21. In the most recent federal survey of schoolchil-

dren, 16.6 percent of eighth graders reported having been drunk at least once in the past year, and by the tenth grade, that number is 39.9 percent.[11]

Despite nearly universal agreement on the potential dangers of underage drinking, alcohol continues to be marketed to young people through magazines and through radio and television programming, sometimes in subtle, yet powerful, ways.

CAMY has published three highly relevant reports dealing with the active marketing of alcohol to individuals under the legal drinking age of 21. Their reports deal with magazine, radio, and TV alcohol advertising to youth. Some of the highlights are as follows:

- *Magazines.* Alcohol beverage ad dollars are spent on youth. "Ten magazines with underage audience compositions at or above 25 percent accounted for nearly one-third of all alcohol advertising expenditures." Twenty-five brands selected only youth-oriented magazines for their marketing efforts.
- *Radio.* Sixty-three of 160 alcohol brands delivered more radio advertising to underage youth than to adults of legal drinking age.
- *Television*—"Alcohol's vast adland." The alcohol industry's voluntary guidelines for ad placements on television are so lax that they allow the substantial exposure of youth to alcoholic beverage advertising, including advertising on programs with disproportionate numbers of young people in the viewing audience.

For the full and disturbing scoop on age-inappropriate marketing of alcohol to youth, we encourage readers to go to CAMY's Web site at http://camy.org.

Lighting up our youth—here and abroad. While TV advertising of tobacco products is no longer allowed in the United States, and while ad strategies found to specifically target young people (such as the Joe Camel character) have been outlawed, tobacco products are still being marketed to today's youth. Tobacco companies are as aggressive with this type of advertising as they can be, while still remaining within the law.

Facts from the Campaign for Tobacco-free Kids Web site (http://www.tobacco.freekids.org)[12]:

- Twenty-eight-and-a-half percent of all high school students are current smokers.
- About 90 percent of all adult smokers began at or before the age of 18.
- More than a third of all kids who ever try smoking become regular, daily smokers before leaving high school.
- Eighty-seven percent of youth (12 to 17) smokers prefer Marlboro, Camel, and Newport—the most heavily advertised brands.

Have legal bans on tobacco advertising to youth been effective? Not according to this July, 2003, report by the Campaign for Tobacco-free Youth. As part of the 1998 state tobacco settlement, the tobacco companies promised not to "take any action, directly or indirectly, to target youth." But the evidence shows that if Big Tobacco has changed at all, it's for the worse: "In the three years after the settlement, tobacco industry marketing expenditures increased by 66.6 percent to a record $11.2 billion in 2001, according to the Federal Trade Commission. This amounts to $30.7 million every day to market their deadly products. Most of the increase was in retail store marketing, which is highly effective at reaching kids. Studies show that 75 percent of teens shop at convenience stores at least once a week, and they are more likely than adults to be influenced by convenience store promotions."

So as legal restrictions and government fines chase after the tobacco companies, these companies have to become increasingly clever in reaching a young audience. Tobacco companies have greatly increased their ad dollar expenditures in convenience stores,[13] for example, and have redoubled efforts to sponsor sporting and concert events—where in some countries they pass out free samples. Tobacco companies also have stepped up their offerings of branded merchandise, some of which function as walking advertisements. After all, how cool is it to sport a Marlboro T-shirt in school?

A growing number of young people are successfully purchasing cigarettes over the Internet. The *Journal of the American Medical Association* (*JAMA*) reported alarming evidence that the Internet is an almost completely unchecked source of cigarettes for kids. The study found that kids as young as 11 were successful more than 90 percent of the time in purchasing cigarettes over the Internet.[14]

Restrictions on actively marketing tobacco and antismoking campaigns have to some extent reduced the number of smokers in the United States. Corporate Accountablitiy International (CAI), a nonprofit organization, reports that the tobacco industry currently loses almost 5,000 customers every day (including those who quit and those who die). The vast majority of smokers start while they're still under the age of 21; nearly half begin before they're 14 years old. And restrictions on advertising haven't dampened the tobacco industry's spending; CAI reports that tobacco companies in the United States spend $11 million each day in advertising and promotion.[15]

In part because of this reduction at home, Big Tobacco has moved beyond the U.S. borders to find new customers/victims. It's redoubled efforts in many regions of the world. Again from CAI:

> Transnational tobacco companies such as Philip Morris, RJR Nabisco, British American Tobacco (BAT) Industries, and American Brands are also making their presence felt in other countries. In the developing world, per-capita cigarette consumption has risen on average by more than 70 percent during the past 25 years. Smoking rates among male Korean teenagers rose from 18 percent to 30 percent in one year after the entry of U.S. tobacco companies. Among female teenagers, rates increased from less than 2 percent to nearly 9 percent.

Can you believe this? In 1999, Philip Morris commissioned a study conducted by the Arthur D. Little Company for the Czech Republic that determined that the Czech government actually would save $1,225 per early death of its citizens due to smoking![16]

Particularly deplorable is the fact that Big Tobacco is capitalizing on the rich-and-famous image of America as portrayed in all the TV programming and films we export. Young people in particular are vulnerable to wanting to identify themselves with America and its many enticing attributes and goodies. CAI cites:

> Outside the United States, central messages are wealth, health, consumption—in short, "USA." . . . . U.S. tobacco companies capitalize on this by associating smoking with affluence.

It's not uncommon to hear children say they start because of the glamorous lifestyle associated with smoking."

In emerging markets from Eastern Europe to Southeast Asia, transnational tobacco giants Philip Morris, RJR Nabisco, and BAT Industries aggressively hawk cigarettes with slogans like: "L & M: The Way America Tastes," "Winston: The Spirit of the USA," and "Lucky Strikes: An American Original."

As the preceding evidence suggests, the aggressive marketing of tobacco to the world's youth is both alive and deadly. As parents and youth caretakers, and as responsible citizens of the world, we all share concerns about these marketing practices, even when they are not directly aimed at our own children.

Guns

High on the list of irresponsible marketing to children is the promotion of gun use to preteens and teenagers. More than 20,000 people under the age of 20 are killed or injured by firearms in the United States alone each year. Gun violence is the second leading cause of death to young people ages 10 to 19. Despite these alarming realities, many individuals—especially National Rifle Association (NRA) advocates—promote the use of guns to and by children. According to the 2002 "Future of Children" report:[17]

The NRA is investing $100 million in a campaign to bring together children and guns. Former NRA President Marion Hammer has declared that the organization is in "an old-fashioned wrestling match for the hearts and minds of our children and we'd better engage our adversaries with no holds barred."

We must teach our children . . . to resolve
their conflicts with words, not weapons.
William J. Clinton

In his monthly column in *Guns & Ammo* magazine, NRA President Charlton Heston has exhorted gun owners to "consider how you can help preserve freedom for future Americans by introducing a young person to the fun and satisfaction of shooting . . ."

. . . Major manufacturers including Colt's Browning and Remington have begun to use video games as marketing tools. "What we need is a computer game that combines the use of the real handgun . . . with state-of-the-art graphics and a real story . . . a game like that would be an extremely effective vehicle to introduce safe, recreational shooting to the video games generation."

Violence-Centered Electronic Games

High on our list of products and programs that are inherently dangerous is the category of video games. With as much as 70 percent to 80 percent of all electronic games containing violent content, including those played on the computer, on handheld devices, and on dedicated systems, it's not difficult to see the potential dangers involved. How extensive is video-game play? A recent article in the *New York Times* reported some eye-opening facts including the $28 billion earned by the videogame industry in 2002. The article also reported that according to *Fortune* magazine, Americans will spend more time playing video games this year—about 75 hours on average—than watching rented videos and DVDs.[18]

There's no longer room to debate whether ultraviolent video-game play leads to more aggression in real life. Study after study has proved that engaging in violent entertainment—the kill cops, bash prostitutes, blast apart bodies kind favored by many electronic games—has the "carryover" effect of leading to more aggressive behavior.

TV and Film Violence

In Chapter 1, we touched on the potentially dangerous impact of viewing TV and film violence. After the Columbine killings, another high school student was arrested just before he and a buddy were about to create a Columbine-style massacre at their own high school. The two of them wore black floor-length leather coats like Keanu Reeves wore in the movie, *The Matrix*. In another example of the influence of media violence on teen behavior, two teens killed and dismembered their mother after viewing an episode of the *Sopranos* in which a guy's hands and head were chopped off to prevent his identification.

Again, we are not arguing for total censorship of this kind of violent fare on TV or in theaters. Our mission is to alert us all to the real dangers of allowing young people to have unlimited access to violent and age-inappropriate media content, so we can take appropriate steps to eliminate or dramatically reduce that access. Viewing these types of shows must be limited to mature individuals who are able to process the information without experiencing undue negative effects on their psyches or behavior.

Some of the irresponsibility on the part of certain producers and marketers of violent TV and film content, however, borders on criminal. In an interview, Quentin Tarantino encouraged kids to see his blood-bath film *Kill Bill Volume 1.* "If you are a 12-year-old girl or boy," he said, "you must go and see *Kill Bill,* and you will have a damn good time. Boys will have a great time; girls will have a dose of girl power. If you are a cool parent out there, go take your kids to the movie." Mr. Tarantino, what were you thinking?

Mick LaSalle, movie critic for the San Francisco Chronicle described the gore: The film contains . . . "seven arm severings, five foot or leg severings, two hatchet deaths, two beating deaths (including a guy getting his head smashed in a doorway), one attempted rape, myriad corpses, one nails-through-the-brain death, one hunting knife stabbing (a mother killed in front of her daughter), one quick shot of a man split in two, and one graphic depiction of a scalping. In addition, there are 45 sword-related deaths, more or less, and a scene of a pregnant woman getting shot in the head."[19]

Make no mistake about it, parents are responsible for monitoring and censoring their children's involvement with all media. But the mere fact that such reprehensible violence is promoted as "fun" for our children is a sad statement on this director's values, his lack of awareness of the special vulnerabilities of children, and his sense of responsibility to society.

Jane Healy has observed and researched the impact of media and technology in our society. The titles of her highly recommended books tell the story.

- *Endangered Minds: Why Children Don't Think and What We Can Do about It*[20]
- *Failure to Connect: How Computers Affect Our Children's Minds and What We Can Do about It*[21]

- *Your Growing Child's Mind: A Guide to Learning and Brain Development from Birth to Adolescence*[22]

Healy emphasizes a variety of "hazards in a media culture" and what she calls an "epidemic of attention deficit disorder, behavioral problems, faltering academic abilities, language difficulties, and weak problem-solving skills."[23]

Internet Violence, Age-Inappropriate Content, and Web Marketing

There's no question that the Internet and access to information and communication via the World Wide Web has been and will continue to be a tremendous technology with life-altering and enhancing benefit. It's hard to imagine commerce or day-to-day living without it. At the same time, however, the Internet occupies a place on any list of potentially dangerous places for young people to hang out. The most pressing dangers are fourfold:

- IIIO. The time spent in front of the computer screen itself adds to the negative effects of IIIO (Invisible and Intangible Information Overload), leads to stress, and, used in excess, displaces other healthier activities.
- Exposure to physical/mental harm occurs from connections made on the Net.
- Age-inappropriate exposure to pornography exists (12 percent of all Web sites are pornographic, consisting of more than 260 million pages).
- Violent video games such as Counter-Strike, a popular game in which players work together to use weapons and explosives to fight terrorists, are accessible. (After 19-year-old Robert Steinhaeuser killed 16 people in his school in Ehfurt, Germany, before turning the gun on himself, sources reported that he was an avid Counter-Strike player.)

We aren't advocating that children be prevented from accessing the Internet entirely. As we have established, used responsibly, the Internet can be a tremendously valuable tool for gathering information and communication. We do believe, however, that parents and teachers simply must know where the children in their charge are traveling on the Internet. They must discuss the dangers with their children and make every effort to restrict access to inappropriate sites.

The World Wide Web also represents a whole new world of marketing to children. First of all, most of the restrictions for marketing to kids using television are not applicable to the Internet, so almost anything goes in that medium. As Jane Healy notes in *Failure to Connect,* parents don't pay much attention to Internet marketing. Says Healy, "... because many parents have abdicated computer control to the youngsters, advertisers have an unprecedented crack at their young audience."[21]

Two other Internet marketing monsters have popped up as well: invasion of privacy and unfair and deceptive advertising. Young people are offered free gifts like T-shirts and CD players in exchange for filling out online surveys. The goal is to be able to "microtarget" individual youngsters. Because the likes of AOL, Compuserve, and the World Wide Web aren't regulated like TV broadcasters, advertisers have free reign to capture hours of children's attention at their Web sites where commercials and content including branded cartoon characters and games are seamlessly interwoven.

Setting Freedom's Boundaries

In any discussion of censorship, people are quick to raise the issues of First Amendment rights to freedom of speech and self-expression. The need for censorship emerges, however, when it comes to children. Here is the truth: If adult porn producers were allowed to broadcast in the after-school hours, they would, and kids, left without supervision or censorship, would watch. In any civilized society, freedom must have its boundaries. The lives and well being of our children are at stake. The ex-mayor of New York, Rudolph Giuliani, has been quoted as saying:

> Freedom is about authority. Freedom is about the willingness of every single human being to cede to lawful authority a great deal of discretion about what you do and how you do it.

Up until now, a good deal of confusion has existed on the part of parents and others regarding where to draw the line. "How do I answer my 12-year-old," one very concerned mom recently complained. "He says all his friends are into all these violent video games and he doesn't see any real danger in them. He's got the game posters plastered all over his room. How can I just tell him he can't play them anymore?"

Our message to this mother and to all who share her uncertainty is this: If you without a doubt knew that something your child was eating everyday was extremely toxic and poisonous, you would immediately stop him. In the case of each of the inherently dangerous products and programs we detail in *Kidnapped*–extreme violence in the media, music, and electronic games; alcohol, tobacco, and drugs; guns; and the Internet–STOP or REGULATE your children's involvement with them as soon as possible. Restructure their days and weeks to replace negative involvement with positive activity. Do everything you can to separate them from these negative influences. If your children kick and holler– and they most likely will–so be it. They'll thank you for it in the end.

Parents of the very young have a distinct advantage in establishing these boundaries. Armed with knowledge of the "good," the "neutral," and the "inherently dangerous" product and program categorizations, they can consciously and carefully design their child's environment and experience for maximum healthy growth and development right from the start.

TIME FOR ACTION

Although we all run the risk of becoming desensitized to the ever-present threats posed by common products, programs, and activities that occupy our children's lives, if we've presented it clearly and accurately, you may be greatly disturbed by the information contained in these first chapters. The pursuit of profit and a love of easy solutions have blinded manufacturers and the audience to whom they market their products to just what we're doing to our world's most precious resource, our children. It's time to extract our heads from dark places and take action to counter the very damaging effects of the products and programs threatening the well-being of young people everywhere.

As you will learn, there is a huge difference between a 4-year-old's brain and the brain of an 11-year-old or an 18-year-old. In later chapters of this book, we discuss the developmental capabilities and limitations of children's minds as they mature from birth through the teen years, and we will explore the implications these developmental stages have for the child's ability to effectively translate and filter marketing messages. These chapters help you to understand how to identify both positive and negative products, programs, and marketing practices for each age group. In every case, we'll be providing suggestions, tools, and strategies for minimizing negative influences and mitigating their harmful effects.

The tools and techniques we offer represent an objective and scientific approach to these different youth stages of development, based on sound brain research and child and teen development principles. To synthesize the enormous amount of information inherent in developmental psychology, we have focused it on what we call the Three Dimensions of Development: Developmental Elements, Developmental Blind Spots, and Dynamics of Communication. In Chapters 4 through 8, we explore these developmental dimensions and their implications for a child's vulnerabilities to marketing and media messages. We devote the next chapter, however, to an overview of the "three dimensions of development" so that you as a parent, other caretakers, and marketers can build a solid foundation for decision making on your way toward guiding your child's healthy development.

> *Nothing is fixed, forever and forever and forever, it is not fixed; the earth is always shifting, the light is always changing, the sea does not cease to grind down rock. Generations do not cease to be born, and we are responsible to them because we are the only witnesses they have. The sea rises, the light fails, lovers cling to each other, and children cling to us. The moment we cease to hold each other, the sea engulfs us and the light goes out.*
> James Baldwin

c h a p t e r

3

THE THREE DIMENSIONS
OF DEVELOPMENT

Q: What do psychologists mean by development?
A: First of all, development means change–change in quantity (e.g.,
increase in vocabulary) and in quality (acquiring the concept of rhyming
words). Special concerns are given to distinctive new thought and behavior
patterns. Secondly, developmental psychologists are concerned with not
only identifying what the changes are during the human life cycle, but also
finding out why these changes take place, and how they take place.
Finally, psychologists study development in many aspects, including
perception, cognition, emotion, relationships, language, and social skills.[1]

Shelly Wu, Ph.D.

Before we begin to seriously evaluate the products and programs marketed to children from birth through the teen years in the chapters that follow, we need to establish an objective basis for the distinctions and categorizations we'll be making. Without a scientific approach to this categorization, all recommendations and observations we make in these chapters would be subjective opinions. In order to establish this objective approach, we have drawn most heavily from the disciplines of child development and the evolving brain. Throughout *Kidnapped* we will approach this exploration from three interrelated developmental "dimensions," which shed the most light on the paths we need to follow as we guide our children toward more positive and appropriate products, programs, and experiences. These three development dimensions are:

1. *Developmental elements.* Key aspects related to your child's development, especially to brain development.

2. *Developmental blind spots.* A biologically or psychologically based condition beyond awareness or understanding that can limit children from realizing their developmental potential.
3. *Dynamics of communication.* The interaction between the child as a consumer and a product, program, or marketing/advertising strategy.

DIMENSION ONE: DEVELOPMENTAL ELEMENTS

Key facts about the developing brain have direct implications for how your child is able to perceive the world, to think, and to learn values. Most important, these brain facts have implications for how your child learns—and this has everything to do with how you and other caretakers navigate through the choppy seas of youth marketing.

The human brain is the core foundation of human development. Children do not come into this world with their brains fully developed. In fact, the near full development of the brain is not in place until the end of the teen years and it continues to develop and change to some degree throughout life. For our purposes, however, we'll consider the development of the brain relatively complete by age 19.

Brain Architecture

A simplified model of the human brain is shown in Figure 3.1. The largest part of the brain is the *thinking brain* or cerebral cortex at the top of the brain. This section of the brain is critical to planning, learning, thinking, and problem solving. In addition, the cerebral cortex is critical to understanding what you hear and see, and for your ability to move.

The second part of the brain can be referred to as the *emotional brain.* This part of the brain is the primary seat of emotion, attention, and affective (emotion-charged) memories. Physiologically, it includes the hypothalamus, hippocampus, and amygdala. Marketing has much to do with making an emotional impact, and your children's "connections" with products and programs are highly emotional.

At the base of the brain is the *reflex brain* or brain stem, which connects to the spinal cord. This section of the brain takes care of basic

FIGURE 3.1 *The Three Main Parts of the Brain*

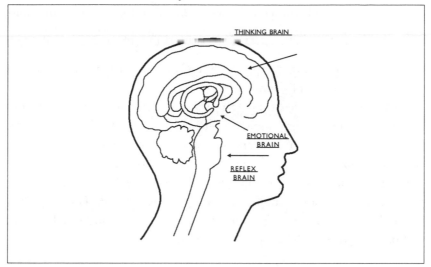

involuntary, unconscious functions such as breathing and the heartbeat that respond automatically to changes in the environment, constantly adapting to our survival needs.

Neural Networks and Brain-Based Learning

Your child's brain is made up of billions of nerve cells called *neurons*. Each neuron connects to thousands of other neurons and accepts signals from other neurons through tree branchlike structures called *dendrites*. Whenever messages arrive from surrounding neurons, a neuron sends an electrical signal down its trunk, which is called its *axon*. When the electrical impulse arrives at the end of the axon, it causes the tiny sacs at the end of the axon to release chemical messengers called *neurotransmitters*, which then travel across tiny little gaps—*synapses*—to arrive at and excite other neurons.

Stimulated by the passage of electrical current along the neurons, your child's learning takes place with the growth of new neural connections, which form the neural networks within the child's brain. This growth is enhanced by the chemicals (neurotransmitters) that are discharged into the gaps (synapses) between the neighboring cells. When this discharge of chemical neurotransmitters occurs, neurons grow more dendrites to reach other neurons. The more activation of the neurons that occurs, the stronger these connections become. As pathways are used, additional connections create more and more flexibility and ease of use for the same neurons. Because learning consists of the development of connections between the cells in these neural networks, then enhanced learning requires repetition and practice of activities that sparked the initial connections.

Your children are learning every waking moment. We could cite any activity, but let's select a simple one—learning to open a door by using a doorknob. First the child observes others, then reaches up and touches the doorknob. The neurons fire away and make connections. Then the child "gets" the idea of turning the knob, practices it, and is successful at opening the door. A neuronal *circuitry* has formed. The child has learned the skill of opening a door using a doorknob, and that learning will be reinforced with every subsequent door opening.

Understanding Neural, Experiential, and Reflective Intelligence

In his book, *Outsmarting IQ: The Emerging Science of Learnable Intelligence,*[2] David Perkins states that there are three different kinds of intelligence: neural, experiential, and reflective. Perkins defines *neural intelligence* as the nerve networks we are born with. *Experiential intelligence* is modified through experience and open to change, as is *reflective intelligence,* which relates to developing our metacognitive or higher-order abilities to think critically, solve problems, and respond to unique and novel situations with flexibility and resilience.

Why are these distinctions important? Because the ultimate goal of any parent is to raise a child who is capable of using all these types of intelligence to make positive, healthy, growth-producing choices on his or her own. The full development of your child's neural, experiential, and reflective intelligence will "arm" him or her with all the tools your child will need to accurately translate marketing and product "messages," and thus make healthy consumption choices.

Recent scientific developments in brain imaging have given us the means to understand more about the brain and how learning occurs.

These technological innovations include such advances as positron emission tomography (PET) and magnetic resonance imaging (MRI) that allow us to map sections of the brain and to understand more clearly how various forms of brain activity and input affect us and our children.

A fundamental understanding of the brain is key to comprehending youth marketing and children's choice-making processes. Your child's brain is the "control center" for the product and program choices he or she makes, and the task of marketers is to impact both the emotional and logical centers of your child's brain to create the desire to have and to purchase.

Brain-Based Learning and Development

The concept of *brain-based learning* is another critical component of our discussion on your child's developing brain and especially relevant to child-targeted marketing. Research in brain-based learning is built upon both the architecture (or *structure*) and the *function* of the brain. At the core of brain-based learning is the view that *the brain actively seeks stimulus input because it is hardwired to learn, learn, learn!*

Learning goes on throughout your child's life unless it is blocked or prohibited by biological or environmental factors. Because of the inherent nature of the brain's learning appetite, a child cannot "not" learn. These 12 brain-based learning principles are founded on scientific research about how the human brain operates:

1. *The unfolding structure of the brain correlates* directly with a child's age and stage of development.
2. *The brain is a living system.* It is a collection of parts that function holistically. Even though each part of the brain has a specific function, the parts interconnect as a whole and the brain is intimately linked with the mind and body.
3. *The brain actively "seeks" information* in order to establish meaning and to "make sense" of its environment.
4. *The brain is social.* It does not stand apart from the social context that surrounds it and changes as a direct result of its interaction with people.

5. *The brain, in its search for meaning, learns* by actively discovering patterns in the world, not as an "empty vessel" being filled with information.

6. *Emotions play an integral role* in discovering patterns and are not separate from the mental process of knowing or cognition (awareness, perception, reasoning, and judgment). The two dimensions of cognition and emotion interact, energize, and shape each other.

7. *Brain architecture is designed to process both wholes and parts* at the same time. Split-brain research indicates that the two separate halves of the brain interact in the learning process with different specialties.

8. *Brain-based learning involves both focused attention and peripheral perception* at the same time. Research indicates that information entering the brain in the background of awareness is still being learned.

9. *Learning involves both conscious and unconscious (out-of-awareness) processes.* The brain can register and record information without an individual having any knowledge or understanding of how this learning has taken place.

10. *There are two different systems for organizing memory.* The first is where static information is stored and the second is the ongoing experiential system that processes our moment-to-moment experiences.

11. *Learning is enhanced by challenge and inhibited by threat.*

12. *Each person is unique* by way of his or her individual genetics and environmental influences, even though different individuals all have a similar set of brain systems.

You will want to consider these principles for they are critical to the key decisions you make regarding your children's consumption habits. Responsible marketers take these principles into account as guidelines, while less scrupulous individuals ignore them or exploit them for their own advantage.

Age and Brain Stage Milestones

We have organized children's development into five specific age segments, based on the architecture of the brain and the principles of
brain-based learning and their correlation with human development. As
we mentioned earlier, those segments include birth through the second
year of life, ages 3 to 7, 8 to 12, 13 to 15, and 16 to 19.

For each of these age segments there are milestone brain developments that directly correlate with the evolving capabilities (and vulnerabilities as we shall see) of babies, kids, tweens, and teens. French child
psychologist Jean Piaget and others[3] pointed to several of these milestones:

- *From birth to two,* the child is predominantly in the "sensorimotor"
  stage, mapping in basic survival skills such as learning to crawl
  then walk, to "ask" for what he or she needs, and to successfully
  interact with parents.
- *Before age six,* children lack sophistication in primary logical thinking tools and in the ability to distinguish, in many cases, between
  reality and fantasy; thus, children in this age group are vulnerable
  to age-inappropriate approaches of persuasion.
- *When the child is at the age of six or seven,* research indicates that activities associated with the left hemisphere (language skills, logical thinking, detail) become integrated and developed.
- *Around age 12,* the brain, in most cases, is developed enough to
  allow for higher forms of abstract reasoning, which are required
  for complex forms of thinking and problem solving. Before this
  time, the abilities necessary to perform these tasks are not yet
  fully developed.

Parents need to be aware of both the capabilities and vulnerabilities
of their children as they grow through each of the stages of development. For example, because pre-six-year-olds have not yet sufficiently developed the ability to reason or think logically, parents need to take
extra precautions with the kinds of media and marketing strategies
these children are exposed to. As for the marketers themselves, any attempt to market products and programs to children and teens at their
different stages of development *must* take these developing brain abilities into account.

As we move through our discussion of responsible and irresponsible marketing, we will integrate key facts from both brain research and child development to provide the neurological and psychological rationale to help you understand how we have arrived at our categorizations and recommendations, so you can better understand how to make decisions about your children's consumption of products and programs, and to what types of marketing they can safely be exposed.

The Whole Child

To fully understand what is occurring with young people as they interact with the multitude of products and programs that either enhance or threaten their lives, we need to take the "whole child" into consideration. With each age and stage of development, each of a child's core aspects matures and evolves, making up what it is to be a human being. In each of the age segment chapters that follow, we will focus our attention on these seven key developmental elements as they relate to the growth of young people:

1. *Physical.* The growth and development of the body
2. *Emotional.* A gradual increase in the capacity to express the full gamut of emotions
3. *Cognitive.* The development of thinking processes of all kinds, such as perceiving, remembering, concept formation, problem solving, imagining, and reasoning
4. *Self/social.* The gradual acquisition of attitudes, relationships, and behavior that enable the individual to function as a member of society
5. *Moral.* The gradual development of an individual's concepts of right and wrong, conscience, ethical and religious values, social attitudes, and behavior
6. *Transpersonal.* The development of behavior that transcends personal identity and individual immediate desires. (This developmental element begins to develop late in childhood.)
7. *Needs.* This developmental element refers to human needs that we seek to satisfy at the various ages and stages of our development.

While the basic needs remain relatively constant, their priority changes with each new developmental stage

Throughout *Kidnapped,* we will integrate relevant information from these core developmental elements with leading edge child and brain development research. With information about how the brain operates coupled with enough details related to the whole child's makeup, anyone who is committed to the well being of today's children as consumers will be "armed" with what they need to understand the key dangers pressing in on children and to make the important decisions necessary to nurture and protect the young people in their charge.

DIMENSION TWO:
DEVELOPMENTAL BLIND SPOTS

Key facts of brain development and information related to the core developmental elements, give rise to what we term *sitting-duck psychology.* As we have explained in previous chapters, when your child is incapable of defending himself or herself from the onslaught of marketing messages because the child has not yet developed the capacities to do so, he or she is a sitting duck for whatever is being "aimed."

As we stated early in this book, sitting-duck psychology refers to the interplay between how an individual child processes incoming information and the child's brain architecture and developmental stage. Another critical contributor to a child's susceptibility to deception or manipulation is the child's specific "default systems" or "blind spots"—biological and psychological gaps or limiting conditions that children cannot recognize or understand. We use the term *blind spots* because children often automatically respond to advertising and marketing messages designed to take advantage of these limitations in developmental capabilities.

In the chapters that follow, we detail key developmental blind spots for children at each stage of their development. It's important to note that these blind spots are cumulative and can remain with a child throughout successive stages of development.

Downshifting and Thinking Limitations

To help you begin to understand blind spots, let's briefly look at the thinking process and downshifting. *Downshifting* is a metaphor for the kind of brain activity that is prevalent in processing information, much like shifting gears of an automobile. This metaphor can be used to explain how your child "shifts" from a more cerebral, rational state (thinking brain) to a more highly emotional brain state (emotional brain) of functioning. A scary movie or a violent video game, for example, can downshift a child, putting the thinking brain "on hold" and into an almost trancelike receptive state, making the child very vulnerable to highly charged emotional impressions and emotionally laden messages. We've all witnessed children so immersed in an activity they appear to be "swept away" or in a trance. Parents and other caretakers need to be able to identify ahead of time the media that has the potential to downshift their children into this more vulnerable state, especially if the child is in a passive, receptive, or emotional state with limited reasoning and critical thought.

A second example of a developmental blind spot is a child's inability to understand levels of abstraction. We refer to this inability as *restrictive reasoning*. If a product or program is communicating positive or negative messages at an abstract level that cannot yet be understood by the child, we really can't be certain how these messages are being processed. Let's say you take your six-year-old to see *Lord of the Rings*. It's loaded with highly symbolic content and metaphors that provide the *mature* viewer with a wealth of positive storytelling information and cinematic excellence. This layer of abstraction provides additional storytelling meaning to the message.

What happens, however, when this layer of information passes through the psyche of your six-year-old? What does he see and feel? How does the incoming information affect him? Will he be capable of receiving and digesting what he's experiencing without negative impact? Children younger than seven will be unlikely to effectively process emotionally charged, scary, and violent images and sounds, including monsters, evil villains, epic battles, and killing in the same manner as an adult, who can integrate more complex layers of information. Young viewers are likely to be left—at least on an unconscious level—confused and somewhat frightened by what they've experienced. Many children have nightmares and experience other troublesome effects after being exposed too early to threatening experiences. Their development simply is not advanced enough to shield them from age-inappropriate, highly charged, negative emotional content.

Protecting Children by Acknowledging Their Developmental Blind Spots

We propose a system of categorizing products and programs as good, neutral, or inherently dangerous, based on their potential impact on children at each age and stage of development. That categorization carefully takes into consideration the developmental blind spots applicable to a child's growth. In the chapters that follow, we will be looking at developmental blind spots for the powerful roles they play in how your children interact with ad strategies and marketed products and programs. These critical elements are either overlooked or misunderstood by those marketing to children, leaving our children highly susceptible to information that is not created to support their healthy growth and development.

DIMENSION THREE: DYNAMICS OF COMMUNICATION

Marketing is all about communication. A communication model is an effective way to assess the impact of marketing communications on the young. A basic marketing communication model is relatively simple.

The marketer's goal is to attract your consumer child's *attention,* to have the child *comprehend* (at whatever level it is developmentally possible) what's being offered, and to engage the child by creating a positive emotional response to the message. Once this emotional *involvement* has occurred, your child begins to *yield* to the message, forming a positive attitude toward it. Simultaneously, marketers seek to create *retention* (memory) so your child begins to develop brand and product awareness. The next step the marketers hope for is *action,* when the child either purchases the advertised item or asks someone else to buy the item. The marketer's design for a successful communication doesn't stop there. The ultimate goal is for your child to have a positive *reaction* to the product or program once it's used or consumed, so that the child wants to buy/use/view it again, and then finally *communicate* positively to others about the product or program (positive word of mouth). From top to bottom, this communication flow can be mapped like this:

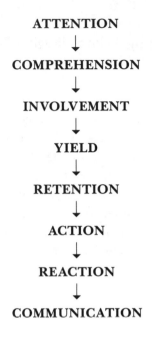

ATTENTION
↓
COMPREHENSION
↓
INVOLVEMENT
↓
YIELD
↓
RETENTION
↓
ACTION
↓
REACTION
↓
COMMUNICATION

Marketers, of course, know this model well and use it strategically to advertise and sell their products and programs. In each of the age segment chapters, we explore how a child's mind and perception tracks him or her through the model so that parents and other caretakers will be able to effectively counter any negative market messaging aimed at young people.

PUTTING IT ALL TOGETHER

In summary, developmental elements, developmental blind spots, and the dynamics of communication make up the objective "tools" we will use to assist us in our quest to categorize marketing, products, and programs as good, neutral, or inherently dangerous. These guidelines will help you determine whether your child is being exposed to irresponsible marketing that might exploit his or her vulnerabilities at different ages and stages of development, and products and programs that might be inappropriate and harmful, based on the nature of the product itself.

In the chapters that follow, we'll point out instances where specific marketing practices exploit or ignore these developmental dimensions and, therefore, put the development of your children in jeopardy. As you read through these chapters, you'll also find a wealth of information that we've drawn from a variety of other disciplines and content areas that have to do with identification, modeling, and other forms of learning. We begin with the first age segment, birth to the age of three. This is a relatively short chapter, because of the relatively minor marketing activity slated toward this age.

> *The most important human endeavor is the striving for morality in our actions. Our inner balance and even our very existence depend on it. Only morality in our actions can give beauty and dignity to life.*
> Albert Einstein

4

THE INNOCENT YEARS
Birth to Age Three

*Babies are necessary to grown-ups. A new baby is like the
beginning of all things—wonder, hope, a dream of possibilities. In a
world that is cutting down its trees to build highways, losing its earth to
concrete . . . babies are almost the only remaining link with nature,
with the natural world of living things from which we spring.*

Eda J. Le Shan

As we have indicated, each age and
stage of a child's development is accompanied by its own developmental elements, developmental blind spots, and dynamics of communication. Using the communications model you learned about in Chapter 3, we will explore direct implications for marketing efforts aimed at children from birth to the age of three. We'll also offer some examples of products and programs within each of the good, neutral, and inherently dangerous categories, so you as a parent will be able to make the most nurturing choices for your young ones.

DIMENSION ONE: DEVELOPMENTAL ELEMENTS

Renowned French child psychologist Jean Piaget termed this earliest stage of development the *sensorimotor* stage. The newborn-through-toddler period is a time of "mapping in" key sensorimotor skills such as gross motor grasping, eye-hand coordination, and learning all the sensory building blocks necessary as a foundation for survival, further learning, and growth. In addition, touch and the role it plays in establishing the emotional bond between the infant and caretaker assumes a primary role in the building blocks for effective development. Higher-order cognitive capabilities are supported later in the developmental journey.

Bonding, Attachment, and the Development of the Prefrontal Lobe

In earlier chapters, we explored the ways that learning helps the development of neuron connections within the brain. The hardwiring of neuronal connections is what keeps these important newly learned circuits in place. This hardwiring is referred to as *myelination*. Myelin is a white, fatty substance that forms a sheath around nerve fibers as they become reinforced with use—much like a rubber sheath around an electrical wire protects the wire and allows for efficient electrical travel along the wire. Regarding early abilities related to myelination and sound, Pfizer[1] states:

> At first, following your genetic blueprint, your brain makes more neurons and connections than you'll ever need. But it only keeps the ones you use. That's why a variety of experiences is so important for children. Early experience designs your wiring just right for you.
>
> While much of an infant's brain isn't yet wired, the sound areas are already developed at birth. Babies can distinguish all sounds of every known language. But if you grow up hearing only your own language, your brain strengthens those circuits and lets the others go. By the end of your first year, it's harder to recognize differences between sounds of other languages.

YES!

Every day make a high priority of quality, positive interactive time with and for your infant or toddler. Reading and playing together, and talking with your child while he or she is eating, bathing, and so on, will promote emotional well being as well as foster the child's intelligence.

The prefrontal lobe is the result of the longest "journey" of neuron connections and is the last part of the brain to completely develop. According to the work of Joseph Chilton Pearce,[2] Marian Diamond,[3] Allan Schore, and Daniel Siegel, a strong caretaker/child connection is essential, especially during the earliest periods of childhood, for the healthiest and fullest development of the prefrontal lobe. Research by Schore[4] and Siegel[5] has focused on the relationship between bonding, attachment, and brain connections. Their research helps us understand how the process of *attunement* takes attachment to the next level for infants. Attunement refers to a "dialog" between the caretaker and the infant in which the caretaker models and mirrors the newly developing child's emotions. For example, if the child is experiencing frustration or discomfort, the "attuned parent" responds with sympathetic facial expressions and tone of voice. In Siegel's words, attunement occurs when the infant "feels felt." Schore contends that attunement is essential to promoting maximum brain development.

Other Core Developmental Elements

Beyond the development of a child's prefrontal lobe, a number of other important developmental changes take place from birth to age three.

- *Physical development.* Especially during the first months of life, babies are engaged in gross motor activity and orienting themselves to their environment. As they progress into toddlerhood, they learn a broader variety of physical skills, from grasping to walking and running.
- *Emotional bonding.* The emotional need for bonding especially with mother, dad, and other close family members is paramount. Babies have a strong need for love and the ability to trust in their emotional safety.
- *Cognitive skills development.* In terms of brain development, this stage is a sensorimotor, prelogical stage—that means that the child's brain is processing things based strictly on the senses of touch, sight, sound, taste, and smell. A child of this age is emotional, reacting to his or her environment rather than evaluating

the things within it. While the infant and toddler comes to know what he or she likes and dislikes in certain categories, such as food and toys, the child is not yet able to use logical thinking to compare and evaluate them or to be very discerning in choices.

YES!

Your infant and toddler are not capable of making considered, healthy choices. Choose wisely for them by controlling the kinds of foods, beverages, toys, situations, and people they are exposed to.

- *Developing a concept of self/social.* These earliest years are extremely dependent years. In fact, this is a symbiotic period, for the child's ability to differentiate himself or herself as a separate entity from the people and world around him or her forms only toward the latter part of this age period.
- *Ethical/moral values development.* Children of this age are essentially premoral. Without the necessary cognitive ability to distinguish between good or bad and right or wrong, children depend on the ever-present "that's OK" and "no no" training to guide them toward acceptable behavior and away from unacceptable or dangerous activity. Loving interpersonal relationships now, however, will play a role in the child's later development of moral behavior.

What babies and toddlers need most is the satisfaction of very basic physical (food, comfort, rest) and emotional (love, bonding) needs. Beyond this, they need stimulating sensory activity so they can learn effectively and, in turn, develop a love for the learning process.

Given their emotional survival needs and the limited ability to understand and evaluate their surroundings, these very young children are also particularly vulnerable to negative emotions. Children between birth and age three simply don't have the skills necessary to process the anger, fear, sadness, and depression of others. Therefore, if children at this age are exposed to large doses of emotional negativity or if they lack sufficient nurturing human contact, they can suffer ongoing emotional and developmental effects, including a permanent slowing down of some important aspects of brain development.

The Child's Basic Human Needs

Because the satisfaction or frustration of basic human needs is critical to healthy development and personal happiness, we all should be aware of those needs as they apply to children within this age group. In our secondary research efforts over 25 years, we have identified these 10 basic needs shared by all human beings:

1. *Safety.* The need to be and feel safe
2. *Growth.* The need to continue to grow and develop
3. *Physical needs.* The need for basic survival necessities such as shelter, food, and drink. (Beyond these are the needs for well being, such as proper diet and exercise.)
4. *Love.* The need to be and feel loved as well as to grow to love oneself
5. *Acceptance.* The need to be and feel accepted by others and to grow into self-acceptance
6. *Reality.* The need to know what's so in order to be oriented to what's real and what's not
7. *Control.* The need to be able to cause to happen what one needs or wants to happen
8. *Release.* The need to express pent-up emotion
9. *Stimulation.* The need to avoid boredom through experiences
10. *Success.* The need to succeed physically, emotionally, mentally, socially, and ethically

Whether you are 1 month old, 9 years old, or 90, you have these needs pushing and driving your behavior. What's important to note, however, is that the hierarchy or prioritization of one's needs is determined by one's stage and condition of life. It's easy to see, for example, that while a 90-year-old may still need to grow and develop to a degree, a 9-month-old is engaged in a flurry of neuronal growth and learning. (Brain research indicates that despite the loss of billions of neurons by old age, the brain still grows to some extent as it learns new things. In fact, at around the age of 60 the brain generates a special type of glial cell that encourages new circuits to form. These support cells may help your brain compensate for the losses of aging. There's hope for the over-50 crowd!)

DIMENSION TWO: DEVELOPMENTAL BLIND SPOTS

As you learned in Chapter 3, a child's developmental blind spots determine the way the child automatically and instinctively responds to any stimulus, based on developmental capabilities and limitations. Children from birth to age three are especially vulnerable to these three blind spots:

1. *The mind-mapping blind spot.* The infant has no control of the brain-mapping process and will respond to the stimulus input that is provided. This, then, is a primary blind spot. Positive mind mapping is the core responsibility of parents and caretakers. Your child is making a brain map of the world that he or she experiences. Information entering through the senses becomes part of this mind map. This neuron map is extremely critical in early infancy because these important brain connections set the stage for unfolding other skills, abilities, and behavior that follow. Neurons or nerve cells that fire together, wire together. The stronger and more powerful the map is formed, the better the possibility for future development. If the opportunity for successful wiring is missed, interrupted, or diminished through exposure to toxic or harmful environmental influences, it will be difficult, and often impossible, to compensate for this missed opportunity at later stages of life.

2. *The social blind spot.* Children depend on social interactions with nurturers and caretakers. The human brain is a social brain and its neurons are hardwired for the need to touch and be touched. If this sense of positive physical contact is neglected during this age and stage of a child's development, the child could be in danger of suffering from arrested growth and behavior in later stages of life, according to research studies. Media cannot take

YES!

Create the most positive, loving, and learning environment possible for your infant or toddler. Fill his days with fun learning experiences (toys, books, nature walks, new experiences, other kids), loving touches, phrasings ("I love you"), and nurturing care.

the place of the interpersonal dynamic. The child who has more social contact with media than positive human social interactions will pay a price in the way the child's mind map is organized regarding emotional well-being, the ability to communicate, and social skills.

YES!

Maximize loving physical touch through holding, stroking, hugging, playing—while minimizing your child's time with machines and media.

3. *The attention blind spot.* As a parent, it is important to note that attention is one of the first steps in the learning process; whatever grabs or holds your child's attention can quickly be absorbed and stored within his or her newly expanding mind map. The power of a novel attraction for an infant or toddler is sometimes described as the *orienting response* for it orients the child's attention toward a single object of focus. The orienting response occurs quite unconsciously and automatically when the child encounters something new and different, or when the child encounters something that's familiar yet presented in an unexpected way. The key to the attention blind spot is novelty. A curious new kitten following a fly, then veering off after an ant, then turning to chase a piece of yarn being pulled across the floor is a perfect example of how a child's attention blind spot is constantly orienting to anything new or novel in the environment. Television and other media have an unlimited potential for triggering the orienting response in infants and toddlers. You will learn more about

how these developmental blind spots play a role in your child's sitting-duck psychology later in this chapter.

In summary, because of the way that your child's brain is naturally wired, his or her attention will shift to anything in the environment that is novel and different. This new information is being hardwired into your child's mind map. The infant needs love, safety, bonding, attunement, and social contact to form a foundation for healthy development, so parents and caretakers must be sure that what fires together and wires together in their children are loving, nurturing, human interactions and experiences, rather than technological or mechanical actions or events.

DIMENSION THREE: DYNAMICS OF COMMUNICATION

If we follow the progress of a two-year-old's communication and interaction with the world around him or her, including the products and programs that child is exposed to, we can expect to follow the "steps" of the communication model. You'll recall that the communication model follows this path for all children:

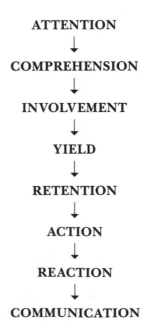

ATTENTION
↓
COMPREHENSION
↓
INVOLVEMENT
↓
YIELD
↓
RETENTION
↓
ACTION
↓
REACTION
↓
COMMUNICATION

The following sections cover each phase of the communication model as it applies to children during these early years.

Attention

As we've established, the birth through two-year-old age segment of a child's development is referred to as the sensorimotor stage. The child's brain at this stage is busy mapping in his environment and all his sensory experiences. His attention is quite local, for it focuses on his immediate surroundings and events ideally populated by multitudes of loving, nurturing moments and lots of stimulating things to see, touch, hear, and explore.

Millions of neuronal connections are being established as the child learns with each experience. At this stage, the child wants to repeat experiences she's already had as well as have new experiences. While we caution against overexposure to too much technology and media—especially for the very young child—certain entertaining media content may also contribute to a toddler's positive development. Just to cite one example, the *Teletubbies* TV program uses the repetition of character behavior to its positive advantage—like showing the characters giggling and falling down and getting up again over and over. When the visual images are positive in their emotional messages and present age-appropriate behavior, children can benefit from this type of repetition for it reinforces what they are learning during their own developmental journey. The Baby Einstein series of videos and DVDs are also watched over and over again by babies and toddlers. They have titles such as *Baby Mozart,*™ *Baby Van Gogh,*™ and *Baby Bach.*™ If you could peek inside your child's brain as she experiences one of these programs, you would see that with each repetition of the musical and visual information, neuronal circuits are reinforced. The visual images and actions on the screen can contribute to your child's mastery of fundamental concepts. While it's not clear just how classical music impacts, the consensus is it soothes and perhaps contributes to emotional well-being. In addition, the nonverbal nature of classical music is devoid of potentially negative concepts and language.

Research on early learning, brain-stimulating products and their effects on babies from birth to approximately eight months indicates that high-contrast visuals and objects can capture a baby's attention and stimulate the brain. Originally, it was thought that red, black, and white patterns on cards or on toys and baby accessories such as crib mobiles were the best approach to this. Now it's generally accepted that any high-contrasting color patterns can stimulate neuron growth, especially in the visual area of the cortex.

Comprehension

While certainly being able to understand basic communications from parents, for example, and while mastering basic levels of speaking and listening, the young child's brain simply doesn't have the tools in place yet to comprehend most complex messages, such as those used in marketing. Although a child of this age cannot translate the intended verbal and conceptual messages of the marketer, the child is, however, absorbing other subliminal parts of the messages. As we have mentioned, comprehension is not essential to effective marketing. A child is constantly engaged in unconscious learning—especially when the information being learned has emotional impact—and this emotional learning often creates far more impact than does cognitive understanding.

Involvement (Valuing/Wanting) and Yielding

By the age of two—and even earlier—children can be very emotional about what they need, want, and don't want. Anyone who has ever tried to feed green beans to a baby who doesn't want green beans knows what we mean. We've all been subjected in a store or restaurant to the eardrum-piercing screams of a toddler who isn't getting what he or she wants. In our communication model, the idea of yielding is the formation of a positive attitude toward a product, brand, program, or character. We recommend that parents be particularly vigilant regarding the tastes, attitudes, and preferences their children are developing.

Retention

As established, the child is an insatiable learner at this early stage of development. The child is going to retain in memory his or her sensory and motor experiences as well as visual and verbal concepts (such as certain brands, product cartoon character icons) and emotional events.

This retention will occur both consciously and unconsciously. Particularly substantial will be the retention of strong emotional experiences.

Action and Reaction

Babies and toddlers don't purchase items themselves. They do, however, take the action of asking for things from their parents. This phenomenon is sometimes referred to as the "nag factor." James McNeal, a pioneer in the arena of marketing to kids, calls it "kidfluence."[6]

As you'll learn later, some direct marketing is aimed at children of this age via, for example, the ads that appear on certain TV programming, such as cartoons. When a two- or three-year-old sees these ads, they may communicate the involvement response of "I like that" and the action response of "I want that."

Identification

Identification is the process by which a child makes a connection—especially emotionally—with a character or person. For the most part, few red flags are hoisted regarding the ways kids of this young age identify. The fact that a two-year-old, for example, starts to identify with and like Mickey Mouse is a natural part of growing up in today's quite entertaining world. If the child then asks for a stuffed Mickey Mouse plush doll at Disneyland, you shouldn't assume that your child has been exploited or exposed to irresponsible marketing.

YES!

With your "Yeses," "Nos," and setting limits, infancy and the toddler years are the perfect time to begin to "train" your children in a healthy and balanced approach to materialism. By standing firmly behind your decisions, often despite your child's strongest objections, you will be establishing important boundaries for the kinds of products and activities to which your child has access.

It is clear, however, that conditioning is occurring along with iden-tification. Although they are virtually impossible to avoid, parents need to be clear about the messages that are embedded in the objects of iden-tification. It's also up to the parents of that two-year-old to say "Yes" or "No" to that stuffed Mickey—and to all other requests—in an effort to nurture the child by training him in a balanced approach to consumer-ism and materialism. A "spoiled child" is definitely one who is too often said "Yes" to—or worse, one who learns to throw tantrums and who is appeased with parents caving in.

MARKETING MESSAGES, SCREEN TIME, AND SITTING-DUCK PSYCHOLOGY

As you learned in Chapter 3, a child's brain and other core develop-mental elements give rise to what we term *sitting-duck psychology*. A child who hasn't yet developed the capability to defend himself or herself from a barrage of marketing messages is a sitting duck for whatever mes-sage or influence is encountered.

Keeping in mind this factor and the three developmental dimen-sions we've just discussed for children from birth to age three, parents and caretakers can assess all the messages that are being communicated to their infants and toddlers through television and other means. The following sections discuss products, programming, marketing, and mes-sage techniques and explore their impact on this age group. By under-standing this influence, caretakers can better meet their responsibility for managing their baby's and toddler's time so that TV and other tech exposure plays only a small part of the child's busy learning and discov-ering day. Caretakers will then be better prepared to say "No" to little Johnny's and Jessica's requests when it's in their child's best interest.

The Toddler's Relationship with Brands

Toddler's brains are not yet developed enough to clearly compre-hend advertising messages. While it's true that brand icons, characters, and images may attract these little ones, this early exposure constitutes direct marketing to this age group only in a limited way. Some of this exposure may form early brand awareness that later leads to brand preference, but this is not typically the result of a direct-marketing effort.

Nevertheless, children as young as six months are the target of some marketing efforts, both direct and indirect. In an article entitled "Designing Valued Relationships between Kids and Their Brands,"[7] Bill Goodwin talks about how kids start relating to brands:

> Kids' relationships with brands begin at a very early age. At six months of age, babies begin to recognize brands by forming mental images of corporate logos and mascots.
>
> Brand loyalty may begin as early as age two. By age three, one out of five American children makes specific requests for brand-name products.
>
> The desired perception is "This brand is for ME!"
>
> By age five, children are ready to make their own (parent-financed) purchases. By age seven, they are totally in control. With this control comes power—a power to make their own decisions. Add the complexities in a seven-year-old and older child's life . . . and prepare yourself for potentially turbulent brand relationships.

PROGRAMS FOR CHILDREN FROM BIRTH TO AGE THREE

One would be hard-pressed to find many cases of marketing that promotes products or programs that can be classified as inherently dangerous to this age group. First of all, the vast majority of the products and programs companies are attempting to sell for this age are not marketed to kids at all; they are marketed to mothers. In addition, these products and programs are, for the most part, healthy, wholesome items that contribute to the positive development of babies and toddlers. They include such items as healthy food and beverages, early learning toys such as blocks and stacking toys, early reader books, products and programs designed for brain stimulation, room decor items and accessories, strollers, baby safety products, and apparel.

> **YES!**
>
> Guide your child toward valuing items and experiences that are the most enriching. This guidance is provided through your "Yeses" and "Nos," as well as through your conscious efforts to surround your child with positive experiences.

Even though marketers don't typically target infants and toddlers directly, this doesn't mean that these very young children don't consume unhealthy products or that they aren't exposed to harmful programs. Far too many infants and toddlers, for example, are initiated into a diet of french fries, soft drinks, candy, and sugary cereals by the age of three. By contrast, healthy food and beverage consumption during these early years can become the foundation for healthy eating and drinking habits later on. Parents can also influence their children's eating habits by modeling healthy consumption in their own diets.

> **YES!**
>
> Give your infant to three-year-old a healthy head start in life by providing the healthiest food and beverages possible and the most nurturing media experiences. Remember, your own dietary choices are setting the example for your child's future dietary behavior.

Technology and the Impact of Screen Time on Babies and Toddlers

Much like the damage caused by secondhand smoke, very young children's exposure to negative programming such as loud and nerve-grating music, and TV and video game violence can only result in harmful impact. There is some basis for the concern that manufacturers are beginning to technologize our babies via a whole host of tech toys and early learning software. As we mentioned earlier, technology becomes an issue when children are immersed in screens (computers and TV) that are used as *substitute forms of reality* and that take the place of real play and interactive communication with loving parents and caretakers.

Some baby development experts are antitechnology of any kind for children of this age or stage of development. They argue that children of this age are too young for tech exposure and instead need lots and lots of social interaction and free play. The healthy growth and development of the whole child is most critical according to these experts, and very young children who are overly technologized can suffer from a variety of negative effects, including stress, frustration, and the less tangible absence of human interaction.

While we believe that allowing absolutely no tech exposure for children within the birth to age three range is carrying this precaution too far, there is definitely reason for caution when the *newborn* is taken into consideration. We agree with Dr. Penelope Leach who says in her book, *Babyhood: Stage by Stage from Birth to Age Two: How Your Baby Develops Physically, Mentally and Emotionally*: ". . . an infant needs what it is hardest to give him. Calm. His physiological needs are few, simple, and repetitive. He needs food, warmth, tactile comfort, and a modicum of cleanliness. . . . Everything needs to be done for him as gently, as calmly, and as slowly as possible."[8] The noise and visual information produced by technology and electronic media can offer precisely the opposite atmosphere, overloading the newborn's sensibilities. A great rule of thumb is to never force a baby or toddler to engage in activities he doesn't relate to, is not interested in, or gets tired of. The child will typically let you know when he or she is not appropriately involved in an activity. Be careful, however, of the child's "orienting response" and what the child is paying attention to.

Children learn by interaction with their environment. The ideal environment for maximum growth and development includes safe settings with lots of appropriate opportunities to interact with toys, books, other kids, adults, animals, nature—and limited forms of supervised and positive media. When indications are that the majority of children under six years are spending around two hours a day in front of TV, video game, and computer screens, and a great many of them have TVs in their bedrooms, there is definite cause for concern.

Barbara Meltz of the *Boston Globe* in an article aptly titled, "With TV So Loud, No One Is Listening," cites research and evidence that indicates that screen time for children—even if it involves "educational" programs or technologies—may do more harm than good.[9]

"It threatens to erode aspects of childhood that are crucial to social, emotional, and cognitive development," says Temple University psychologist Kathy Hirsh-Pasek. She is the author of *Einstein Never Used Flash Cards: How Our Children REALLY Learn*[10]

The downside of increasing screen time—especially for the very young child—is that the neuronal circuits responsible for social interaction and deductive reasoning get short changed. "Those circuits are stimulated by direct interpersonal connections with parents and the environment: eye contact, gesture, responsiveness, trial and error," according to Jane Healy, author of *Failure to Connect, How Computers Affect Our Children's Minds*[11] As a result, these children become passive learners who must depend on television or computer screens or other sources of spoon-fed information for any type of intellectual stimulation. This type of individual won't develop the cognitive skills necessary for solving problems or coming up with innovative ideas.

Meltz also reported on a variety of related problems associated with excessive TV viewing at a young age, including becoming dependent on "canned" entertainment rather than learning to entertain themselves, shortened attention spans, and secondhand exposure, which can contribute to increased irritability and aggression.

No one may know the definitive impact of this trend toward increased screen time for children yet because studies have not been completed. We believe that limited forms of technology, if properly used as part of a child's *balanced* routine that includes free play, social bonding, love, and plenty of healthy human interaction, could enhance a child's growth and development. A supply of healthy technology exposure for toddlers might include limited viewing of positive TV such as *Barney & Friends, Teletubbies, Dora the Explorer,* and *Jay Jay, the Jet Plane* and perhaps very limited time with toddler-oriented computer learning software. It might also include certain tech learning "toys" such as Leapfrog that the child is most likely to self-regulate. These are our views, but remember: the jury is still out on the subject of how much infants and toddlers should be exposed to television and technology.

Without question, however, time spent passively in front of the TV cannot accomplish what free and interactive play and exploration accomplishes, and takes time away from loving, emotionally bonding experiences with parents, other caretakers, and siblings. At the least, more tech time means less reading time, and studies abound that point to the benefits of reading to infants and toddlers both for the development of the imagination and for the development of cognitive/thinking skills.

As we've discussed in earlier sections of this chapter, healthy emotional, cognitive, and other core developmental elements are essentially an "interactive dance" that demands strong human commitment and contact. By regulating the emotional bond, the caretaker is also regulating the release of essential hormones in the child's brain that are critical to maximize neurological connections. Children raised with strong daily dosages of media will be handicapped in important ways compared to children raised in nontech and low-tech environments, and they may suffer from excessive IIIO.

YES!

Minimize screen time overall—no more than one hour a day—and carefully select the media content you *do* expose your child to. Better to opt for minimal tech time for your infants and toddlers rather than succumb to the temptation of using technology as a babysitter.

We believe that ongoing studies using brain-imaging techniques will clearly show the advantages of raising children in a low-tech environment that is filled with positive emotional dynamics between parent and child.

KEY VULNERABILITIES OF
INFANTS AND TODDLERS

Much of this chapter has been devoted to analyzing the developmental dimensions of children in the years from birth to age three. In play with each of these dimensions is the child's age and stage-related vulnerabilities. Here are the key vulnerabilities of children in this age group.

- *They are dependent.* More than any other stage, the infant, toddler, and child up to age three is extremely dependent on his parents for all of his needs—in particular, his physical, safety, and love needs. Patterns of emotional stability, types of food and beverage preferences, and allowed entertainment experiences begin here.

- *They have limited comprehension.* Because their left-brain dominant rational capabilities have yet to form, children of this age cannot understand logic-based, complex, or abstract communications. They tend to believe what they see or hear.

- *They are emotional.* This stage is marked by emotionality. Without developed rational abilities, the infant to three-year-old uses his emotions to survive and get what he wants and needs. Emotional memories are powerful and formative at this early age. Scary things, upsets, or trauma can leave lasting impressions. Quiet time is valuable at this age. TV and other screen-time activities are no emotional substitutes for strong, positive bonding and loving interaction. In addition, the foundations for the formation of relative inner tranquility and emotional safety occur during this stage—or its opposite, the beginnings of emotional insecurity and stress.

- *They are nonethical.* Children this young do not yet have the capacity to understand the ethical foundations of right from wrong or distinguish good from bad on their own. They need to be guided and told what's right or wrong and good or bad. This is not to say you shouldn't explain these issues; just don't expect young children to fully comprehend them.

A WEEK IN THE LIFE OF A TODDLER

By way of summary, let's look at a week in the life of a hypothetical two-and-a-half-year-old to provide some guidelines for what would be positively empowering in her life. In our example, we call the toddler Joanie:

EXPERIENCE	EMPOWERING	DISEMPOWERING
Parents/ Home Life	Joanie's mom made the choice to quit work for four years to stay at home with Joanie and her older brother, Mikey, who is five. She has positive and loving interactions with Joanie each day, playing with her, reading to her, taking her to the park and on walks. Each Tuesday, mom takes a "day off" and brings Joanie and Mikey to a day care facility where they have fun interacting with the other kids. Dad also enjoys his special times with Joanie and Mikey after work and on weekends.	During the workweek, Joanie's mom drops her off at a day care facility and her brother at pre-school. Joanie interacts with the other kids, but misses her mom. Mom tries to make up for it on her weekend with the kids, but is too tired to organize many outings that include exercise. Children of an early divorce, Joanie and Mikey spend every other week-end with their dad who isn't very knowledgeable about children's needs and little quality dad/child time together is the result. Dad pretty much just buys them things to keep them occupied.
Friends	Knowing that interaction with other little ones her age will help Joanie's social development, Joanie's mother makes sure they have regular visit times each week with her friends and their children.	Contact with little friends Joanie's age outside her preschool is occasional but not consciously planned.

EXPERIENCE	EMPOWERING	DISEMPOWERING
Toys/Electronic Games	Joanie has a moderate amount of toys, from plush animals on her bed to lots of books, fun learning puzzles, and baby dolls. There are no electronic games allowed yet for either Joanie or Mikey.	Joanie and Mikey have tons of toys and they are perpetually scattered about their room. Mikey has a Nintendo set that he shares with his dad. Both Joanie and Mikey are exposed to some of the fast-action and combat games their dad plays.
Learning Hardware & Software	None except for a couple of electronic toys that make music and assist with the early learning of colors and shapes.	Joanie's dad bought her a learning-type computer toy and even though she doesn't naturally have much interest in it, he sits with her in front of it for about 30 minutes and insists that she "play with it."
Room Décor	Joanie has her own room decorated with soft and childhood themes such as Strawberry Shortcake and Disney characters like Winnie the Pooh.	Joanie has her own room when she's with her mom. It's relatively bare-walled and devoid of any themes. When she's with her dad she has to share a room with her brother and it's decked out in a Power Rangers theme.
Television/ Film	Joanie is allowed to watch one half-hour show every day during the week on the family TV. She has no TV in her room. She can choose between three preapproved shows.	Joanie watches as much TV as she wants between the morning hours and eight PM. She has a TV in her room with Mikey and he has it on all the time. They have a VCR also and a stack of videos. Average hours in front of the TV is 25 to 30 per week.

EXPERIENCE	EMPOWERING	DISEMPOWERING
Television/ Film (cont.)	On Saturday morning, she is allowed to watch one hour of TV and none on Sunday, which is "family day."	On weekends, dad rents movies, some of which are appropriate for Joanie and Mikey, and some that aren't. Joanie cruises in and out and watches them as she pleases.
Food and Beverage	Joanie's parents are careful to prepare only the healthiest food for her at home. When they go out, there's only the occasional fast-food purchase, and then mom and dad avoid fries and sugary drinks and treats as much as possible. Mom packs Joanie and Mikey a healthy lunch on Tuesdays when they're at day care.	Because of mom's work schedule, she stocks the fridge with frozen dinners and lots of snack food. Twice a week, she brings home fast food. Weekends with dad are worse, with sugary cold cereal for breakfast, peanut butter-and-jelly sandwiches for lunch, and fast food for dinner. Mikey is already ten pounds overweight.
Music and Radio	Joanie's mom, believing in the potential positive influence of classical music on children's development, often has it playing in the background during the day. She has also purchased a variety of kid song audiotapes and sings along with Joanie and Mikey.	At mom's house, nobody listens to music or the radio. The TV is almost always on. At dad's house, he often plays hard rock and jazz music very loud.
Publications/ Books	Joanie's mom and dad have both read to her from picture books ever since she was about six months old.	There's one or two picture books in Joanie's room and when she asks her mom to read them, her mom sometimes does.

PARENT AND CARETAKER TOOLBOX
FOR YOUTH ENRICHMENT STRATEGIES

Here is our toolbox of key dos and don'ts for parents and other care-takers to help serve as good gatekeepers for the children in the birth to age three group. You've seen these Youth Enrichment Strategies through-out the chapter, but we've gathered them here to give you easy and im-mediate access to our recommendations. To help guide these infants and toddlers in their healthy consumption of and exposure to products, pro-grams, and advertising, follow these recommendations.

- Every day make a high priority of quality, positive interactive time with and for your infant or toddler. Reading and playing together, and lots of talking with your child while he's eating, bathing, and so on, will promote his emotional well-being as well as foster the child's intelligence.
- Your infant or toddler cannot make considered, healthy choices. Choose wisely for her by controlling the kinds of foods, beverages, toys, situations, and people she is exposed to.
- Create the most positive, loving, and learning environment possi-ble for your infant or toddler. Fill his days with fun learning expe-riences (toys, books, nature walks, new experiences, other kids), loving touches, phrasings ("I love you"), and nurturing care.
- Maximize loving physical touch through holding, stroking, hug-ging, playing—while minimizing your child's time with machines and media.
- With your "Yeses," "Nos," and setting limits, infancy and the tod-dler years are the perfect time to begin to "train" your children in a healthy and balanced approach to materialism. By standing firmly behind your decisions, often despite your child's strongest objections, you will be establishing important boundaries for the kinds of products and activities to which your child has access.
- Guide your child toward valuing items and experiences that are the most enriching. This guidance is provided through your "Yeses" and "Nos," as well as your conscious efforts to surround your child with positive experiences.
- Give your infant to three-year-old a healthy head start in life by providing the healthiest food and beverages possible and the

most nurturing media experiences. Remember, your own dietary choices are setting the example for your child's future dietary behavior.

- Minimize screen time overall—no more than one hour a day—and carefully select the media content you *do* expose your child to. Better to opt for minimal tech time for your infant or toddler rather than to succumb to the temptation of using technology as a babysitter.

MOVING ON TO AGES THREE TO SEVEN

The developmental stage of birth to the age of three is a critical formative period marked by the child's needs for love, bonding, and emotional safety. Fortunately, children within this age group aren't subjected to as much direct marketing as are those from age three and up. The world is filled with not only great varieties of positive products and programming, but also with numerous potential product and program land mines for these older children. Step carefully, kids, we're off to see the marketing wizards who target three- to seven-year-olds.

The birth of every new baby is God's vote
of confidence in the future of man.
Imogene Fey

5

THE IMPRESSIONABLE YEARS
Ages Three to Seven

*"I'll tell you what, husband," answered the woman, "early tomorrow
morning we will take the children out into the forest to where it is the thickest;
there we will light a fire for them, and give each of them one more
piece of bread, and then we will go to our work and leave them alone.
They will not find the way home again, and we shall be rid of them."*

Hansel and Gretel's mother

Fairy tale lore is chock full of examples of stories meant to put the fear of God into little ones during these most impressionable years. It was no accident that Hansel and Gretel got thrown out of their house by a selfish mother as their weakling father stood by, were lured into a candy-coated hut in the forest, and almost got eaten by a witch. Humpty Dumpty broke in a fall and couldn't be fixed, two of the stupid little pigs and Little Red's grandmamma were eaten, Mary lost her lamb, and naughty little Jack had to sit in a corner. Even to this day, many adults, like many fire-and-brimstone religions, use fear and guilt as methods of control.

Bruno Bettelheim in his classic book, *The Uses of Enchantment*,[1] suggests that perhaps children need violent or scary imagery to learn and that's why so many fairy tales are filled with frightening and violent content. While it appears to be true that children—and all of us—learn some things more effectively when negative emotions such as fear are part of the experience, that doesn't mean that fear is the most effective motivator for learning. And using fear as a learning tool is certainly not the most loving and emotionally supportive approach to child rearing. Throughout time, people have chosen fear as an instructional tool, however, because it is most effective with those individuals who are most vulnerable. In a very real sense, far too many of our most innocent and vulnerable children—like Hansel and Gretel—are "left alone" to emotionally fend for themselves as they attempt to sort out a world filled with mixed messages of love and hate, innocence and sexuality, peace and violence.

No other stage of development is marked by such psychological vulnerability as those years between the ages of three and seven. A child's abilities to think logically and to reason begin their most focused development only at the later period of this age group; therefore, children during the majority of this stage are open to believe just about everything that is presented to them and are vulnerable to all experience. When it comes to marketing to your three- to seven-year-olds, they are in many ways the most vulnerable sitting ducks.

In this chapter, we outline the three dimensions of development for children between the ages of three and seven, and we explore each step of the communications model for children in this age group. Then, we offer specific descriptions of good, neutral, and inherently dangerous products and programs your children will encounter at this important age and stage of their development. Along the way, our Youth Enrichment Strategies (YES!) will provide you with specific ideas and techniques for guiding your children toward the types of toys, games, and other items that will help nurture healthy emotional, physical, and psychological growth and avoid potentially dangerous pitfalls.

DIMENSION ONE: DEVELOPMENTAL ELEMENTS

Anyone who has spent much time around children knows there are huge differences between a three- or four-year-old and a six- or seven-year-old. There is one key similarity, however, and it's the reason we classify three- to seven-year-olds into one age segment: In children of both age groups, logical, more left brain–based reasoning capacities have not yet fully matured. This three- to seven-year-old stage of development is often referred to as the "fantasy stage." Your child's "right brain" is on the front burner of development during these years, for it controls such important abilities as imagination, creativity, nonlinear thinking, and visualization. While some precocious six- and seven-year-olds may show signs of rather highly developed logic abilities, the majority of children in this age group are smack-dab in the middle of the fantasy period.

Their day-to-day world is filled with discovery and learning with each new and repeated experience.

If you could see into the brains of children in this age group, you'd see the neuronal synapses firing away like crazy. The trillions of neurons they were born with (they developed about 250,000 a minute during the 9-month gestation period) get a workout during these years. Many of these neurons—the ones important to survival functions such as breathing, hunger responses, and the like—are hardwired at or shortly after birth. The remaining trillions are ready for action—the action of learning. With each new experience, millions if not billions of neurons fire away and, as we've mentioned in earlier chapters, neurons that fire together, wire together. Through this action, the brain develops memories of both events and emotions.

Dr. Joe Carver explains emotional memory this way: "Much like a modern day computer, the brain stores memories in a system of files. In a manner that is still partially unknown, the brain has the ability to store not only memories but emotions—as they occurred at the time the memory was made. Memory files thus contain two parts, the information about the event and the feeling we had at the time of the event. Graphically put: Memory file = Information + Feelings at the time."[2]

Why is this understanding of emotional memory important for our exploration of the impact of potentially harmful products or marketing to children—particularly to children below the age of seven? Because they, more than adults, are dominated by emotion. These children have far less command of the logic, discernment, or problem-solving skills necessary for understanding and filtering incoming information. The experiences, products, and marketing messages your children are exposed to at this age directly constitute learning. The more those experiences and exposures are repeated, the stronger their influence becomes. The ideas and experiences your child is exposed to during this stage of his or her brain development will be filed in an "emotional memory" bank and could have long-reaching impact on your child's beliefs, habits, and behavior.

> ## YES!
>
> Be hyperalert to those occasions when your three- to seven-year-old is exposed to or engaged in negative emotionality at home, in school, or through the media. Whenever possible, eliminate or lessen the extent of this exposure; and always be sure to communicate simply and completely with your child, to help guide him or her through any negative experience.

Core Developmental Elements for This Age Group

In addition to the development of "right-brain" abilities and emotional memory, children within the age range of three to seven share these core developmental capabilities, experiences, and limitations.

- *Physical.* Gross and fine motor skills and capabilities are fast developing during this stage. It's one of the most active physical periods of childhood, with a constant dance of activities such as running, skipping, hopping about, tumbling, riding play vehicles, squirming in one's seat, and learning sports. Not only are these activities critical to the healthy physical development of the three- to seven-year-old, they also involve interactive play with others, which promotes the child's healthy social development.
- *Emotional.* This is perhaps the most highly emotional period of development (although many parents of teenagers might disagree). Because she is learning so many social-interactive lessons, and because her rational mind hasn't fully developed, the three- to seven-year-old wears her emotions on her sleeve. If she's happy, you'll know it, and if she's upset or frustrated, you'll know that, too. Part of the emotionality of this stage comes from this child's need for autonomy; she's trying to establish some sense of her own independence and thus can challenge the rules and restrictions laid down for her.
- *Cognitive.* We've discussed this age group's lack of rational, logical capability, a developmental state known as *prelogical.* Children in this age group are also *preoperational*—meaning that they haven't

yet developed key cognitive abilities. For example, the preoperational child can't grasp the notion of volume in liquids. When
asked which glass has the most water in it, he will invariably point
to the taller glass rather than a shorter but wider glass with more
volume. This can be called *black-and-white* thinking, because it is
unsophisticated and operates strictly on the surface of the reasoning faculty. Especially when at the younger end of this three- to
seven-year-old age group, children also are highly intuitional and
imaginative. Because children lack logical skills during this phase,
anything goes—a stick can become a sword, short tree branches
can become wings, and a superhero really does have the power to
leap tall buildings or shoot spider webs out of his wrists.

- *Self/social.* Regarding her developing sense of herself as an individual, the three- to seven-year-old is busy separating herself and
gaining autonomy as much as authority allows. This is a period of
impulsivity and self-centeredness—as it should be. The three- to
seven-year-old is learning how to take the interests of others into
account, but doesn't have most of the brain tools yet in place to
do so. This age range also is very much an "It's all about me" period. By the age of two or three, the child knows his or her gender
and is busy being taught and learning all the attitudes and behavior that gender implies.

- *Ethical/moral.* As with the previous age group, children between
the ages of three and seven are essentially premoral. Without the
necessary cognitive abilities to distinguish between good or bad
and right or wrong, children depend on being trained into acceptable behavior and away from unacceptable or dangerous activity.

- *Transpersonal.* Transpersonal capabilities or experiences refer to
those that demonstrate an ability to go beyond—or transcend—the
personal. Children at this age and stage are narcissistic, seeing the
world as a tiny sphere that revolves around their existence and
needs. These children have a very limited concept of the world
and have not developed the ability to entertain ideas beyond the
self, such as abstract conceptual spiritual notions.

The Prioritization of Needs

Needs prioritization is the final developmental element we must consider for this group. Many of the ten needs we outlined for infants to three-year-olds also apply to children in the three- to seven-year-old age group. Here is the needs prioritization for this age group.

1. *Love.* Study after study shows the critical importance of a child receiving lots of positive physical and emotional strokes and attention at this early stage. Starting even before birth and extending into the early years of a child's life, the healthiest parent-child relationship is one of consistent experiences of love and emotional bonding.

2. *Stimulation.* A bored child is an unhappy child. Because of the child's intense need to learn at this stage, both new and repetitious experiences are extremely important to him. Related to this need for stimulation is the child's desire for yummy sensations through food and beverage—especially those that are sweet or otherwise pleasurable. By the end of the third year of life, most children in the developed world have come to trust that their basic physical needs of food and drink will be supplied, so "treats" beyond the basics are perceived as tasty and fun.

3. *Growth.* Directly related to the need for stimulation is the child's need for growth and success. Learning is an extremely high priority at this stage.

4. *Safety.* Children need a high degree of safety at this age. A child who feels unsafe—either physically or emotionally—cannot be fully free to learn.

5. *Reality.* Very important to this stage of development is the need for things in the child's real environment to be predictable and stable. This stable reality serves as a base for growth, with healthy forms of slight unpredictable change serving to challenge the capacities for learning.

6. *Control.* Beginning with what many refer to as "the terrible twos," children begin to "test" parental limits in their pursuit of becoming more independent. This testing is a normal part of healthy development so long as it occurs within loving and safe boundaries.

7. *Release.* With the often intense emotionality that is characteristic of this age range, and without reasoning skills in place, the three- to seven-year-old needs to be able to—and typically is quite proficient at—letting out pent-up emotions. In fact, children in this age group most often express emotions immediately, through crying, bursts of temper, playful activities, and laughter.

YES!

Love, emotional safety, and stimulating learning experiences are key to early positive development, well being, and happiness. Fill your three- to seven-year-old's days with lots of positive, loving interaction and stimulating learning experiences, including free play indoors and outdoors, and creative activities such as art and music. Include quiet time as well, for such things as reading and walks.

Based on this set of needs, it's easy to gauge the priorities of children in this age group and to predict what they are most likely to pay attention to. Little Johnnie and Jessica need and want to feel safe (safety) and have things be predictable (reality) while they get lots of attention (love) and have lots of experiences (stimulation, growth, success). They need to gain a degree of independence (control), and when frustrated or hurt they need to be allowed to let out their emotions (release) in acceptable ways.

DIMENSION TWO: DEVELOPMENTAL BLIND SPOTS

With the preceding developmental elements in mind for the three- to seven-year-olds, we turn to their developmental blind spots. By becoming aware of these developmental "defaults," we can better understand the key vulnerabilities of children in this age group, and how those vulnerabilities make them sitting ducks for products, programs, marketing messages, and other information targeted to influence and persuade them.

The following sections describe three key blind spots for children in this stage of development. As we proceed through each new developmental age and stage, keep in mind that the previous set of developmental blind spots are still in place, creating a cumulative set of vulnerabilities as we continue through the teen years.

The *Bipolar* Blind Spot

Children at this stage of development polarize or "split" information into simple black-and-white categories and cannot integrate or process information that falls into "gray" areas of reasoning. For example, the concept of good guys and bad guys makes great sense for the preoperational child. A character who is both good and bad, or who has more subtle qualities of both goodness and negativity, however, is problematic for this age and stage. (Unfortunately, some adults fail to grow past this immature stage of development in their own thinking process, and feel most comfortable clinging to these simple black-and-white categories of reasoning.)

YES!

Before your child reaches the age of five, begin introducing her to "shades of gray," for example, by asking the question "Why?" Even though dealing with subtle areas of reasoning may be difficult for your child, learning to do so is critical for the development of higher-level thinking capabilities. Speak in simple and concrete terms at first, but constantly try to expand your child's range of thinking. This core skill will help your child become more discerning about advertising and marketing messages, especially those designed to manipulate more simple thinking processes.

The *Thinking/Feeling* Blind Spot

This developmental blind spot reflects the brain's unique system for coding incoming information. Thinking contains an emotional component and is inextricably linked to the feeling dimension, just as emotion can contain a thinking and/or meaning component. This neurological "bond" raises serious implications for your child's vulnerability to emotion-laden programs, products, marketing, and advertising. Your four-year-old, for example, just happens to be in the room when his older sibling is watching a horror movie or violent cop show. Perhaps a six-year-old sees an ad for a particularly violent video game. The emotions that are associated with the product or program will be accompanied by the unique set of thoughts and ideas this child is capable of at the child's level of cognitive development. Given the child's developmental limitations, such exposure could result in confusion or an unpredictably negative impact.

The *Immersion* Blind Spot

This blind spot is directly related to a process mentioned previously: *downshifting*. When a child is overwhelmed with sensory and emotional stimuli, he or she often becomes immersed in the compelling emotional aspects of the stimuli that are driving the attention default.

YES!

Avoid allowing your child to become immersed in powerful, potentially negative entertainment experiences such as films or television programs laden with violence and negative emotional content.

Where downshifting is the brain *process* that occurs, immersion is the *response* to this brain process. During immersion, the cognitive or thinking part of the brain is rendered less effective, or in a sense "put on hold." Some video games, for example, are designed to first downshift the player into a powerful emotional state by encouraging that individual to identify with the game's characters, content, and actions. As the identification occurs, the player becomes more "immersed" in this emotionally gratifying fantasy, which often leads to hours and hours of playing time. To cite another example, some films immerse the child in

20 or 30 minutes of fear-inducing negative images, accompanied by music and special effects that add even more impact to the message. The implication of this age group's immersion blind spot is that the emotions associated with these experiences are being coded and stored in memory, devoid of reasoning or a thinking component that can counter any negative or age-inappropriate images and messages. The child is vulnerable to these emotional messages and may store in memory any emotional reactions to them.

DIMENSION THREE: DYNAMICS OF COMMUNICATION

We've looked at the communication model in earlier chapters of this book. A step-by-step examination of this model tells us about the way three- to seven-year-olds process product, marketing, and program messages.

Attention

Three- to seven-year-olds—like all of us—are going to pay attention to what they need, want, and like. The motivation toward paying attention to X stimulus rather than Y is based on X having the potential to satisfy some basic need or desire (even if that desire has been "manufactured" and incorporated into the child's memory bank). Children within this age range will attend to almost anything placed in front of them—especially if it's something they've not experienced before. As they have been since birth, children in this age group are "learning machines," hardwired to explore and learn. A key difference at this stage, however, is their ability to sustain attention for longer periods.

Comprehension

Children between the ages of three and seven are not yet able to comprehend information as fully as older children. They simply do not have sufficient cognitive reasoning tools in place to be able to comprehend complicated or abstract messages and communications.

Children of this age typically cannot understand communications that are beyond their experience or are too abstract, nor can they fully discriminate between reality and fantasy. As a result, they are particularly vulnerable to experiencing as real the events, messages, visuals, attitudes, and behavior portrayed in the media. Children in this age group learn from everything they experience, even when they can't accurately comprehend the full meaning of the experience. For example, when children of this age are exposed to products and programs associated with aggressive, violent, or other age-inappropriate content, they will be affected by the themes, messages, and behavior being conveyed, even though they don't fully comprehend their meanings.

Involvement and Retention

The involvement communication dynamic involves wanting, and at this stage of development, when cognitive discrimination tools are not yet in place, your three- to seven-year-olds want just about anything and everything that has a modicum of appeal. Watch a three- or five-year-old with mom at the grocery store and you'll see the child reaching out to touch, experience, and ask for a variety of colorful and enticing food and beverage items, typically packaged in colorful and entertaining ways, complete with bright, eye-catching symbols and entertaining characters.

In general my children refuse to eat anything that hasn't danced on television.
Erma Bombeck

Because learning of both a cognitive and emotional nature is particularly intense during this period, the three- to seven-year-old is highly impressionable and will retain a great deal of what he or she experiences.

Action

Remember, by "action" we mean either the action of purchase or the act of asking for something. Children in the three- to seven-year-old age range have limited amounts of their own money to spend, so throughout most of this stage children are limited to asking for things. The "nag factor," which may have begun in the earlier age range, is the name of the game during these years. Marketing for children in the three- to seven-year-old age range is targeted toward getting them to ask for the items being promoted.

In particular, the three- to seven-year-old age range is the prime target for toy advertising. Watch most cartoon shows and you'll typically see a proliferation of toy ads promoting everything from trucks that transform into monsters to dolls that wet themselves and burp to megasquirt rifles and video games. Because the typical three- to seven-year-old only participates in small self purchases, and because mothers generally make the purchase decisions for this age group, marketers also frequently target mothers through TV ads during kiddie-type programming and print ads in parenting magazines. These types of advertisements usually don't offer harmful messages to either parent or child, as long as the product is age-appropriate and there is no deception or emotional manipulation involved.

Reaction

In our communication model, "reaction" has two meanings. The first meaning relates to the way the consumer child feels about the product or program or commercial just experienced. The child's reaction might be positive, negative, or totally unconcerned. Because of developmental defaults present at this stage, the child's reaction may be either overt or below her awareness.

The second meaning is related to the child's consumer behavior after the experience. Will the child ask to have another such experience? Will the child re-act?

Communication

The absolute best result that any marketer wants is for consumers to be so satisfied and happy with his or her product that they will form a positive attitude toward it and ideally even go so far as tell others about it. If it's a consumable item, the marketer wants repeat purchase. Three to seven-year-olds' social development in this regard, however, is yet to develop fully. At this stage of their development, children don't typically care if anyone else has one of the products or programs they use.

Because of their cognitive stage of development, three- to seven-year-olds live for the most part in the here and now. This means they don't spend time thinking about the next purchasing or use event. When they are again presented with a product, they may ask for it—especially if their previous experience was a satisfying one. As children reach the upper stages of this age range (around age six), their here-and-now orientation begins to shift toward the ability to think of the future and to think of sharing with others.

GOOD PRODUCT AND PROGRAM CHOICES FOR THREE- TO SEVEN-YEAR-OLDS

Parents and all child caretakers must carefully and critically examine the products, programs, and marketing messages that bombard their young daily. This watchfulness is key to separating the products and programs that are good for children from those that need monitoring and those that are inherently dangerous and must be avoided.

Many products and programs for the three- to seven-year-old, of course, provide important learning opportunities and healthy entertainment. Books are at the top of the list, whether they are being read to or by the child. Both picture books and nonpicture books encourage children to use their imaginations. Throughout this age range, books and healthy magazines represent great bonding and learning opportunities; even though most six- and seven-year-olds read for themselves, many love to be read to from time to time.

YES!

Educate yourself through parent magazines, books, and the Internet about age-appropriate, growth-producing products and programs for your three- to seven-year-old. Some recommended magazines include *Parents, Parents Talk, Family Fun,* and *Fathering Magazine.*

Toys and games that are devoid of violent conflict are also healthy choices. Beyond obvious entertainment value, play with toys can produce a variety of learning experiences, including dexterity and problem-solving skills, and an increase in imagination. A variety of sources are available to discover which toys are highest in play and learning value. We recommend http://www.worldsbesttoys.com and Dr. Stevanne Auerbach's Web site at http://www.drtoy.com.

In addition to publications and toys, a variety of learning software products are in the marketplace that—in limited use—could provide healthy child involvement. Other healthy product and program categories include carefully selected and limited TV programming, some PG feature films, school supplies, personal hygiene items, and sports equipment.

PRODUCTS AND PROGRAMS IN NEED OF MONITORING FOR THIS AGE GROUP

The following categories of products and programs include those that require careful monitoring by parents and other caretakers. As we've previously described, these neutral products can be healthy and empowering when used appropriately and in the right quantities. But your three- to seven-year-old, however, should not be allowed uncontrolled and unmonitored access to any of these items.

Food and Beverages

Given the reality of major increases in childhood obesity, diabetes, and ADHD (Attention Deficit and Hyperactivity Disorder), parents and caretakers must be especially cautious about monitoring the food and beverages consumed by children. Children in the three- to seven-year-old age range have particular vulnerabilities when it comes to making food choices. Their cognitive skills aren't advanced enough to help them choose healthy food, and they are particularly prone to preferring pleasure food and drink and to modeling the behavior of others. Without good guidance and positive models, children in this age group are likely to suffer symptoms related to poor nutrition as well as to develop dangerously poor eating habits.

Managing food choices. While certainly the three- to seven-year-old will have his preferences about which cereal to eat, which peanut butter he likes, which soft drink or fruit juice or snack food item should go into the grocery cart, it really is not his place to have total freedom to choose whatever he likes. "If I don't buy what he wants," mothers often complain in focus groups, "he won't eat it. It'll just sit there until I throw it out."

We acknowledge the sometimes difficult battles over food and drink that inevitably are waged in many of today's households—battles fueled by the proliferation of alternatives lining the grocery shelves; the sugary, greasy, chemical-riddled pleasure foods that abound; and the hurry-up lifestyles that make fast and convenient but really-really-bad-for-you choices so easy to indulge in. At the same time, however, these are battles parents must win. Parents must take charge of purchasing and preparing healthy meals for their children and themselves. Study the contents of a parent's grocery cart and you'll see immediately whether that parent is part of the problem or part of the solution.

Your children are watching: modeling healthy eating habits. When parents make food choices for themselves, they are modeling the food choice process for their children. Monkey see, monkey do. Daddy eats junk food and Mommy's 100 pounds overweight with a sugar and carb habit that would kill most large dogs. In fact, most parents who have poor diets inevitably provide similar poor food and beverage selections for their whole family.

YES!

Create a healthy, family game plan regarding meals and snacks for everyone in the family. Pull together menus for meals and snack options ahead of time, and stick to them.

A typical three- to seven-year-old does not have the cognitive ability or awareness to make good, nutritional choices on her own. In fact, when allowed to choose their own food, most children in this age group will opt for pleasure food. In addition to controlling your child's choices, you need to model healthy eating habits yourself. Good modeling, healthy eating habits, monitoring and censoring choices, and educating and training your child in the basics of good nutrition and good eating and drinking habits are the best ways to teach your child to make healthy food choices. If you don't train your child, the foods she eats will; over time, a person's very cells become "educated"—conditioned and, you even could say, addicted—to the kinds of consumables that feed them.

Supersize kids? A shared responsibility. In a society that proclaims to love its children and to want to provide what is best for their healthy growth and development, parents do not have the sole responsibility when it comes to shaping children's diets. While the task of determining what enters into their children's digestive systems ultimately falls on caretakers (and to the children themselves as they mature), food and beverage manufacturers and marketers must step up to the plate and do their part. This responsibility includes providing healthier products and options, and eliminating or substantially limiting aggressive unhealthy food and beverage marketing—especially to the very young and vulnerable.

As stated, boys and girls below the age of approximately seven, with limited cognitive discernment capacities in place, want just about everything they see marketed on TV. Food and beverage marketing has even invaded our schools through TV in the classrooms, vending machines, in-school advertising, and fast-food retailers on campus. While many food and beverage marketers may think it heretical to suggest the curtailment of marketing efforts for unhealthy items, it's time for them to do their part in protecting the health of our society's children.

YES!

Fight for healthier food and beverage options in groceries, restaurants, and schools. Communicate your views to manufacturers, restaurant owners, and school boards. Write letters and e-mail, contact the presidents of companies, bring the issue to school board meetings, hold concerned parent meetings/support groups, and—if necessary—consider nonfrivolous lawsuits to push for change.

Retailers, such as fast-food restaurants, also must be responsible for encouraging healthy eating habits, and they should make sure their ingredients and preparation processes are as healthy as possible. Some fast-food restaurants prominently display posters listing the ingredients—fat, sugar, and caloric content—of their menu items. We'd like to see that posting of such information becomes mandatory.

Kudos and congratulations to those restaurant chains starting to provide at least somewhat healthier alternatives—fruit juice instead of soda, applesauce or fruit rollups instead of candy—in their kids' meals. Special acknowledgment also goes to organizations like the Kid Power Xchange (http://www.kidpowerx.com), which organizes and hosts marketing conferences such as the Kid Power Food & Beverage Marketing Conference. The conference focuses on the rapidly growing problem of obesity in today's children and boasts such food-industry participants as McDonald's, Nestlé, Dole, and Coca-Cola. Other participants include healthy nutrition advocacy organizations such as the National Institute on Media and the Family, the Department of Nutrition of New York University, and the Eat Smart, Play Hard campaign of the USDA.

Parents, in the meantime, can't afford to wait to see if marketers and retailers are going to step up. Marketers are in the business of selling, so the burden of controlling our children's access to products at the end of the day falls to us as parents and caretakers. When it comes to most day-to-day purchases for kids of any age, parents need to understand and pay attention to the types of products their children consume and what advertisements they are exposed to. There's nothing wrong with parents indulging their kids in a fast-food treat occasionally. But when the daily menu is sugary cold cereal for breakfast; hot dogs, hamburgers, or bologna sandwiches for lunch; and pizza, fast food, or frozen dinners at night followed by ice cream—Houston, we've got a problem. (Houston, Texas, ranked #1 on the *Men's Fitness Magazine* "Top 25 Fattest Cities" list for 2005!)

The responsibility of healthy food and beverage consumption by our children is definitely shared. Marketers might want to reevaluate their jobs when the products they are attempting to get parents and kids to buy are inherently unhealthy—especially food and beverages with damaging ingredients such as trans fats that are unhealthy even when consumed in moderation. But only when parents begin to learn more about food and beverage ingredients, and pay more attention to the food marketing their children are exposed to, and voice their concerns at levels that get the attention of corporate decision makers, will it affect the profit incentive of the manufacturers and marketers. Only then will things begin to change. Until that time, children will continue to pay the price of poor choices.

Television

As we mentioned earlier in this chapter, children between the ages of three and seven have a number of cognitive and emotional characteristics that make television a particularly powerful influence. Three- to seven-year-olds are extremely impressionable; they believe most of what they're presented with and trust in its veracity. Children are charmingly naive at this stage and are not yet able to weigh differences effectively, determine relative values, or make comparisons when it comes to relatively complex communications such as those contained in TV ads. They are, however, able to distinguish between items of direct interest to them such as foodstuffs and toys—especially as they reach the upper end of this age range.

Three- to seven-year-olds also are oriented toward fantasy. Because of the emotional impact of programs, as we discussed earlier, children may very well come away from intense film, video, or TV experiences having formed upsetting irrational conclusions based on what they experienced. Their aggressive behavior may increase. In addition to the potential dangers of age-inappropriate and violent TV programming for children of this age group, excessive TV watching displaces many more healthy and growth-oriented activities.

Most kids will merely enjoy programs like the *Power Rangers* and will take away some good from their viewing time. Others, especially those kids with emotional troubles, suffer from involvement in media themes with aggression and violence, and from identification with the characters who carry out that aggression. Such programs and characters add to the negativity that afflicts these children and may just be the "tipping point" that pushes them over the edge and into antisocial acting out—in dangerous acts of copycatting.

Parents are chiefly responsible for all the activities of their children at this age and should carefully screen all TV programming for appro-

A *Closer* L*ook at the* P*ower* R*angers*

Your children becoming involved in a show such as the *Power Rangers*
isn't all negative. Watch any *Power Rangers* TV episode and you will find
positive messages that promote the benefits of teamwork and loyalty;
and the good guys always win. But at the same time, problems in this series are typically solved with martial arts–type fighting and gunlike rockets and machines. In Canada, Y-TV (which airs children's programming)
took *Power Rangers* off the air because of actual incidents of children using martial arts–type kicks and hits on the playground.

priateness. Parents should mirror some of the more influential entertainment celebrities and icons, including Steven Spielberg, Arnold
Schwartzenegger, and Tom Cruise, who are outspoken about TV viewing for their own children, limiting viewing time to a few hours per
week.

YES!

Sit down with your children and decide on and post a weekly schedule
of television programs that you will allow them to watch. Initiate a discussion about *why* you are choosing these programs to establish a foundation for good choices and for early stages of "shades of gray"
reasoning.

TV producers and the outlets that broadcast the programs are, however, also responsible for developing content that at a minimum does
not negatively impact three- to seven-year-olds and at its maximum positively contributes to their cognitive, social, and emotional growth and
well being. In addition, they are responsible for informing parents and
child caretakers of the potential impact of their programs on young
viewers.

Computer Software

Viewed and used in moderation, and balanced with other healthy activities, early learning software programs can contribute to the development and growth of children in the three- to seven-year age range. We have evolved beyond the information age into the age of technology, and there's no turning back. Tomorrow's children will not only benefit from a limited and balanced "early start" with technology, they will need key technological skills to survive and thrive in that future world.

A variety of early learning programs are designed for the three- to four-year-old preschool child. The Learning Company offers several titles, including *Strawberry Shortcake: Incredible Cookie Machine, Reader Rabbit Toddler 2002,* and *Reader Rabbit Preschool 2002.* Also available are *Clifford the Big Red Dog Thinking Adventures,* by Scholastic, *Blue's Clues Preschool,* by Atari, and *JumpStart Advanced Preschool 2003,* by Knowledge Adventure. Many of the software programs developed for this age group promote early learning of colors, shapes, letters, numbers, and simple vocabulary.

YES!

Limit learning software involvement to a few hours a week of only the best programs. Too much screen time with even the best learning software is not a good idea. Remember, interpersonal and relationship time is *always* better than tech time.

Even more titles are available for five-, six-, and seven-year-olds as they enter school. Examples of these programs include the Learning Company's other Reader Rabbit titles and Arthur the Aardvark series, and Knowledge Adventure titles such as *JumpStart First Grade Fun Pack* with activities for reading, music, and math.

The caution of the IIIO (Invisible and Intangible Information Overload) phenomenon is still an important one, however. A child who is overloaded with too much exposure to technology at too early an age may be excessively bombarded with stimuli and electronic emissions. Maintaining a balance of activity types is essential; a half an hour or so a day and no more than two or three hours a week should be the limit.

Feature Films

As with television, film holds an especially strong power to influence children between the ages of three and seven, because of this age group's emotional and developmental characteristics. Many in today's world have become lax regarding which media experiences to allow their children to participate in. Far too many parents take their three- to seven-year-old children along to PG and PG-13 movies—a classification that suggests parental guidance and caution because "Some material may be inappropriate for children under 13."

Don't be misled by the fact that a film is produced by Disney Studios or is marketed as a "family" film. Adults are the ones who are making the films and they don't always know (or care) about the potential for a film's negative impact on a child's brain and psyche. Parents must be prepared to censor films and to help their children understand and process the films they do see. Even soft-conflict films for children, such as Disney's *Snow White and the Seven Dwarfs* (1937), *Sleeping Beauty* (1959), *Beauty and the Beast* (1991), and *The Lion King* (1994), can be upsetting, or even traumatizing for the three- to seven-year-old who has yet to develop the comprehension and emotional coping skills to offset the fear and potential threat the films present. When viewed through the eyes of a child, these films can contain some quite violent threats, acts, and potent villains: hunters with guns who kill mothers (*Bambi*), Queens that shout "Off with their heads!" (*Alice in Wonderland*), sword-wielding pirates who capture children (*Peter Pan*), evil witches who poison people (*Sleeping Beauty*), frightening beasts (*Beauty and the Beast*), mean animals who kill dads (*The Lion King*), and predator sharks with huge teeth that can snap up a small and vulnerable fish in a split second (*Finding Nemo*).

YES!

Check out reviews of films ahead of time for child-appropriateness and limit your child's film experiences to only those you are certain will be positive. Make a list of dos and don'ts themes that you can look for when viewing films. Afterwards, always talk through the thoughts and feelings your child "takes away" from films.

Parents have access to a variety of resources to assist them in determining age-appropriateness before allowing their children to view a film. With resources such as http://www.filmvalues.com available, any parent with Internet access can check out a film for harmful content before taking his or her child to see it. To check movies that are already on video, *Leonard Maltin's Family Film Guide*[3] provides clear-cut information on movie rental content for a multitude of family-type movies produced over the past decades.

While it's recognized that a parent doesn't always know exactly what's going to happen in a film once the credits begin to roll, if age-inappropriate or upsetting scenes do occur, it would be wise for that parent to discuss those scenes with his or her child afterward to diffuse any possible negative impact. We recommend you talk about the content and characters with your children after seeing such films together. Probe for hidden fears and irrational conclusions they may have made. Assure them that it was "only a story"; make sure they separate the film from the reality of their own lives. Help them take away positive messages of love and hope and courage. And, of course, don't take your children to films that contain age-inappropriate material.

YES!

Limit your child's time spent in front of screens and with technology of any kind in favor of free play, reading, and human interaction and communication. Remember, technology often does the thinking for the child. Imaginative and creative activities, such as reading and free play, allow the child to do the thinking and to exercise the "shades of gray" muscle.

Technology

The three- to seven-year-old in most cases is below the age when technological devices such as cell phones, calculators, electronic notepads, and desktop, portable, and handheld computers serve as integral parts of daily life. If there is a concern about exposure to technology at this age/stage of development, it is with excessive time spent watching television and perhaps with some forms of computer and video games that contain excessive violence and inappropriate sexuality. Again, problems from these activities can be demonstrated as subtle forms of stress caused by IIIO and by tech time replacing more physically active and otherwise beneficial activities.

If their child is younger than six or so, most parents aren't faced with the problem of having to watch over the child's Internet activity. At six or seven years, however, some children begin to actively use the Internet, and for those children, parental cautions are a must. Parental restrictions and content blocks should be put in place so that Junior can't access sites with age-inappropriate content. It's quite appropriate to prevent children within this age range from having any Internet involvement at all. There will be plenty of time for that later.

YES!

Consider allowing Internet access to children only at the upper end of the three- to seven-year age range, and then only under strict supervision.

Toys and Products Associated with Characters

There is another neutral category that may be below the radar in its impact. Especially when exploring the power of different stimuli for three- to seven-year-olds, we need to look at the world of cartoon characters as they appear in different media, including TV animation and film as well as on the front and back panels of cereal boxes and other food, snack, or beverage packaging. Beginning in the baby's crib and room, this "space" becomes occupied with all kinds of human and animal "characters." What starts out as cute and fuzzy bunnies to cuddle and love ends up as Bugs Bunny whose antics keep a seven-year-old glued to the screen.

Soon little purple dinosaurs populate the room and when the child is around five years old—for good or bad—the latest cartoon and toy characters creep onto the walls and invade the bedsheets. From stuffed toys and dolls, to the menagerie of characters that populate children's breakfast cereal packaging and lunchboxes, and the clowns and cartoon-like kids that welcome children to fast-food restaurants, our children's world is populated with an unending series of commercial characters designed to appeal directly to them as consumers.

The strategy of using characters to promote one's brand is likely here to stay. The title of Michael Wolf's book, *The Entertainment Economy*,[4] makes the point that we are in an economy that attracts by entertaining, and cartoon characters are fun. How children identify with characters is the key to whether that connection is good, neutral, or potentially harmful.

YES!

Be especially aware of any "emulating" on the part of your child. In particular, be careful of the celebrities, sports stars, or cartoon characters your child starts to identify with and imitate. Make sure the child is emulating only positive characteristics as much as possible.

Because identification is such an important part of a child's learning experience, let's take a moment to look at it in more detail. An "identification pattern" is essentially the relationship that the child has with an animated character, a celebrity or sports star, or a doll or stuffed toy. We have identified five identification patterns that children become involved with in their relationships to characters of all types as they progress through the stages of development.

- *Nurturing*. In this relationship, the child either perceives himself as the "nurturer" of, for example, a doll, animal, or other character (Stanley, Charlie Brown, or a baby doll), or the child is nurtured by the character (Big Bird, Mr. Rogers, Barney).
- *Like me*. A "like me" relationship or identification pattern with a character or a doll or other object of identification means that the child sees the character, doll, or animal—or some attributes of them—as like herself (Strawberry Shortcake).
- *Emulatory*. In an "emulatory" identification pattern, the relationship is one in which the child emulates or wants to be like the human or animal character/object (a Pokémon character, a Barbie

doll, Xena the Warrior Princess, a Power Ranger, Tiger Woods). This form of identification is very potent.

- *Entertaining.* In this type of identification, the target audience is merely "entertained." The child does not particularly want to be like the character, nor does he necessarily see aspects of the character that are similar to himself; he merely finds this character's antics, demeanor, looks, or behavior entertaining.
- *Disidentification.* This is a different type of identification by which the child does not want to be like the character, animal, or person, but is attracted to and involved with it because of its "dark side" or "edge"—its negative attributes and the threat they represent. Villains such as Darth Vader of *Star Wars,* Team Rocket of Pokémon, many of the World Wrestling Federation wrestlers, or "soft" villains such as Wile E. Coyote or Elmer Fudd are typical objects of disidentification.

Given a child's power of identification with characters, is using cartoon characters as advertising tools irresponsible? Is it deceitful or exploitative or manipulative? It depends. Here's how we assess the good, neutral, and bad categories for character-related products, programs, and advertising for children between the ages of three and seven.

- *Character-based products, programs, and advertising are good* when the entertaining and fun effects of having the characters adds to the quality and enjoyment of life for our children—and all of us—so long as there are no inherently harmful effects. While we might imagine a world without advertising that involves cartoon characters, many wouldn't find it as fun to live in. Having stated this, caution and limits should be applied when it comes to allowing very young children to view advertising using these characters to undue advantage.
- *Character-based products, programs, and advertising are neutral* when they have a potential for harming the child's emotional, physical, or psychological development, and therefore are acceptable only in limited or controlled amounts. For example, parents might occasionally yield to their children's requests for a sugary cereal promoted by the Alpo the Alligator character, but the parents should do so only rarely.

- *Character-based products, programs, and advertising are inherently dangerous* if the characters have negative, violent, or otherwise unhealthy attributes or associations, such as when used to promote unhealthy or dangerous products. These characters include those who appear in violent video games and to a lesser extent in the *Power Rangers.* Although Joe Camel has been removed from advertising, his character was used to lure our young toward the inherently dangerous tobacco habit. This kind of character use must not be allowed.

Radio, Room Decor, and Apparel

Of less concern but still needing a watchful eye are these other products within the neutral category.

- *Radio.* Parents need to monitor age-inappropriate content such as violence and sexual references in music lyrics and censor such content to prevent their three- to seven-year-old children from listening or being exposed to it.
- *Room decor.* Watch for inappropriate messaging transmitted through wall posters and room accessories for children within this age group.
- *Apparel.* Censor inappropriate messages that may appear on clothing as logos or slogans, as well as the values inherent in different styles of dress. For example, be on the alert to steer your children in this age group away from dark, gothic-type clothing or T-shirts carrying hard rock music group messages and associations.

INHERENTLY DANGEROUS PRODUCTS TO BE AVOIDED FOR THIS AGE GROUP

During each of the developmental stages, children incorporate habits, attitudes, values, and ways of being. We call the three- to seven-year stage "the impressionable years" because children only begin to develop left-brain, logical capacities toward the end of this age span. Children between the ages of three and six essentially operate from emotion, rather than reason. As we have established previously, emotional memory is typically stronger than is cognitive memory.

The products and programming content that we've red-flagged in this section represent, therefore, a real and present danger. It's too easy in these busy times to go with the flow and let your kids participate in whatever activities are popular with their peers and society at large. But, even if it makes you the bad guy, you must carefully monitor your child's activities and involvements, and impose appropriate restrictions, guidelines, and censorship. Your children may or may not thank you someday, but you can rest at night knowing you provided them with the safest, most nurturing environment possible. In this section, we highlight some of the products and programs you should be most careful about screening and prohibiting for children within this age group. Other product categories that become problematic for older age groups—categories such as cosmetics, publications, drugs, alcohol, and tobacco—are nonissues for three- to seven-year-olds, and therefore aren't covered in the following sections.

Toys That Promote Aggression and Violence

You should make every effort to avoid aggressive and violence-provoking toys for your children between the ages of three and seven. While it is natural for children (especially young boys, who are by nature more aggressive) to play fighting games with whatever toy or "pretend" weapons are available, we recommend that you disallow any use of manufactured toys with aggressive or violent associations by children of any age. This group of toys includes water pistols and other toy guns that resemble real guns, as well as combative action figures, swords, knives, missiles, bombs, grenades, and vehicles with weapons as accessories.

Numerous studies have indicated that toy gunplay is positively associated with real aggression in boys, including rough-and-tumble play. You can expect children to pick up a stick and pretend it's a gun; but to deliberately arm children with practice weapons is irresponsible. We support the banning of all such toys.

"Wow," you might say, "I played with guns and weapons when I was a kid and it never affected me." Our answer to this type of thinking is that times have *dramatically* changed since most of us were children. When it comes to violent play with toys, as a culture we've moved way

> ## YES!
>
> Despite your child's possible preferences for aggressive toys and games, consider disallowing all of them—even against the child's protests. Send a strong message and value for nonviolence.

beyond the toy pistol stage. A few decades ago that was the extent of it—small squirt guns, some little plastic army men, cowboy holster and gun sets, and bows and arrows to play cowboys and Indians. Today, our toy pistols have evolved into every kind of weapon from simulated guns and rifles to fantasy megacannons and monster squirt rifles—some of which have a stream so strong that it could be damaging to the eyes. Military toys abound, complete with arsenals of guns, rifles, missiles, bombs, rockets, grenades, and futuristic weapons of doom and destruction. Army men have evolved into both realistic and fantasy-based fighting figures with specializations like flame throwing, grenade launching, and bombadeering.

Far too many highly aggressive toys are in the marketplace to detail, but here's a sample of some action figures with aggressive themes and values.

- Wrestling figures with names like Sid Vicious (Galoob), Pallbearer (Hasbro), and Ripped and Ruthless Undertaker (WWF)
- Fantasy characters like Overtkill (from McFarland's Spawn line) and Red Cloak Blood Queen (Wetworks)
- TV, movie, and music figures such as Stalker Predator (Kenner), Morpheus from the movie *The Matrix*, the KISS musical group, and would you believe a Warrior Nun named Areala?

For these and other details about what kinds of toys and games to avoid, we refer you to the Lion & Lamb Project Web site at http://www.lionlamb.org.[5]

Particularly irresponsible is the inherent contradiction and danger in making toys based on characters from PG-13, R-rated, and NC-17 movies. *The Matrix* movie is a prime example. While the movie industry rates this film R, which requires anyone under the age of 17 to be accompanied by an adult to view the movie, companies designed and marketed action figures and toy play sets based on the movie and its characters. While it's true that many of these "toys" are purchased by older collectors, they are toys and the prime age for playing with and collecting toys is three to seven! After age seven, some boys may still collect action figures, but they are past the stage where they are actually playing with these action figures.

Extreme "hawks" might encourage play with violence-based action figures and toys based on killing machines as necessary preparation for the realities of the post-September 11th world; they and others with a laissez-faire attitude toward the potential dangers of violent play may discard our indictment here as overreactionary. Nevertheless, the results from hundreds of studies on the effects of exposure to violent and aggressive themes and play couldn't be clearer: Children identify with and learn by modeling after the real and fantasy characters that populate our screens and stores. The "copycat" phenomenon couldn't be more real, and is a particular threat for children in the three- to seven-year age range.

Violence-Based Electronic Games

Many of us grossly underestimate the negative impact of children's exposure to and participation in violent electronic games. There are three key dangers:

1. *Influence on aggressive predisposition.* Research has clearly shown a relationship with playing violent video games and possessing tendencies toward more aggressive and violent thoughts, feelings, and actions.
2. *Increased stress.* Only now are we beginning to comprehend the little-known effects of the release of cortisol and other stress-related hormones.
3. *Time spent away from healthier activities.*

Game players identify with and assume the role of the perpetrator of violence within most of these games. Because of electronic game-play processes that involve active and stress-producing participation, the cumulative negative impact is more dramatic than forms of passive viewing. This negative impact can extend to children between the ages of three and seven even when they aren't playing these games but are exposed to them through the play of older siblings, friends, and parents, or in mall play zones and arcades.

In summary, no child in this age group should be allowed to play or be exposed to others playing electronic games with sexual and violent content. In a nation in which some estimates suggest more than half the population (approximately 140 million people) at one time or another becomes involved in video game play, this may seem like Dark Ages moralization. Nevertheless, we stand by our recommendation. Plenty of nonviolent games are available to select from. Parents need to become informed of game content and act knowledgably.

KEY VULNERABILITIES OF THE THREE- TO SEVEN-YEAR-OLD

Here are the most important vulnerabilities of this stage of development.

- *They are nonlogical in their thought processes.* Without the cognitive (thinking) ability to effectively reason and discern in place, children at this age are susceptible to believing almost anything they're told. This applies to all advertising they witness as well.
- *They are impulsive in their involvements.* Because these children follow their emotions rather than logic, they are likely to want most of the attractive things they see.
- *They are ruled by their emotions.* Without the dampening effect of logic, the three- to seven-year-old is more susceptible to negative emotions such as anger, fear, guilt, and depression. Emotional memory is highly active during this stage and has a lifelong impact.
- *They are prone to emulation.* Being highly impressionable, three- to seven-year-olds want to emulate—to be and act like—older siblings, peers, adults, and the role models they see in the media.
- *They often cannot distinguish fantasy from reality.* Especially at the younger end of this three- to seven-year-old stage, children are not able to distinguish between fantasy and reality. Cartoons, TV shows, and advertising content based on fantasy in many cases are likely to be experienced as what's really so.

A WEEK IN THE LIFE

As we did for the birth through the age of two stage, we present a hypothetical overview of a week in the life of a child in the three- to seven-year age range. We hope that this synopsis of a representative child's life during this stage of development will help to illustrate the warnings, guidelines, and solutions we've offered in this chapter. In this hypothetical example, we're looking at a week in the life of Luis, age six.

EXPERIENCE	EMPOWERING	DISEMPOWERING
Parents/ Home Life	Luis enjoys the benefits of a loving and enriching home life. His parents and nine-year-old brother, David, share dinner together almost every night, and when there are problems they sit down together and work things out. Sunday morning is church time for everyone. Luis is in a Cub Scout Den, which his mom helps run, and older brother David is in a Boy Scout Troop that his dad heads up.	Daily life in the Rodriguez household can be an isolated experience. Meals are seldom shared together except at holidays. Luis and his older brother, David, spend most of their free time in their separate rooms watching TV or playing video games.
Toys	Being a teacher, Luis's mother has made sure that his toy collection includes a good variety of educational toys and games. Friday nights are family game night, and each family member takes a turn selecting the evening's game.	By the age of six, Luis has gone through just about every possible toy that's made it to the market. Gone are any signs of babyish toys such as Barney. His current favorite toy is a snap-together set that he uses to construct action figures and fighting scenes.

EXPERIENCE	EMPOWERING	DISEMPOWERING
Toys **(cont.)**	Luis has a Nintendo game system, which was passed down from his older brother, but Luis is only allowed to play carefully screened games and only on the weekends for no more than one hour each day.	Luis's dad bought the latest electronic game system for both boys (and for himself). At first, there were restrictions on certain games Luis was allowed to play, but as time went by, no one enforced the limits. Luis is "hooked" on two of the rather bloody games and plays them for more than 16 hours a week.
Learning Hardware & Software	Under Luis's parents' guidance, and using their computer, Luis plays and works with three different educational software programs to enhance his math, vocabulary building, and reading abilities. His time with these programs is limited to 45 minutes each session.	Luis's parents believe that anything that says "learning" or "educational" on the packaging is good for the child. Because they also need to keep Luis busy, the "learning" alternative can appear overly seductive.
Room Décor	Luis's relatively neat and organized room has no particular theme. On one wall is a large world map and on the other is a large corkboard filled with school drawings and starred papers. There is a poster of Superman and next to it a picture of Christopher Reeves in a wheelchair. There's also a poster of Nolan Ryan. Luis's bedspread is themed to baseball. His stuffed animals from earlier years are in a narrow box under his bed.	The walls of Luis's room are filled with posters from his favorite action movies. Cartoon character posters have been taken down, and replaced with video game posters of monsters and heroes fighting bad guys. Luis has a pet coral snake in one terrarium and a tarantula in another. There's a big sign outside his bedroom door that reads "Keep out!"

EXPERIENCE	EMPOWERING	DISEMPOWERING
Television/ Film	There's no TV in Luis's room. He's only allowed TV time on Saturday morning and can only watch three shows that are approved by his parents. He is only allowed to go to G-rated films and then only with his family, relatives, or friends his parents approve of. As a family, they often rent all-family movies on Sunday night and watch them together. Afterwards they discuss the movies.	During the week, Luis can watch as much TV as he wants so long as he swears his homework is done. (In the first grade there's very little homework.) He's not allowed to tune in the cable channels, but he and his older brother often watch questionable programming in David's room. His mom doesn't like action movies, but Luis goes to lots of PG-13 movies with his dad and older brother.
The Internet	Luis isn't allowed to access the Internet yet. Under supervision, his older brother does access it for schoolwork and learning purposes.	Luis has a hand-me-down computer in his room and is already chat-rooming on the Net and frequently communicates with one of his first-grade buddies. His parents put parental blocks on as much as they could figure out, but have long since stopped paying attention to where Luis goes on the Web.
Food & Beverages	Luis's mother is a nut about healthy food and drink for herself and her family. She allows Luis to eat at the school cafeteria for lunch only because she became president of a committee of the PTA to reform the nutritional value of school lunches. When the family goes out to dinner, they typically	Luis's parents are both overweight. When they're not bringing takeout food home from fast-food joints, their kitchen refrigerator and cabinets are stocked with carbohydrate-heavy foods for the most part. Frozen meals quickly prepared in the microwave are the typical order of most evening meals,

EXPERIENCE	EMPOWERING	DISEMPOWERING
Food & Beverages (cont.)	avoid fast-food establishments in favor of places with healthier menus. (They do have a pizza and root beer float–night once a month!)	although every Friday night they have a meat-and-potatoes type of sit down–together meal. There's well-frequented sugar bowls in both the kitchen and dining room.
Music & Radio	Luis isn't allowed to have his radio on during the weeks school is in session. On the weekends when he does listen to it, he's only allowed to listen to Disney radio. He doesn't have a CD player, but David has one and what David listens to is carefully screened by his father who is into music.	All kinds of music from hard rock to gangsta rap can be heard coming from older brother David's room at just about any waking hour. Luis listens to music on the rock stations in the mornings when he's getting up. He also has a portable CD player with all kinds of CDs and takes them to school in his backpack.
Apparel	At Luis's school, wearing school uniforms is mandatory through the sixth grade. Luis's mom is careful not to buy clothing items with inappropriate icons that might carry negative associations—such as *violent or raunchy* characters or movie or TV icons related to objectionable messaging.	Luis's favorite sweatshirt is a heavy metal rock group themed pullover passed down from David. His parents don't pay much attention to what either of their boys wear so long as the clothes are clean enough.
Publications	Luis's mom orders three different publications for her boys: *Boy's Life, Disney Adventures,* and *National Geographic Kids.* Luis's dad takes them to the library every other Saturday to check out one or two new books.	Luis doesn't read any publications. He knows David has a couple of his dad's *Playboy* magazines hidden in his room but as yet has not been able to find them.

It's an easy task to compare these two environments and to predict the critical learning and habit formation that would result in each scenario. As a parent or other caretaker, how would you have filled in a week in the life of your children? As an exercise, go back and respond to each category yourself in writing, or at least think them through.

PARENT AND CARETAKER TOOLBOX FOR YOUTH ENRICHMENT STRATEGIES

Here, again, is our toolbox of key dos and don'ts for parents and other caretakers to help serve as good gatekeepers for children within the three- to seven-year age group. You've seen these Youth Enrichment Strategies throughout the chapter, but we've gathered them here to give you easy and immediate access to our recommendations. To help guide children between the ages of three to seven in their consumption of and exposure to products, programs, and advertising, follow these recommendations.

- Be hyperalert to those occasions when your three- to seven-year-old is exposed to or engaged in negative emotionality at home, in school, or through the media. Whenever possible, eliminate or lessen the extent of this exposure; and always be sure to communicate simply and completely with your child, to help guide him or her through any negative experience.
- Love, emotional safety, and stimulating learning experiences are key to early positive development, well being, and happiness. Fill your three- to seven-year-old's days with lots of positive, loving interaction and stimulating learning experiences, including free play indoors and outdoors, and creative activities such as art and music. Include quiet time as well, for such things as reading and walks.
- Before your child reaches the age of five, begin introducing him or her to "shades of gray," for example, by asking the question "Why?" Even though dealing with subtle areas of reasoning may be difficult for your child, learning to do so is critical for the development of higher-level thinking capabilities. Speak in simple and concrete terms at first, but constantly try to expand your

child's range of thinking. This core skill will help your child become more discerning about advertising and marketing messages, especially those designed to manipulate more simple thinking processes.

- Avoid allowing your child to become immersed in powerful, potentially negative entertainment experiences such as films or television programs laden with violence and negative emotional content.

- Educate yourself through parent magazines, books, and the Internet about age-appropriate, growth-producing products and programs for your three- to seven-year-old. Some recommended magazines include *Parents, Parents Talk, Family Fun,* and *Fathering Magazine.*

- We suggest the creation of a healthy, family game plan regarding meals and snacks for everyone in the family. Create menus for meals and snack options ahead of time, and stick to them.

- Fight for healthier food and beverage options in groceries, restaurants, and schools. Communicate your views to manufacturers, restaurant owners, and school boards. Write letters and e-mail, contact the presidents of companies, bring the issue to school board meetings, hold concerned parent meetings/support groups, and—if necessary—consider nonfrivolous lawsuits to push for change.

- Sit down with your children and decide on and post a weekly schedule of television programs that you will allow them to watch. Initiate a discussion about *why* you are choosing these programs to establish a foundation for good choices and for early stages of "shades of gray" reasoning.

- Limit learning software involvement to a few hours a week of only the best programs. Too much screen time with even the best learning software is not a good idea. Remember, interpersonal and relationship time is *always* better than tech time.

- Check out reviews of films ahead of time for child-appropriateness and limit your child's film experiences to only those you are certain will be positive. Make a list of dos and don'ts themes that you can look for when viewing films. Afterwards, always talk through the thoughts and feelings your child "takes away" from films.

- Limit your child's time spent in front of screens and with technology of any kind in favor of free play, reading, and human interaction and communication. Remember, technology often does the thinking for the child. Imaginative and creative activities, such as reading and free play, allow the child to do the thinking and to exercise the "shades of gray" muscle.
- Consider allowing Internet access to children only at the upper end of the three- to seven-year age range, and then only under strict supervision.
- Be especially aware of any "emulating" on the part of your child. In particular, be careful of the celebrities, sports stars, or cartoon characters your child starts to identify with and imitate. Make sure the child is emulating only positive characteristics as much as possible.
- Despite your child's possible preferences for aggressive toys and games, consider disallowing all of them—even against the child's protests. Send a strong message and value for nonviolence.

ON TO THE 8- TO 12-YEAR-OLD "RULE-AND-ROLE" STAGE OF DEVELOPMENT

OK, if their parents and other caretakers have done a good job, little Benjamin and Lauren are thriving as they move happily through the three- to seven-year-old impressionable years, having benefited from proper management of marketing exposure, what and who they play with, how they learn, what they eat, and in what forms of entertainment they participate. Their next hurdle is the 8- to 12-year stage. We call it the "Rule-and-Role Stage" because it is a very formative stage of development—perhaps the stage most filled with making both empowering and disempowering decisions about oneself, others, and the world.

I think we need to give them (our children) too much love and not enough money . . . too much time and attention and not enough privilege . . . I believe that overindulgence is one of the most insidious forms of child abuse known to man.
Dr. Phil McGraw

6

THE "RULE-AND-ROLE" STAGE OF DEVELOPMENT

Ages 8 to 12

Don't worry that children never listen to you.
Worry that they are always watching you.

Robert Fulghum

In between childhood and adolescence, your children reach a stage of development that makes them the inhabitants of a very special territory. Many of these budding consumers no longer want to be referred to as "kids." No longer babies and not yet teens, they have come to be dubbed "tweens." While some expand this group to include early adolescents ages 13 and 14, we do not—primarily because of the way the developing brain is progressing during those years.

Tweens today represent a lucrative market for advertisers, for they initiate the expense of millions of dollars of goods and services. In this chapter, we focus on just what makes a tween tick and how the strategies and techniques used by marketers can impact and influence children as they pass through this important stage of their physical, emotional, and cognitive development.

DIMENSION ONE: DEVELOPMENTAL ELEMENTS

Having established a degree of psychological independence from his parents by this time, and armed with developing cognitive skills, including a good start on rational thinking and the ability to distinguish between fantasy and reality, our tween is very much becoming his own person.

Three brain developments distinguish this age group from the others:

1. *"Left-brain" development.* During the previous three- to seven-year stage, the right hemisphere of the brain (seat of intuition, visual thinking, and imagination) was on the developmental "front burner." Around the age of six, the left hemisphere maturation becomes prevalent. Cognitive abilities such as comparison, sequencing, and elementary logic are now evolving, as the left brain begins its accelerated development. The result is a more rational child at the expense of some spontaneity and innocent fantasy.

2. *"Housecleaning."* Around the age of 11, the brain goes through a "housecleaning" process to make it more efficient. Millions of unmyelinated neurons are "swept away," leaving the strongest neuronal connections and "circuits." This housecleaning makes for a more efficient brain.

3. *New capabilities of abstraction.* Because of the brain's natural evolution, growth, and increased efficiencies, tweens are able to deal with complexities and abstractions that were more difficult or impossible before. This new capability accounts in part for an increase in independent thinking as tweens begin to merge into the fast lane of adolescence.

These latter two brain developments occur toward the end of this 8- to 12-year age range and contribute to the uniqueness of the 13- to 15-year early adolescent stage that we'll deal with in the next chapter.

Core Developmental Elements for the Tween Years

When examining any developmental age, it's important to look at how the whole child is developing. In previous chapters, we described a series of developmental elements that we labeled as physical, cognitive, emotional, social, moral/ethical, and transpersonal.

For children below the age of eight, physical and emotional development are of primary importance. As children move into their tween years, their physical and emotional development continues, but the cognitive, social, and ethical developmental elements move to center stage. We refer to this stage as the "rule-and-role" stage of development because the tween is developing the capability to formulate personal rules for living along with an understanding of his or her role as an individual and as a part of society. As a result of these rule-and-role developmental changes, the tween is:

- *Cognitively evolving.* Jean Piaget refers to this stage as a time of "concrete operations," when, with brain growth and learning, the tween begins to perform many thinking operations, such as sequential thinking and elementary forms of logic, which were impossible before.

YES!

Be careful not to talk down to your 8- to 12-year-old. In fact, include your tween in conversations you might have assumed were beyond him or her. Asking her for her views on different subjects will reinforce the idea that you respect her opinion.

- *Formulating ideas, beliefs, and a sense of self.* The child this age is formulating stronger personal ideas, beliefs, attitudes, and values regarding himself, others, and all of life. This is an important age for the design of one's self-concept and self-esteem.

YES!

Feed and nurture your child's formation of positive self-esteem by offering praise directly and in front of others.

- *Socially vulnerable.* Peer influence is very much on the rise during this stage of development. The need for acceptance is always present, but now that the social situation is dramatically changing and peer pressure is critical, it takes on a much higher level of importance. Tweens also typically tend to be conformists during this period and are looking around for role models to imitate and model themselves after. Although research suggests many tweens still look to their parents as role models, tweens are susceptible to adopting negative attitudes and behavior modeled both at home and by sports and media icons and celebrities.

- *Ethically aware.* Most tweens are attempting to figure out the rules of life—what's acceptable to parents and peers and what's not. The great majority of tweens want to be good; they want to figure out the right way to behave so they will be accepted. Problems can arise, however, as the tween seeks approval from peers, who sometimes might have troublesome beliefs, values, and behavior.
- *Transpersonally aware.* Tweens are moving beyond the intense self-centeredness and narcissistic attitudes of their previous developmental stage and begin developing the cognitive capacity for an awareness and concern for others. The primary reason for this shift is that the tween has developed the ability to think more abstractly and is therefore better able to see things from a perspective outside of the self. This is also an important time spiritually, for many individuals at this age formulate and imprint numerous attitudes and beliefs.

Prioritizing the Needs of Tweens

If we look at the prioritization of needs for individuals between the ages of 8 and 12, we can begin to discover important patterns that correlate to the rule-and-role stage. Here is the needs prioritization for this age group:

1. *Safety.* By the time children reach the age of eight or so, most will have begun to feel safe emotionally and physically. Exceptions include children with ADHD and other psychological and psychiatric disorders, problems of obesity, and the victims of abuse or extreme poverty, to name only a few.
2. *Growth.* The 8- to 12-year stage is dynamically charged with learning and growth. All kinds of physical, mental, emotional, social,

and ethical growth and learning is taking place during this period.

3. *Love.* While parental and familial love is still the critical emotional "rock" for tweens, they begin to look for and depend on love and support (hard to separate from the need for acceptance) from outside the family, particularly from their friends. Most important of all, individuals in this age range need to form their own positive self-love.

4. *Acceptance.* Tweens also have a strong need to be accepted—liked, approved of, and included—which is distinct from, but related to, their need for love. Tweens often struggle with this need; they may often behave in uncharacteristic ways to earn acceptance. Conformity is very high at this stage of development, related to particularly strong needs for approval and acceptance at home, at school, with peers.

YES!

Your child's need to feel "OK" and accepted is particularly strong during this period. Do everything you can to communicate this acceptance verbally ("I love you," "Good job," "I'm proud of you") and nonverbally (through hugs, pats on the back, reassuring touches, and so on).

---

5. *Success.* Achieving success to gain peer approval becomes a very big deal for most tweens. Self-esteem, in our view, is made up primarily of the satisfaction of the individual's needs for love, acceptance, and success. Tweens are very busy making key decisions about what they can and cannot do successfully. The 8- to 12-year stage of development is an extremely formative period in the pursuit of fulfilling the need for success, and a critical period for the development of self-esteem.

6. *Reality.* The 8- to 12-year stage is filled with sorting out fact from fiction, reality from fantasy. The child also struggles with making meaning out of the fast-paced world that surrounds him or her. More equipped than before with the cognitive abilities to distinguish between fantasy and reality and between deception and

YES!

Avoid situations that impose on your child tasks he or she is not yet ready to tackle. Do not demand too much too soon. Consciously place your child in situations in which success can be met physically, mentally, emotionally, socially, and morally by behaving and doing the right thing.

the truth, tweens are becoming savvy consumers. This is not to say they are not vulnerable to irresponsible marketing and manipulative advertising, but they at least are developing some tools to distinguish those types of unethical messages for themselves.

YES!

We recommend discussions at home about commercial messages and marketing strategies. In addition, we strongly suggest parents and educators insist on media education in school.

7. *Control.* While tweens do enjoy a greater degree of independence than ever before, they still remain very much under the thumb of parental, school, and other authorities. They both need and enjoy the emotional safety of limits placed upon them (and, in fact, are busy learning the rules), and at the same time they are nudging against those limits and rules in order to grow in independence and self-determination. Some psychologists refer to this stage as "the quiet before the storm" preceding the turbulence of adolescence.

YES!

Tweens are very alert to exactly what rules, guidelines, and limits they are expected to adhere to. Make sure that rules are crystal clear and that they are enforced in a loving and consistent manner.

8. *Release.* Tweens need to express pent-up emotions. They have basic rational capacities in place as a sort of "throttle" that can inhibit raw emotional expression. At the same time, tweens also are trying to figure out the right things to say and do in order to be loved and accepted, which also can repress the tween's self-expression. This phenomenon of repression is most present perhaps during these oversensitive years, and continues throughout life.

9. *Stimulation.* Their increased capacity for boredom makes tweens particularly hungry for new experiences. They've experienced enough by way of entertainment and consumer goods to start to have a sense of "been there, done that." In a crowded marketplace, this creates a tendency toward fickleness and perpetually wanting what's new and different.

DIMENSION TWO:
DEVELOPMENTAL BLIND SPOTS

Now let's take a look at the developmental blind spots for this age group; these are built-in vulnerabilities, especially relevant to this age, that can make this group sitting ducks for negative images and influences and unscrupulous marketing tactics. As individuals proceed through this new developmental age and stage, all the developmental blind spots present during the previous years of their lives remain part of the individual's *cumulative* set of vulnerabilities.

The *Needs/Identification* Blind Spot

Given the powerful needs for acceptance, love, and success, the tween patterns of identification are typically directed outward, as the individual looks to the outside world for models and for validation that will provide the positive feedback necessary for navigating this vulnerable stage. In addition, today's tween will reject childlike behavior in favor of being "cool" and grown-up. To accomplish this, the 8- to 12-year-old typically looks to the older teens and celebrities who are prominent in pop culture and with peers in order to "fit in" and feel like one of the crowd.

YES!

A growing tween's self-esteem can be dramatically undermined by his or her conclusion of "not being good enough." In fact, most adults feel they are "not good enough" in one way or another. To instill the belief "I'm good enough" in your child, avoid undue criticism and find every opportunity for praise.

The *Making Meaning* Blind Spot

A person *must* make sense out of his or her experiences; the process is fundamental to the very act of survival in society. Importantly, if the cognitive developmental level of the child is immature, as is the case with the youngest tweens, then the ability to make meaning from the incoming information is also immature. When the attention blind spot of the child's infancy and early youth is combined with the *making meaning* blind spot, the tween becomes especially vulnerable to advertising and other outside influences.

Today's media is all about grabbing the "eyeballs" of potential consumers. Advertisers use various technological advances to flood the child's senses with information designed to capture the attention and drive the "orienting response." Once the orienting response has been elicited, the child will create meaning from the information that he pays attention to.

The tween will make inner representations of his experiences, interpret incoming information, and add these meanings to his developing mind map. The making meaning blind spot has direct implications for the marketing to tweens of age-inappropriate products and programs that promote violence, alcohol, sexuality, and drugs.

The *Peripheral Perception* Blind Spot

The brain of the tween is immersed in an avalanche of incoming images and messages and, at the same time, several dimensions of the child's attention and perceptual process are occurring simultaneously. While the child is focused on the images and messages that are designed to attract her attention, she is also absorbing other parts of the incoming stimuli that lie outside her immediate field of attention. The "background" images and messages being presented are also being absorbed into the child's mind map in a process referred to as *peripheral perception*. The dual process of focused attention and peripheral perception is part of the brain's inherent biological makeup. Therefore, children are being "programmed" by the multiple dimensions of the information that they are exposed to whether they are intently focused and paying attention to it or not.

This peripheral perception blind spot has profound implications for the effect of negative influences over time and their ability to modify beliefs and influence the values of our youth. As we look at contemporary youth issues such as entitlement or consumerism, it is easy to see how thousands of hours of age-inappropriate messaging are going to impact both the brain and the thinking and valuing process, with or without the individual's awareness. For example, when the tween goes into a local convenience store to buy a soft drink, he or she may also be absorbing information being relayed by the images of "cool" models depicted in cigarette and liquor ads throughout the store, even if those ads are not a focus of the child's attention.

DIMENSION THREE: DYNAMICS OF COMMUNICATION

The implications of these emerging developments during the tween years are next to be examined. Again we rely on the communication model you first learned about in Chapter 3's, "Dimension # Three: The Dynamics of Communication." The following sections detail the elements of the communication model, as they apply to the 8- to 12-year-old child's developmental stage.

The Attention Dynamic

If you've ever watched a nine-year-old intent on getting her parents to buy her a video game system, you know how focused attention can become. People essentially focus their attention on those things they need, want, or like.

A tween's capabilities at this stage of development coupled with her needs and wants, drive her to pay attention to particular things more than others. For example, during the rule-and-role stage, the needs of love and acceptance are high on the tween's list of priorities, so much of her waking time is preoccupied with this pursuit. Of course, the character of this focus of attention will vary from individual to individual, and the needs for love and acceptance may become prominent sooner for some individuals than for others.

Comprehension and Involvement (Emotional Valuing)

With his left brain maturing and most rational cognitive functions and capabilities in place, the 8- to 12-year-old can comprehend most communications within his vocabulary range and his abstraction abilities. As a result, the comprehension dynamic is in full force for the tween.

The tween's demonstration of involvement and emotional valuing may be somewhat less immediately forceful than in earlier years, even though those aspects of the communication dynamic also are quite strong for this age group. As we have pointed out, the child's developing rational mind can act as a sort of "throttle" on the full display of his emotions. When their needs and wants are strong, however, tweens will most certainly let you know what it is they are after. This also can be a highly sensitive period, as the tween's developing ego is at times quite fragile. Tweens may not communicate their insecurities or upsets, however, choosing instead to internalize their feelings.

YES!

With the knowledge that it may be difficult for your 9- to 12-year-old to share and articulate feelings, we suggest you establish set times either daily or weekly during which you and your child talk about feelings. And remember, these feelings can be positive—as in happiness, joy, excitement, satisfaction, love, or peace—as well as negative—for example, anger, sadness, hate, anxiety, worry, disappointment, frustration, guilt, depression, or fear.

Yielding to Wants and Desires

There is a direct correlation here between the way tweens communicate, their core developmental elements, and their prioritization of needs. Because they are passing through the rule-and-role stage, and because their needs for acceptance, love, and stimulation are so high, tweens have particularly strong desires related to the satisfaction of those needs. If a certain brand of clothing is "in" with her friends, that's what Cheri wants. If Zachary's buddies have the latest electronic game system, Zach is beside himself asking for it. The rule-and-role stage is a very powerful beginning for the drive to be one of the "in" crowd and to do, buy, and have what your peer group is doing, buying, and having.

YES!

So many products and activities are available for the 8- to 12-year-old age group that you must be careful not to overindulge your tween. Be particularly alert to the message or content of the things your tween is asking for and the values associated with those things. As a rule of thumb, before making any purchase ask yourself, "Is this going to contribute positively to my child's life?"

Retention, Action, and Reaction

Tweens will tend to remember what most appears to satisfy their needs—especially the needs for acceptance, success, and stimulation (fun). Because their "context" for living is still quite localized in the sense that they are focused mostly on their immediate world of friends, family, and school, tweens will tend to strongly retain informational and emotional content related to those needs.

The tween's action of either buying what he or she wants or asking for it is, of course, the natural result of the drive produced by the need/want process. The tween also has a significantly greater amount of personal money to spend, which plays a role in the increased importance of the action dynamic for this age.

The reaction dynamic is also more important for tweens than it was in earlier years. The 8- to 12-year-old is by now a relatively savvy consumer. If the product or program doesn't deliver or if it fast becomes boring, like anyone else the tween won't want to continue buying or using the product or program.

Communication

In the previous stage of the child's development, neither the cognitive abilities nor the social needs related to one's peers were in place to allow for much "word of mouth" about products and programs. Because the 8- to 12-year-old is now armed with rationality and the need to interrelate effectively with friends, however, the child is actually driven to communicate about the products and programs in his life. This drive is especially true as it relates to communications about entertainment-related products and programs, sports-related items, apparel, or anything that constitutes something of emotional importance among one's peer group.

MARKETING TO TWEENS

Tweens are a formidable market. As reflected in the title of a book by Dave Siegel, et al., *The Great Tween Buying Machine,*[1] tweens today not only are the recipients of millions of dollars of goods and services purchased for them, they have millions of dollars to spend out of their own pockets. Given the realities of the tween's developmental blind spots and communication dynamics, we need to examine some fundamental questions about the practices of marketing to children within this age group. For example, if a company knows that the need for acceptance is very high on a tween's list of priorities, is it irresponsible, for example, to design products and advertising campaigns specifically to exploit this need? Consider, for example, a cell phone sold under the name "Telepal" or some other name that links the apparatus to friendship and communication, and ad campaigns for this phone that depict lots of tweens chatting excitedly with one another using their Telepals. Is this type of advertising potentially harmful for the tweens who view it?

No, not in our view. A basic principle of marketing is to "know your consumers" and to know what they want and need. If the Telepal delivers on the promises its advertising makes, then great; it's most likely contributing in some way to the quality of life of those who buy and use it. Our guideline in most cases is this: If a company designs or promotes a product or program that in any way harms or otherwise degrades, deceives, or diminishes anyone, then that company is participating in unethical and irresponsible behavior.

But then consider this example: You've no doubt seen ads that use a classroom setting and that make the teacher out to be a dim-witted goofus. Often, these advertisements are attempting to exploit the tween and early teen need to develop more independence (control) from authority figures. Let's say what's being sold is a particular brand of sneakers. The advertisers show all the kids in class wearing that brand of sneakers and defying the teacher by putting their feet up on their desks. The teacher gets flustered and loses control of the class. The kids (and the sneakers) win, but at the expense of making a fool out of the teacher. What's the message? *Teachers can be had by students; you just have to know how to push their buttons. Kids are in control, not the teacher. Defiance works!*

This kind of advertising is irresponsible and could negatively influence the tweens who view it. Not only were teachers—through the use of a negative teacher archetype—cast in a bad light and made to look like fools, but the ad also shows defiance as admired and rewarded.

GOOD PRODUCT AND PROGRAM CHOICES FOR 8- TO 12-YEAR-OLDS

Again, the products and programs that are unlikely to be any cause for concern whatsoever make up a very short list. They include personal hygiene items, sports equipment, school supplies, and most card and traditional board and party games. Games of this healthy variety are particularly popular with the 8- to 12-year-old, for they provide plenty of opportunities for fun social interaction with friends and family at a time when self-expression can be sometimes tentative and self-conscious.

PRODUCTS AND PROGRAMS IN NEED OF MONITORING

Most categories of products and programs available in the market-place and media will need some degree of parental monitoring, super-vision, and guidance. As an effectively protective and nurturing parent, you must pay daily attention to what products and programs your tweens are becoming involved with, which is, perhaps, a daunting but necessary task.

Toys and Some Board Games

A couple of decades ago, you wouldn't find it out of the ordinary for eight- and nine-year-olds to peruse the shelves of toy stores looking per-haps for the latest fashion-doll phenomenon, new construction-toy ac-cessories, or new action figures to add to a military action figure set. Today, most traditional "toys" are beneath boys and girls 8 to 12, who consider themselves beyond that "kid stuff."

There are exceptions, such as the highly stylized Lego accessories and Pokémon soft conflict–themed character sets, trading cards, and "battle" games. In the late spring of every year, you'll see ads for high-powered squirt guns and outdoor toys such as Frisbees—toys that fre-quently appeal to children in this age group. Traditional board games such as Monopoly are very popular during this stage—in part, because of the drive to socialize with friends and family.

Barbie? Most girls are finished with Barbie by this stage except for some who continue to be involved—not with play patterns of dress-up so much anymore as with collecting and displaying their many dolls and accessories. Doll play is most definitely "out" except for an occasional return for nostalgia's sake.

Fashion is in, however, for 8- to 12-year-old girls. Clothing and accessories such as jewelry rank high on tweens' wish lists. The make-your-own-Barbie-clothes software has what it takes to attract and involve the eight-year-old and older girl because of its complexity and the creativity involved in using it. Nail and hair care items along with jewelry display products also hit the bull's-eye at this stage—products that allow tween girls to work and play with their nail, hair, and jewelry accessories, as well as display and store them in unique carrying cases.

Inappropriate games and toys. In our view, parents should be wary of programs and advertising that market toys and games that promote negative values, age-inappropriate sexuality, or violence. Examples include guns of any kind (even squirt guns that resemble realistic guns and rifles) and fantasy-based or futuristic war-based action figures, vehicles, and accessories.

Two cases in point: Remember the Garbage Pail Kids collector card series that entertained by calling attention to mucus, stench, and mild forms of gore? While tongue in cheek and mild in its offensiveness compared to some toys and games, Garbage Pail Kids certainly could not be classified as wholesome fun.

Jumping from mildly offensive to a major attack on human sensibilities is the game Ghettopoly. While it could be argued that Ghettopoly was never intended for 8- to 12-year-olds, board games are very popular with children of this age group, and many tweens could come in contact with this game. In a *New York Times* article, Bob Herbert describes some of the demeaning and reprehensible content of this game, stating that it promotes negative racial stereotypes. "It presents blacks as murderous, thieving, dope-dealing, carjacking degenerates. Instead of the familiar Monopoly pieces, like top hats and thimbles, Ghettopoly players get to move around the board as pimps, machine guns, and rocks of crack cocaine."[2]

Ghettopoly and similar games are inappropriate for children. In these dangerous and violent times, the last thing we need as a society is more people making light of the very illnesses we are trying to eradicate—maladies that are undermining efforts toward peace, respect for our fellow man, and common decency.

Soft-conflict characters. When it comes to 8- to 12-year-old kids, we cite Pokémon (Pocket Monsters) as one example of the borderline limit between a concept that's acceptable and one that crosses the line. In our view, Pokémon is an acceptable product and program for 8- to 12-year-olds. We would categorize Pokémon and similar toys as acceptable for this age group for several reasons.

- *Soft fantasy.* All the characters and settings are fantasy and nonrealistic. While the characters transform from less scary to more scary, even the most threatening dragons and other characters are within acceptable parameters. (Remember that children at this particular age and stage of development are able to discriminate more between what is real and what is fantasy, especially with clear fantasized visual images.)
- *Soft conflict.* We define soft conflict as using inherently nonviolent objects, such as water balloons, air, and sticky stuff, that pose no major threat if their use is emulated in real life. The battles between Pokémon characters are typically soft conflicts: One character might overpower the other using his superability to shoot frozen blasts of air at him, for example, while another wins by exuding sticky stuff to trap his opponent.
- *Good triumphs.* Ash Ketchum, the Master Trainer of the Pokémons, and his friends win in the end over Team Rocket, a pair of male and female soft villains who are up to no good. In the process, the villains' bad behavior is shown up as undesirable and ineffective.

A good deal of controversy surrounded the Pokémon phenomenon when kids started taking their collections of Pokémon cards to school and playing "battle-trading" games. Kids who lost cards in the skirmishes got upset, and cards were becoming a distraction at school. The problem was ameliorated when teachers and schools banned Pokémon cards from school—a good example of authority intervention. But the trouble caused at schools does not, in our view, constitute grounds for labeling such a product as inherently dangerous.

Television

Children younger than eight watch a great deal of television but are so physically active that their attention spans direct them into lots of different directions at once. Their entertainment time is more varied. After the age of 15 or so, teens have access to cars and their mobility increases, taking them out of the home and away from TV sets to some degree. But for the 8- to 12-year and the 13- to 15-year stages of development, TV takes up major portions of their days and evenings and is a major influencer.

Violence and sex on the screen. We're all aware of the obvious types of shows 8- to 12-year-olds should not be permitted to watch. These include programs, movies, and music videos depicting graphic sexual content, blood and gore, hack-'em-up violence, and other inappropriate images and ideas.

You'd be alarmed if you knew how popular sexually inappropriate TV programs are with this age group. In 2004, for example, one of the most popular new shows was *Desperate Housewives*. Guess which age segment according to surveys most tuned in to *DH*? Nine- to 12-year-olds! If you want more evidence, watch half a dozen or so of the steamiest music videos available; many tweens will be tuned into these videos as well.

In an AOL poll of 463,248 people who were asked the question "Does violent TV make children more aggressive?" approximately 76 percent answered yes. Some 18 percent said no, and 5 percent were undecided. These poll results indicate that many people are aware of the potential harm of allowing young children to watch this kind of programming. Even some of the stars who deliver violent content are aware of its potential for harm and don't let their own children watch the shows they star in. *Shield* star Michael Chiklis wouldn't allow his nine-year-old daughter, Autumn, to watch the show *even though she's in it.* (Don't be relieved if *Shield* or any other examples we cite are no longer on the air; new and even more objectionable offerings will always be taking their place.)

> **YES!**
> _____
>
> We strongly recommend that you strictly prohibit your tween's viewing of television programming with excessively violent and sexually explicit content.

Television role models. During the rule-and-role stage, the drive to figure out right and healthy ways to behave is particularly strong and therefore gives adult role models a powerful influence over tweens.

Beyond looking to their parents and other family members for role models, tweens also look to their teachers and older kids at school. Tweens also find role models in media personalities and sports stars, watching and learning from their behavior on and off the camera or sports fields. In an age of fallen stars, we commend the celebrities who have remained positive role models for youth; may they continue to do so.

Tweens also learn from the content of the programs and events they are tuned in to. How societal roles are portrayed on television (and in all media) has a substantial impact on children's emerging views of themselves and others. Far too many models are unhealthy to say the least. Many sitcom dads, for example, are made out to be idiots or incompetent in one way or another—Homer Simpson of *The Simpsons* and Al of *Married with Children* are just two examples. The females who appear in these cartoons are far too often portrayed as either la-la airheads or self-centered-nags-in-training; consider, for example, Lucy of *Peanuts,* Miss Piggy of the *Muppets,* Helga of *Hey Arnold!,* and Angelica of the *Rugrats.*

Choosing, monitoring, and censoring your tween's television programming. For the 8- to 12-year-old, we find that some programming is almost always positive, some is acceptable in small doses only, and some is outright dangerous. In general, however, television viewing falls into the neutral category, because—as we've mentioned previously— we believe that excessive time spent viewing *any* television program can have a potentially negative effect on children of any age. From the content of learning channels such as PBS, National Geographic, the History Channel, and the Discovery Channel, to the content of harmless game shows and many cartoons there is much television programming to be glad for. Many sitcoms (at least those appearing before 8 PM, when the "after-family hours" kick in) are not only entertaining, but often carry small life lessons and positive role modeling.

Currently, there are too many great programs that are appropriate for the 8- to 12-year-old to name all of them, but it would be derelict not to point to a few. Positive values messages can be "taken away" from such shows as *Everybody Loves Raymond, 8 Simple Rules, The Hughleys,* and *George Lopez.* While these are definitely not the idyllic days of *The Adventures of Ozzie & Harriet* and *Father Knows Best,* some current television programming can offer valuable lessons for this age group.

Some types of programming should, however, be allowed for tweens only in measured doses. The news is an example of such potentially harmful programming. As with many TV dramas and movies, the news is filled with stabbings, shootings, drive-by tragedies, and wars, and your 8- to 12-year-old doesn't benefit from being exposed to large doses of this negativity. Limit TV news time and then discuss the news and what's happening around the nation and world with your tweens—maybe at those family meals you're heading up. Your child will pick up plenty of what's going on in the world just by passing through; your discussions can help your tween understand and cope with current events.

We'd also caution against excessive cartoon watching—especially those cartoons with violent and otherwise inappropriate content, such as the foulmouthing in *South Park* and the sexually loaded dialogue that helped make *Beavis & Butt Head* famous. We believe that no preadolescent should be allowed free access to cartoons such as the sexy *Drawn Together* or the controversial *South Park.*

Also, some types and aspects of television are inherently dangerous. We cannot overestimate the dangers inherent in IIIO—Invisible and Intangible Information Overload. As a caring parent or guardian, you can train yourself to recognize and combat the hidden stresses that result from too much time with any technology, and be sure your children follow a varied schedule that includes such things as time with pets, out-of-doors activities, sports, clubs, family time, and cultural events.

YES!

In our view, placing a TV in a tween's bedroom is tantamount to giving up parental control. Consider either not allowing your tween to have a TV in his or her bedroom or at least restricting TV viewing to specified hours, such as with certain programs on weekends and no TV after 8 PM.

Food and Beverages

When it comes to your 8- to 12-year-old's food and beverage consumption, there is even more reason for concern than with younger children. New research from the *Journal of the American Dietetic Association* indicates that many children today are spending a lot of time absent-mindedly snacking. A survey was conducted of 615 children, ages 8 to 17, and their parents and it concluded:

- More than 50 percent of children and teens eat—some of them constantly—when they are playing video or computer games or doing homework.
- Kids often eat after school, after dinner, and off and on during the rest of the day.
- Parents significantly underestimate how much their kids are snacking, unaware of some of the foods being purchased at school, convenience stores, and restaurants.[3]

Three key factors come into play during this stage of development regarding food and beverage selection:

1. *Choice.* As the tween ages, he has more of his own money to spend and more freedom from parental control regarding food and beverage choices. Ideally, as this stage progresses, parents and teachers have made an impression on tweens regarding the need for a healthy diet, and the tweens' menu choices reflect what they've learned.

2. *Modeling.* Because the 8- to 12-year-old is in the rule-and-role stage of development, she is actively seeking out role models to emulate their behavior. Modeling healthy dietary choices for your child is perhaps more critical at this stage than at any other. This is the stage when the child's strongest beliefs, values, and attitudes—about diet, exercise, and all other aspects of life—are being formulated.

3. *Character power.* As a tween progresses from 8 to 12, the persuasive impact on the child of cartoonlike characters *used* in conjunction with food and beverages diminishes, but doesn't disappear entirely. While you would not typically see a tween wearing a T-shirt to school that sports a Cap'n Crunch or Tony the Tiger or the Trix Rabbit, in the safety (away from possible peer critique) of their own homes, cereal, snack, and beverage characters like L. C. (Lucky) Leprechaun and the Flintstones continue to add an extra element of fun and entertainment to tweens' eating and drinking experiences.

YES!

Even with more control and choice available for your tween, it's still very much the responsibility of parents to set down guidelines, limits, and rules about food, snack, and beverage alternatives—and, as important, to enforce them. (We're quite aware of how difficult this can be given how many unhealthy food and beverage alternatives are readily available outside the home, but the recommendation remains.)

Technology, Computer Software, and the Internet

Enter the age and stage of technology! The typical 8- to 12-year-old quickly becomes facile with a wide variety of technological devices such as cell phones, calculators, electronic game systems, electronic notepads, and desktop, portable, and handheld computers. With certain cautions in place, such as the need for balance and the concern for IIIO, most of these electric gadgets can add to the child's ability to communicate and to be more effective in the world.

A Fitness Program for Tweens

As stated, obesity statistics are skyrocketing. Child and parent education and action are critical to stop the bulge before it becomes a lifestyle. Programs such as Los Angeles–based Dr. Naomi Neufeld's KidShape® program[4] are healthy steps in the right direction. Dr. Neufeld's foundation offers three curricula designed to teach the entire family how to eat more nutritiously; make exercise a fun part of the daily routine; form new, healthy habits; and to like themselves, regardless of size: KidShape is designed for children ages 6 to 14. The second curriculum is Kinder-Shape for children ages three to five. Under development and trial is TeenShape, a program for 13- to 18-year-olds. Parents can also learn about Neufeld's program via her book, *Kid Shape*.

While a variety of educational software titles provide solid learning experiences for the tween, these are typically incorporated into the classroom and, therefore, are not common consumer items. Parents, it seems, expend a good deal of money and effort to get their children off to a good start during the preschool years with supplemental software learning experiences, but after school starts, they don't feel the need for these programs.

For homework purposes, tweens—like so many of us—rely on the Internet. But the Internet offers danger, as well. If your nine-year-old wants to check out adult porn sites, download the latest violent gangsta-rap lyrics, purchase prescription drugs or cigarettes, or find out how to build a bomb, he or she probably can at the worldwide shopping mall called the Internet.

Parents and educators must use extreme vigilance and take every precaution to restrict and watchdog the tween's Internet activities. Even more dangerous than the access the Internet provides for your tween is the access the Internet offers would-be predators *to* your 8- to 12-year-old. The ostensibly innocent Web site, http://www.myspace.com—"a place for friends"—is a case in point. Children put up their own pages with pictures and personal information on the site and can be contacted by anyone who accesses the site.

Those who promote and market adult-oriented Internet content must do their part to prevent tweens and all young people from accessing their sites. It's also incumbent upon both hardware and software manufacturers to come up with new ways to restrict Internet access and to ensure privacy.

YES!

More than anyone else, parents are responsible for monitoring their children's Internet access and activities and to set strict guidelines and limits for Internet use. Given the Internet's broad array of age-inappropriate content and potential for danger, dogged and consistent enforcement of these limits is a must for any parent whose tween has access to the Internet.

Films

Many parents are careful to shield their younger children from age-inappropriate film experiences, whether in theaters or on home video. As children move through the tween years, however, far too many parents loosen the reins, misguidedly assuming their 8- to 12-year-olds are able to handle most film content (short of R or NC-17 rated films). We recommend, instead, a tightening of the reins, to protect tweens from disturbing or age-inappropriate content that can appear even in PG-rated films.

Tweens also spend a great deal more time hanging out with their friends and their friends' families. Different families have different standards for what is acceptable viewing or entertainment, however, so parents need to work a bit harder as their children move into and through the tween years to stay on top of all the experiences their children are engaged in.

> The Motion Picture Association rating system is . . . "nothing but a smoke screen to provide cover for immoral and unconscionable business practices."
> Arizona Senator John McCain

Choosing appropriate films. An excellent film rating and review resource for parents is the FilmValues.com Web site. The reviews posted on this site are excellent and chock-full of detail. By taking a moment to read through some of the film reviews on this site, parents also can gain some valuable insights into the type of material that is being communicated to children through films.

On the FilmValues.com Web site, a ratings box gives a snapshot profile of the film's age-appropriateness and content (including nudity, blood, profanity, sex, violence, and so on). The site also rates films for the degree of parental guidance they require and their "watchability for adults." In addition to the ratings box, the site also presents lengthy and detailed reviews for parents, detailing Plot Overview, Degree of Violence and Scariness, Types of Crimes committed, Moral Issues and Values portrayed, Sexuality and Gender Issues, and Types of Substances (alcohol, tobacco, drugs) used by characters.

Monitoring films for negative "take-away" messages. Movies with scary content are not going away nor should they. A good horror flick once in a while can provide great viewing fun for older teenagers or adults. Often, however, the problem with these and other violent or stress-inducing films is the character-undermining ideas or sentiments viewers—particularly young, impressionable tween viewers—"take away" from the experience.

A *take-away,* the way we define it, is a clear message imbedded in media content that can have a lasting impact. Negative behavior and values may be promoted in a film and may negatively influence the moviegoer's own personal belief-value system. The demented Woody Harrelson character in *Natural Born Killers,* for example, after violently blowing away dozens of people, escapes from prison and is shown happily motoring away with his family in an RV at the end of the movie. The takeaway from this film tells viewers that the bad guy and his twisted values win.

Equally as insidious is the take-away of excessive doses of stress hormones that assault the brain of the unaware moviegoer, simply as a result of stress-inducing film content.

Film violence clearly has a long-term impact on young people. According to Dr. John P. Murray:

> When children watch violent movies, they know that they
> are watching make-believe scenes, yet their brains process the

images as "real" and store those images in the same place where real-life traumatic events are stored, according to recent Senate testimony. "The brain treats entertainment violence as something significant and something real—and it stores this violence as long-term memory."[5]

As we've said before, your children are learning all the time, whether they are aware of it or not. This "always on" learning can be especially dangerous for tweens when they view violent or otherwise age-inappropriate films.

Although the Motion Picture Association film-rating system ostensibly was designed to guide parents regarding the content and age-appropriateness of any film, this rating system isn't always accurately applied nor are its guidelines consistently enforced. It's time to establish reliable means of monitoring the actions of movie theater personnel and real penalties for infractions. Until then, parents must monitor and control their impressionable tween's exposure to all forms of media, including films.

Publications

Certain publications that target tweens are healthy and advisable, including *Boys' Life, Disney Adventures, National Geographic for Kids,* and *Sports Illustrated for Kids.* Publications to be concerned about include magazines and some comics with objectionably violent or sexual content, some electronic game magazines, adult and teen-targeted sensationalist rags, such as the *National Enquirer, Sun,* and *Star.* As with other media, the degree and frequency of potentially harmful themes and content are on the increase in publications.

PRODUCTS AND PROGRAMS THAT ARE INHERENTLY DANGEROUS

While bad habits can form long before a child reaches the ages of 8 to 12, it's important to be clear that these preadolescent years are rife with potential pitfalls. Tweens are busy during this stage formulating many of the values and the attitudes and the behavior they will carry into adolescence and adulthood. It's particularly important, therefore, to make every effort to guide your tweens away from unhealthy and inherently dangerous products, programs, and activities such as those listed here.

Electronic Games

At the top of the list of greatest dangers to the 8- to 12-year-old are violent electronic games. In previous chapters, we've enumerated the reasons why these games are dangerous, including the interactivity they involve, the first-person nature of play, where the player becomes the shooter or perpetrator, the degree of bloody violence, and a reward system that positively reinforces violent acts. But tweens, because of their developmental realities and vulnerabilities, can be particularly susceptible to the dangers of exposure to violent electronic games. If you think the game-rating system will provide all the guidance you need in reviewing and approving electronic games for your tween, you could be terribly wrong. As you'll see in the following sections, the burden again falls on you to carefully monitor and protect your tween from exposure to these inherently dangerous items.

Game ratings and advertising. A rating system in place for electronic games parallels the rating system for films (you can learn more about this system from the Entertainment Software Rating Board, or ESRB, Web site at http://www.esrb.org). The ESRB uses this system of rating codes:

C   for early childhood
E   for everyone—similar to a G movie rating
T   for teens
M   for mature (ages 17+)
A   for adults only (ages 18+)

We've found no problems with the C- and E-rated games. These include nonviolent chase and fantasy games such as Pooh and Tigger's Hunny Safari, Frogger, Mario Brothers, Harry Potter and the Chamber of Secrets, and the Zelda series. They also include sports games such as Madden NFL 2004 and racing games such as the Hot Wheels racing series.

The problem with the remaining games isn't because of the rating system, but is related to accessibility. The ratings don't actually prevent children below the recommended age groups from actually playing the games. Games rated T, M, and A are easily accessible to tweens. The ESRB rating system also includes "content notes," brief descriptors to tell the type of game content that could be of "interest or concern," such as violence, blood, or sexually suggestive themes. Here are some samplings of T-rated games, and the content notes and descriptions printed on the packaging.

- *Arc the Lad* (Sony PlayStation). √ Violence √ Mild language √ Alcohol Reference
- *Freedom Fighters* (PlayStation). √ Violence ". . . an arsenal of machine guns, Molotov cocktails, and other tools of the revolution"
- *Tomb Raider* (PlayStation). √ Blood √ Violence
- *Dungeons & Dragons Heroes* (Xbox). √ Blood and Gore √ Violence
- *Summer Heat Beach Volleyball* (PlayStation). √ Suggestive themes (on package): "Dress 'em as you see fit."
- *Splinter Cell* (Nintendo). √ Blood and Gore √ Violence (premise from the package): "You are Sam Fisher. You have the right to spy, steal, destroy, and assassinate, to ensure that American freedoms are protected. If captured, the U.S. government will disavow any knowledge of your existence."

Then there are the M-rated games that also end up in the hands of 8- to 12 year-olds, games such as:

- *Resident Evil Dead Aim* (Capcom for PlayStation). √ Blood and Gore √ Violence
- *Bloodrayne 2* (Majesco). √ Blood and Gore √ Strong Language √ Violence (The movie rights have been purchased.) (description on packaging): "Half-human, half-vampire, all-woman. Let this wickedly sexy heroine escort you into the terrifying world of the occult."

When it comes to directly advertising these games, it appears that most manufacturers and game-system companies keep to self-imposed guidelines. (They don't dare violate them.) According to the ESRB Web site:

> The ESRB's Advertising Review Council (ARC) promotes responsible advertising and marketing practices in the computer and video-game industry. ARC's goal is to ensure that software publishers follow standardized requirements for the display of rating information and guarantee that advertising is appropriate, responsible, truthful, and accurate.
>
> ARC implements marketing guidelines that prohibit game publishers from targeting inappropriate audiences. For example, the marketing guidelines prohibit the placement of ads for Mature-rated games in magazines where 45 percent of readers are under 17 years old. Publishers of the leading game-enthusiast magazines have agreed to adopt ARC's Principles and Guidelines and provide joint oversight and monitoring services.

The lack of direct advertising of these games is all well and good for it does assist somewhat in their nonproliferation—but only somewhat. As established earlier, the 8- to 12-year-old stage is a period filled with inter-peer communication and pervasive and effective word of mouth regarding products and programs. It's also a period when far too many parents loosen the reins on their children's activities. These parents and other caretakers are either unaware of what their children are up to with these electronic games or have turned their backs on the very real dangers lurking there. The bottom line is that unless adult limits and censorship are in place, the accessibility of these games and their advertisements to the 8- to 12-year-old is an alarming reality.

We highly recommend that parents familiarize themselves with this electronic game rating system and then view and even play a variety of the different types of games themselves. Working from this firsthand knowledge, parents can best determine which electronic games they can safely allow their tweens to play.

The stealth impact of inappropriate game–play. The impact on young people of age-inappropriate game playing takes the form of "under-the-radar," subconscious teaching and learning. That's the "stealth impact" we're pointing to here and the reason we have subtitled this book: *How Irresponsible Marketers Are Stealing the Minds of Your Children.* Our children's attitudes are being unconsciously shaped by their experiences related to sexuality, violence, and man's inhumanity to man. Previously in Chapter 3, we discussed brain-based learning principle #9: *Learning involves conscious and unconscious processes.* Negative experiences predetermine negative attitudes and behavior and they are learned both consciously and unconsciously.

Barbara Meltz, in a *Boston Globe* article, "Legislation Would Target Violence in Video Games,"[6] points to the fact that video games are, in fact, teaching tools.

> Iowa State University psychologist Craig Anderson is the nation's preeminent researcher on the effect of exposure to violent video games. As Anderson and other researchers see it, . . . : If your 11-year-old spends 6 or 7 hours a week in focused concentration on violent action in a video game, will it make him a rampaging killer? No. Will it mean that when someone accidentally bumps into him at the cafeteria, he's more likely to interpret it as a threat and respond aggressively? Yes.

Responsibility for the often horrendously abusive, violent, and bloody content of some electronic games doesn't stop with the game developers. It includes the hardware/game system companies they develop the games for, the actors who lend their images, voices, and talents; the ad agencies that promote them; and the retailers who sell them—far too often without regard for ratings. In our view, these games are extremely dangerous—rating system or not—and should not be on the market. These games are undermining the morality of our young and the culture they are growing into.

Alcohol, Tobacco, and Sex

As we've established, 8- to 12-year-olds are exploring different ways of thinking, valuing, and behaving. They are making key decisions about themselves—who they are going to be like, and how they are going to act. It's during the latter years of this stage that many young people first experiment with alcohol and tobacco as well as sex in many cases.

YES!

To best ensure that your tween isn't negatively affected by violent or otherwise inappropriate or harmful video-game content, restrict him or her to only "E for Everyone" games. Even then, restrict game playtime because of IIIO and its related stress. If you choose to allow your child access to T- or M-rated games, make sure to review them yourself and discuss the content with your child.

By now there can be no doubt about our point of view regarding the aggressive marketing of violence, drugs, and age-inappropriate sexuality to our children through video games, TV, and movies. We've also made clear our views on the inept and unenforced regulations that continue to support lax approaches at censorship and restriction of access to this violence.

The most abhorrent and reproachable marketing efforts are those that advertise, promote, and glorify the use of alcohol and tobacco. Tweens are very vulnerable to such advertising, because of their strong desire to be "grown-up." They believe that behaving like their music, TV, and film icons will make them "cool." If the latest pop icon smokes, then that must be the cool thing to do. If a TV idol gets drunk, the typical tween response is, *Wow! Can't wait to try the stuff myself!*

Given the government and FCC restrictions on directly marketing to kids, the alcohol and tobacco companies resort to less direct-marketing techniques to reach this audience. Their strategies include aggressive promotional efforts in convenience stores, broad distribution of apparel with their products and logos prominently displayed, and sponsorship of concerts and sporting events. And, as we've mentioned previously, alcohol and tobacco companies have redoubled their efforts in countries that don't restrict their marketing approaches. These companies know habits form early.

And sex? If as much as 70 percent of TV programming has sexual content in one form or another as the Kaiser report[7] claims, then so-called innocent sitcoms, reality shows, and TV movies are pumping in sexual attitudes right and left during the average tween's two to six hours of daily screen watching.

Drugs

It's not too early during the tween years to be concerned about drug use. Toward the upper limit of this 8- to 12-year age range, statistics show that around 10 percent of kids experiment with and/or use drugs (primarily marijuana). That's one in ten—and that one could be your child. Some of the warning signs to be on the watch for include loss of interest in family activities, sudden increase or decrease in appetite, lying, hiding out in their room, verbal and/or physically abusive behavior, disappearance of valuable items or money, depression, and the smell of alcohol or marijuana. Please note that the presence of many of these signs does not necessarily mean drug use—passage through the emotional and hormonal storm of adolescence may in itself account for some of these indicators.

KEY VULNERABILITIES OF 8- TO 12-YEAR-OLDS

We've outlined a number of developmental realities and blind spots that lead to vulnerabilities within children between the ages of 8 and 12. To summarize, here are the key vulnerabilities of this age group.

- *Decision making.* Equipped with concrete rational abilities, children in this age group are busy making key decisions about themselves, others, and the world. Egos are quite fragile at this age and stage. Decision-making skills are still basic and concrete without the higher thinking elements that are necessary for success in an adult, information-based culture.
- *Need for acceptance.* Now that they spend significant time away from home and with their peers, tweens have a particularly strong need to be accepted and liked by others. They want to do what's "in"; they want to be included and approved of.
- *Experimentation.* In the quest to discover who they are and to find their own boundaries as well as possibilities, some children in this age group are open to trying new things.
- *Emulation.* Tweens are looking for and latching on to role models to assist them with their own design of the self. Irresponsible marketers create and promote characters with negative values, attitudes, and behavior specifically with the tween in mind.

- *Seeking morality.* Tweens are actively seeking to figure out right values, attitudes, and behavior. This is their time of greatest need for positive role modeling and guidance.
- *Wants and desires.* Raising kids becomes quite an expensive enterprise once the tween years begin. Wanting and asking for big-ticket items such as video game systems, computers, sound systems, TVs, and cell phones is a weekly if not daily affair.

A WEEK IN THE LIFE

A review of a week in the life of a hypothetical child in this 8- to 12-year age range will shed additional light on problems and provide potential guidelines, examples, and solutions for creating an empowering environment for tweens. In this profile, we'll focus on 9-year-old Marty and his 11-year-old sister, Kristy.

EXPERIENCE	EMPOWERING	DISEMPOWERING
Parents/ Home Life	Both of Marty and Kristy's parents are involved closely in all aspects of their lives. Even though mom works, she has arranged her schedule to be home as they arrive from school each afternoon. They are a close-knit family and once or twice a month they go on outings together to museums or amusement parks, movies, or just to eat out together. Dad makes sure each family member gets plenty of opportunity to share what's going on with each of them.	Both mom and dad work and don't get home until dinnertime. By this time, Kristy is typically over at her friend Shari's house and doesn't get home until almost bedtime. (Kristy loves Shari's mom—she's always available to hear anything that's going on with the girls.) Marty spends unsupervised time on the Internet most afternoons, plays electronic games, and watches cartoons. Everybody pretty much goes their own way on the weekends—dad plays golf, mom catches up on her taped soaps and works in the garden, and the kids hang out at friends' houses.

EXPERIENCE	EMPOWERING	DISEMPOWERING
Toys/Electronic Games	Both Marty and Kristy for the most part no longer are interested in playing with action figures, dolls, or other traditional toys. Marty's collection of *Star Wars* figures sits gathering dust on the bookshelf and Kristy's Barbies are in a box under her bed ready for the occasional nostalgic revisit. Their toys now are more expensive such as video games (both kids are only allowed to have safe, approved games and can play for a maximum of only two hours on weekends). They play a lot of board and card games with family and friends.	Marty has become addicted to electronic games of all kinds. Just about any hour you'll find him feverishly battling away as the cortisol pumps into his system. He also has a collection of fantasy and violence-filled comic books. Kristy isn't interested at all in any of the toys of her earlier years, and the appeal of electronic games has come and gone for her. She's much more interested in music and starting to get quite interested in boys. The "toy" cosmetics her mom bought for her have transformed into adult versions and she spends a good deal of time worrying about looking pretty.
Learning Hardware & Software	Marty uses math software to assist him with his troubles with math. Kristy doesn't use any.	None.
Room Décor	Marty has sports champion posters plastered on his walls—like Michael Jordan, Wayne Gretzky, and Andre Agassi. With the help of her mom, Kristy has decorated her room using a theme of flowers, fairies, and elves.	There's no particular theme to Marty's room. He's got a large *Matrix* film poster on his wall, and overall his room's a mess. Every square inch of Kristy's wall space is covered with posters and clippings from magazines—all having to do with movie, TV, and music celebrities. Her dresser has a huge mirror and is cluttered with cosmetics and jewelry, all in disarray.

EXPERIENCE	EMPOWERING	DISEMPOWERING
Television/ Film	Both Marty and Kristy have TVs in their rooms but are only allowed to watch a maximum of one approved show an evening during the week and only after they've finished their homework. Weekend TV watching has no limits except those that are self-imposed or declared off-limits by their parents. R-rated films are out of the question, along with PG-13 films that their parents screen out carefully, often with the assistance of http://www.filmvalues.com.	Almost any waking hour you'll hear the TVs on in both Marty and Kristy's rooms. There are no restrictions except that they have to turn TVs off by 11 PM. Only R-rated movies are off-limits and Marty and Kristy's parents aren't really tuned in to which kinds of movies their kids are frequenting—much less do they discuss any of them in any way other than superficially: "How'd you like *Scary Movie II*, honey? . . . It was great? That's nice. . . ."
Food & Beverage	Mom has always prepared very healthy meals at home. She still makes Marty's lunch for school as well. Kristy eats at school where lunches aren't as healthy as the ones mom makes, but by now, Kristy has learned to make choices in the cafeteria line that are as healthy as possible. As a family they once in a while enjoy fast-food or pizza treats, but more often when they go out to eat they select restaurants with healthier menus.	Mom and dad rarely think or talk about choosing healthy food and beverages. In fact, everyone is overweight except for Kristy who is actually too skinny because of the beginnings of an eating disorder. She's so preoccupied with looking like the TV, film, and model stars she admires that she eats either too sparingly or centers her diet on junk food with little nutritional value.

EXPERIENCE	EMPOWERING	DISEMPOWERING
The Internet	Marty and Kristy's parents are very restrictive in how their children use the Internet. They are restricted to e-mail chatting with friends on the weekends only and to using the Internet for study-related purposes.	No restrictions.
Music & Radio	Marty doesn't listen to the radio. Kristy listens to music as background while she studies. She only listens to soft rock and avoids music with objectionable lyrics. She also has a collection of CDs, none of which have negative lyrical content.	Kristy and her girlfriends have gone bananas over the latest teen pop music stars and not only listen to their music but watch them on MTV. They look up to them as role models and attempt to emulate them in dress and attitude. Away from home, Marty is almost always seen with earphones and listens to all sorts of music. His favorites are rap, hip-hop, and even some gangsta-rap music with lyrical content that is quite violent and filled with sexuality—content way beyond his years.
Publications/ Books	Marty and Kristy are encouraged to read and, in fact, are happily engaged with their parents' encouragement in a weekly reading program that involves checking out one or two new books from the library each week. Marty and Kristy both still like *National Geographic for Kids,* and Marty loves *Sports Illustrated for Kids.* They've outgrown *Disney Adventures.*	The only publications Marty reads are comic books and magazines dealing with electronic games. Kristy's weekly reading of publications is substantial and includes the *National Enquirer, Globe,* and *Star* publications as well as teen- and adult-targeted magazines having to do with celebrities, style, and makeup.

EXPERIENCE	EMPOWERING	DISEMPOWERING
Apparel	There's no issue here. Both Marty and Kristy wear conventional yet stylish clothing.	Kristy wins most battles with her mom over how to dress. While her mom puts her foot down once in a while, Kristy frequently looks like one of the music icons she so admires. Her dress is often that of girls way beyond her 11 years. In addition, she is into makeup and has double-pierced both ears. She's asking mom to be able to get a tattoo, but mom has won that battle so far. Marty doesn't really pay much attention to how he looks; he's actually relatively sloppy in the way he dresses, (reflective in part of low self-esteem).
Telephone	Time on the telephone is a nonissue for Marty. Kristy has her own cell phone, especially for safety reasons. She chats with her girlfriends on the home phone but is limited to 15 minutes a call.	Marty is pretty much a loner at school so phoning friends is not something he's into. Kristy, on the other hand, is always on the phone with her girlfriends and, in fact, has a boyfriend, Greg, who she talks to every day as well. She also has a cell phone and frequently has gone over her minutes limit, causing dad to have fits when bill time comes around.

EXPERIENCE	EMPOWERING	DISEMPOWERING
Alcohol, Drugs, Tobacco	Family discussions related to the dangers of alcohol, drugs, and smoking have made strong impacts on both Marty and Kristy. Marty and Kristy's parents don't smoke and they drink socially or occasionally with dinner at home. Overall, they are solid models for responsibility regarding alcohol. Drugs are out of the question.	Marty and Kristy's parents are poor role models when it comes to alcohol, tobacco, and drugs. Not only do they both overindulge in alcohol, but dad smokes a pack and a half of cigarettes a day. Kristy has found marijuana paraphernalia in mom's drawers. At the age of nine, Marty hasn't tried anything yet, but two of his buddies are encouraging him to smoke and drink and try pot. Unknown to her parents, Kristy drinks and smokes occasionally with her friends and has already tried marijuana on several occasions. She and her friends have obviously been influenced by the negative modeling of her star icons.

In an ideal scenario, the Martys and Kristys of the world have survived and thrived during their rite of passage through the tween years. They have:

- Emerged with the solid beginnings of positive self-esteem.
- Learned to engage in open and honest communication with their parents.
- Developed a sense of values that includes as much value placed on family, integrity, and friendship as it includes the desire and drive for consumer items.
- Learned through consumer education curriculum and from parental guidance some of the traps inherent in marketing and advertising and are becoming savvy consumers.
- Balanced their use of free time between time with technology such as TV, video games, and the Internet, and time spent with

outdoor and sports activities, with family and friends, and with reading.
- Learned to avoid age-inappropriate products and programs and choose healthy options on their own.
- Learned to distinguish between hyped heroes and the real thing when it comes to the role models they look up to.

PARENT AND CARETAKER TOOLBOX FOR YOUTH ENRICHMENT STRATEGIES

As in previous chapters, here is a summary of all the recommended Youth Enrichment Strategies for the 8- to 12-year-old stage of development you've read in this chapter.

- Be careful not to talk down to your 8- to 12-year-old. In fact, include your tween in conversations you might have assumed were beyond him or her. Asking for his or her views on different subjects will reinforce the idea that you respect that opinion.
- Feed and nurture your child's formation of positive self-esteem by offering praise directly and in front of others.
- Your child's need to feel "OK" and accepted is particularly strong during this period. Do everything you can to communicate this acceptance verbally ("I love you," "Good job," "I'm proud of you") and nonverbally (through hugs, pats on the back, reassuring touches, and so on).
- Avoid situations that impose on your child tasks he or she is not yet ready to tackle. Do not demand too much too soon. Consciously place your child in situations in which succeess can be met physically, mentally, emotionally, socially, and morally by behaving and doing the right thing.
- We recommend discussions at home about commercial messages and marketing strategies. In addition, we strongly suggest parents and educators insist on media education in school.
- Tweens are very alert to exactly what rules, guidelines, and limits they are expected to adhere to. Make sure that rules are crystal clear and that they are enforced in a loving and consistent manner.
- A growing tween's self-esteem can be dramatically undermined by his or her conclusion of "not being good enough." In fact, most

adults feel they are "not good enough" in one way or another. To instill the belief "I'm good enough" in your child, avoid undue criticism and find every opportunity for praise.

- With the knowledge that it may be difficult for your 8- to 12-year-old to share and articulate feelings, we suggest you establish set times either daily or weekly during which you and your child talk about feelings. And remember, these feelings can be positive—as in happiness, joy, excitement, satisfaction, love, or peace—as well as negative—for example, anger, sadness, hate, anxiety, worry, disappointment, frustration, guilt, depression, or fear.

- So many products and activities available for the 8- to 12-year-old age group that you must be careful not to overindulge your tween. Be particularly alert to the message or content of the things your tween is asking for and the values associated with those things. As a rule of thumb, before making any purchase ask yourself, "Is this going to contribute positively to my child's life?"

- We strongly recommend that you strictly prohibit your tween's viewing of television programming with excessively violent and sexually explicit content.

- In our view, placing a TV in a tween's bedroom is tantamount to giving up parental control. Consider either not allowing your tween to have a TV in his or her bedroom or at least restricting TV viewing to specified hours, such as with certain programs on weekends and no TV after 8 PM.

- Even with more control and choice available for your tween, it's still very much the responsibility of parents to set down guidelines, limits, and rules about food, snack, and beverage alternatives—and, as important, to enforce them. (We're quite aware of how difficult this can be given how many unhealthy food and beverage alternatives are readily available outside the home, but the recommendation remains.)

- More than anyone else, parents are responsible for monitoring their children's Internet access and activities and to set strict guidelines and limits for Internet use. Given the Internet's broad array of age-inappropriate content and potential for danger, dogged and consistent enforcement of these limits is a must for any parent whose tween has access to the Internet.

- To best ensure that your tween isn't negatively affected by violent or otherwise inappropriate or harmful video-game content, restrict him or her to only "E for Everyone" games. Even then, restrict game playtime because of IIIO and its related stress. If you choose to allow your child access to T- or M-rated games, make sure to review them yourself and discuss the content with your child.

BRING ON THE HORMONES!

We've arrived. We've made it to that stage of development revered and mostly feared by parents—adolescence. By now, in the best of scenarios, a great many ideals, values, and positive attitudes and behavior are in place to allow the child to self-direct when it comes to daily choices regarding what's beneficial and what's potentially and actually harmful. There remains a strong need for parental vigilance, guidance, and the imposition of limits, however—perhaps greater today than in decades past.

Leaving the tweenagers behind, it's on to an exploration of the teen years and early adolescence, ages 13 to 15.

The test of the morality of a society is what it does for its children.
Dietrich Bonhoeffer

7

EARLY ADOLESCENCE
Ages 13 to 15

Yielding to the worry that our car might break down and leave her stranded somewhere, I purchased a cell phone for my oldest girl to use in emergencies. To me, "emergency" means "You're 52 seconds late for curfew; where are you?" To my daughter, it means, "Oh m'God, Heather like broke up with Derek AGAIN!" My cellular company recently informed me that I've been elected their 1999 "Man of the Year!"[1]

an exasperated parent of a teenager

There's no shortage of adjectives or exasperated cries for help on the part of befuddled parents during this stage of their children's development.

- "I don't know what happened," a mom of a 13-year-old complains. "One day she was the sweetest little thing and now she's transformed into some kind of monster with a will to fight me at every turn."
- "Mysterious, that's all I can say," says the dad of 15-year-old Jennie. "I don't know who my little girl is anymore. She won't speak to me about anything important that's going on in her life. All I get is superficial weather reports like 'I'm fine, Dad.'"
- "I never see Brad and Robin any more," their mom says sadly. "They're always gone somewhere or hanging out at friends' houses. Sometimes I wonder why I had kids in the first place. Maybe I *don't* have kids any more; they're never around."

Adult exasperations with teens don't seem to be limited to current times either, as it is made clear by this quote from Socrates:

> Children today are tyrants. They contradict their parents, gobble their food, and tyrannize their teachers.

Although it's true that increased cognitive abilities and social independence do lead some teens toward radically independent thinking, valuing, and even rebellious behavior, not all teens are rebellious. The majority of teens, in fact, are relatively well-behaved adults-in-training. When it comes to consumption, however, early teens face real challenges. With unfamiliar hormones grabbing the reins of reason, they find themselves galloping toward a quagmire of unsteadiness, especially in affairs of the heart and relationships. They have more of their own spending money, and use it in constant efforts to dump whatever is "out" and get, watch, play, wear, and eat whatever is "in." You learn about these challenges and the vulnerabilities teens face as a result of their developmental age and stage. The information you learn in this chapter will help you spot marketing or program messages intended to prey upon the vulnerabilities of the developing adolescent mind.

DIMENSION ONE: DEVELOPMENTAL ELEMENTS

In the first years of adolescence—during the ages of 13 to 15—teens go through major physical, cognitive, social, and emotional changes. These changes contribute to substantial shifts in how a teenager perceives the world, formulates values and attitudes, and behaves.

The Teen Brain

Adults often assume that the brain of a teenager is complete and has reached physical maturation. In reality, the human brain doesn't reach its full physical size until the individual is in his or her 20s. As we've mentioned in previous chapters, the brain's cortex and other components continue to build in density throughout the individual's childhood, adolescence, and early adulthood, as the brain builds thicker and more extended internal connections, like an expanding web. Of special importance are the connections in the frontal lobe of the brain during adolescence, for this is the area that houses the higher thinking skills of planning, organization, strategizing, judgment, and self-reflection. The frontal lobe is, in effect, the "gateway" to a child's future and to the critical skills for creativity, imagination, self-understanding, self-mastery, and self-management.

The brain's development can be dramatically influenced by the teen brain's *use*. During adolescence, extra, unused neural connections deteriorate and die, and are swept away in a sort of "housecleaning" within the brain. This housecleaning process can have serious implications for the teen's future cognitive development. A typical contemporary teen is mesmerized by today's technological gadgets and immersed in amusing and distracting video games, television, or films. Many teens prefer to spend their time engaged in mindless and passive tasks, rather than tackling those "harder" tasks that require higher order thinking skills of analysis, synthesis, planning, self-reflection, problem solving, critical thinking, and abstract reasoning.

As a result, those areas of the brain that process mindless media get stronger, while the prefrontal lobe can actually lose ground because of the use-it-or-lose-it housecleaning process. Add to this the potential for teen experimentation with dangerous drugs and alcohol and immersion in violent media and you have set the stage for producing a cognitively handicapped child. As parents, we need to do all we can to help our teenage children avoid the risks of incomplete brain development at this critical stage.

Core Developmental Elements

The early teen years are filled with all kinds of new happenings and developments, including physical, cognitive, and social changes.

- *Physical and emotional developments.* While some budding teenagers appear to sail through the hormonal rainstorm of early adolescence, others have a more difficult time. Beyond having to adapt to the physical changes of puberty, many teens are entering into unfamiliar emotional territory. The outward display of this inward turmoil is not always visible, but many teens ride an emotional roller coaster during this stage. The worst outcomes are depression, intimacy problems, eating disorders, negative acting out, and even suicide.

- *Cognitive changes.* Parents and psychologists alike have struggled for years with the question of just what are the underlying causes of increased conflict, aggression, and rebellion during the adolescent years. Some of this "mystery" is resolved in the very insightful work by Pennsylvania researcher Mandy Light as she sheds "light" on the impact of cognitive developments:

> During adolescence, young people develop advances in reasoning. They are more able to think about things abstractly and logically. Adolescents become interested in concepts such as justice, fairness, and rights (Galotti et al., 1991). This change in thinking allows teenagers to question their parents' authority and rules. . . .[2]

- *Social development.* The onset of puberty frequently is accompanied by increased desire for autonomy that expresses itself as an emotional and physical distancing from parents. While most early teens are still interested in obtaining the approval of their parents, they may begin to communicate and confide in friends more than with family.

The emotional, cognitive, and social metamorphoses of early teenagers offer parents both challenges and opportunities. As mom and dad face the challenge of losing control of their children, they also have the opportunity to grow themselves. By understanding and attempting to embrace the shift that occurs as they cease to dominate their child, parents can move toward a more cooperative state of interaction with their teens to reach mutually acceptable agreements.

Peer Power and Its Marketing Implications

The underlying dynamic of the teen's distancing from family and gravitation toward a peer group may very well be a process of supply and demand. Before adolescence, a child's need for love and acceptance is primarily supplied by the child's parents. Beginning in the tween years and crystallizing in adolescence, the child's need for love and acceptance is fulfilled by friends—a teenager's peer group becomes a fundamental support system, a "bridge" over the troubled waters of pubertal changes toward the scary shores of adulthood. It's important for parents to face up to this reality.

Pennsylvania State University researcher Dina Castrogiovanni provides insight into the peer group phenomenon, pointing to the fact that high school students spend twice as much time with peers as with parents or other adults. One's peer group provides a variety of benefits, including support in defining identity, interests, abilities, personality, and autonomy without the control of adults, and emotional support.[3]

From the tween years to early adolescence, there is also a continuous transition from an outward—if feigned—repulsion for the opposite sex to an active attraction toward this group. We should all be quite grateful for the repulsion stage, for it keeps boys and girls apart for the most part until they shift hormonal gears and enter full-scale adolescence. In early adolescence, attitudes toward the opposite gender shift and peer groups become mixed with males and females in many cases. Changes in tastes in certain products and programs occur at this time as well.

YES!

We strongly recommend that parents of teenagers not attempt to guide their charges through the challenging stage of adolescence alone. Many resources are available with advice and tips. In addition to numerous books such as *Your Adolescent,* there are magazines such as *Today's Parent, Parents,* and *Your Teen,* and a variety of Web sites including http://www.parents.com, http://www.parent-teen.com, and http://www.parenting.ivillage.com (for parents of children of all ages).

The implications of the peer-group phenomenon and the influence it exerts on your early teen's response to marketing messages is substantial. With the drive to be liked and accepted by one's peers paramount, the early teen is particularly vulnerable to marketing strategies that play on the teen's desire to be part of the "in" crowd by promoting the belief that to do so, the teen must wear X apparel, eat at Y restaurants, and drink Z beverages.

Teen Depression and Suicide

Increased pressures and stresses brought about by societal changes and shifting cultural values have sadly resulted in increased depression and suicide over the past half century—and their roots can be found in childhood and far too often take a fatal turn for the worse during adolescence. A 2000 National Institutes of Health publication found that more than 8 percent of adolescents in the United States suffer from depression, and that in 1997, suicide was the third leading cause of death for those between ages 10 and 24. Accompanying these statistics, the publication cited the following signs that may be associated with depression in adolescents:[4]

- Frequent vague, nonspecific physical complaints such as headaches, muscle aches, stomachaches, or tiredness
- Frequent absences from school or poor performance in school
- Talk of or efforts to run away from home
- Outbursts of shouting, complaining, unexplained irritability, or crying
- Being bored
- Lack of interest in playing with friends
- Alcohol or substance abuse
- Social isolation, poor communication
- Fear of death
- Extreme sensitivity to rejection or failure
- Increased irritability, anger, or hostility
- Reckless behavior
- Difficulty with relationships

DIMENSION TWO: DEVELOPMENTAL BLIND SPOTS

The developmental blind spots of the early teenage brain can result in a number of development-related issues. If teens fail to develop their capacity for reasoning ability, for example, they become more vulnerable to emotional advertising ploys. Excessive exposure to violent imagery and entertainment, too, can result in a lifelong desensitization to violence.

While, as we've stated, the cumulative blind spots discussed thus far face the young teen at this stage of development, the three described here are particularly potent. Why spend so much time on the psychosocial dynamics of the early teen years in a book exploring the impact on young people of various products, programs, and marketing tactics? Because only by uncovering the needs, abilities, perceptions, motivations, desires, and behavior of the teen, can we understand what types of products and experiences might be in the best interests of these young people and what might be cause for harm.

The *Use It or Lose It* Blind Spot

From our previous discussion on brain development, we know that the brain of the teen is in the middle of a neuron or brain-cell "housecleaning" period. This is a normal brain process, designed to clear away brain cells that have not been effectively developed into functional nerve units to provide the proper foundation for the next phase of a teen's brain development. Unfortunately, this process also sets up the *use it or lose it* blind spot in the early teen brain. If the teen is not using *key* and important areas of the brain, the neurons or nerve cells in those areas may not make the necessary connections and become prime candidates for housecleaning removal.

Let's assume, for example, that a teen spends very little time reading and instead becomes a "screenager" immersed in the world of video games and television. As a result, this teen's "reading sections" of the brain, including those responsible for language comprehension, decoding and linguistic knowledge skills, and reflective thinking—one of the key foundational elements of the higher thinking process—are neglected. Without a sufficient "workout," the neuron connections in these areas of the brain can fail to develop, like a poorly exercised muscle. As the brain's housecleaning process sweeps away incomplete neuron connections, these critical portions of the brain lose those brain cells and are left weak and underdeveloped, making it even harder for the individual to develop stronger reading, language, and associated skills in the future. When the basic foundations of reading development are in jeopardy, based on the activation and use of critical nerve pathways, reading comprehension and abstract reasoning abilities are also in jeopardy.

Because the "use it or lose it" blind spot is unfamiliar to teens, it takes strong adult or parental guidance to oversee the development of the core skills necessary for future success. Some important skill-honing activities may seem "boring" to adolescents, but are neurologically critical to their future success.

The *Restricted Reasoning* Blind Spot

If, through lack of exercise and the subsequent housecleaning process previously described, the teen's brain does not develop fully during this stage, the teen can be left with limited reasoning skills, resulting in the *restricted reasoning* blind spot.

The teen transition is biologically designed to support a major shift in a teen's thinking ability. Jean Piaget calls this new period of higher thinking and reasoning *formal operations*. The formal operations period represents a transformation from simple black-and-white thinking and concrete reasoning to the higher thinking skills of more complex understanding and self-reflection. In other words, the teen has now reached the stage where more mature and "deeper" thought processes are possible.

It is important to understand, however, that just because the higher thinking skills are *supposed* to emerge during adolescence, they often do not, and the child is left with limited thinking skills and the abilities to move beyond concrete black-and-white thinking are restricted. The parts of the brain engaged in higher thinking skills and reasoning need to be challenged and stimulated. The teen that operates in the limited thinking mode will not wire the brain for the higher-level thought processes. The result will be limitations and restrictions in reasoning, critical thinking, creativity, imagination, problem solving, and the necessary skills for future success.

YES!

Because teens are not aware of the "use it or lose it" blind spot, it takes strong adult guidance to oversee the development of the core skills necessary for future success. Sit down with your teenager and map out a plan that requires higher-order thinking—activities such as reading, discussion groups, writing projects. Even learning to play music has been shown to aid brain growth.

The *Desensitization* Blind Spot

Desensitization refers to an individual's reduction to or loss of sensitivity to an incoming stimulus or message, resulting from repeated exposure to that stimulus or message over time. This blind spot is directly linked to the attention blind spot you learned about in Chapter 4. As we discussed there, a child's attention—or orienting response—is easily captured by unique or novel stimuli. But if the same (or a similar) stimulus is presented over and over again, it loses its novelty and therefore the child's attention toward that stimulus is diminished. The person effectively becomes desensitized or habituated to the stimulus that was once "attention-getting" and compelling.

Now apply this same principle to media violence, for example. Continued exposure to media violence makes violence commonplace and even "boring" for some teens. The teen in our contemporary society is so used to seeing murder and mayhem depicted on a screen, that the teen's attention and orienting response toward violence is gradually reduced. Along with this reduction of attention, however, is often the reduction of empathy toward the victims of the violence, and a reduction in response to blood, gore, violence, chaos, and brutality. Children then begin to attend only to higher and higher levels of violence without the original fear and disgust that was once a normal response to it. A new norm or "adaptation level" is established in the child's perception and with it the possibility for a change in the child's norms and values.

The desensitization blind spot has frightening implications for children and adults. Over time, and with thousands upon thousands of negative media messages, something that used to be considered dysfunctional, disgusting, or psychopathic gradually can become more normal. Reprehensible and abnormal forms of negative behavior can become normal and acceptable. At the same time, producers of negatively charged products and programs determine that they must increase the level of the bizarre or dysfunctional message or images to gain and maintain the attention of the desensitized and "bored" receiver. The end result can be that 32 ax or chain-saw massacres have been replaced by 55 or 60 beheadings and dismemberments. (Did you see the film *Kill Bill?*)

In a technological world of increased special effects, powerful images, and surround sound, where will this end? In the midst of it all, the teen, with his desensitization blind spot, is the likely prey of such attention-gathering tactics, and will likely be happy to pay for the opportunity to experience some newly escalated form of media violence.

Can Increased Exposure to Media Violence Increase Bullying?

We don't have to go far to document some of the negative behavioral effects of an increase in our children's exposure to violent themes. Early teens are exposed to violent acts both at home and in the media. One source cites, for example, that 44 percent of the perpetrators of violence in TV programming have some attractive qualities and that 75 percent of violent scenes present no immediate punishment for or condemnation of violence.

Kids have always teased other kids and there has always been the school or neighborhood bully, but bullying itself has increased. Three different studies[5] report that incidents of bullying increase as children move from elementary to middle school, and that as many as 80 percent of students in middle school "engage in bullying behaviors." The studies found that about 75 percent of students had been bullied, victimized, or both bullied and victimized during the 1998–1999 school year.

DIMENSION THREE:
DYNAMICS OF COMMUNICATION

The period between ages 13 to 15 is made up of extremely formative years. To better understand the implications of various marketing programs on this age group, let's again look at key aspects of the communication model and how the communication dynamics are shifting now that children are leaving childhood behind and climbing aboard the seesaw of adolescence.

Attention

As we've established, people pay attention to what they believe will satisfy their needs and desires at a particular moment in time of development. Notably, the need for control and autonomy has moved up within the teen's hierarchy of needs. Your young teen is going to be paying more attention than ever before to opportunities for increased autonomy and control over the day-to-day decisions and activities of life.

Marketing themes, therefore, that promise a sense of increased autonomy will be very attractive to this age group. As peers become the teen's primary suppliers of love and acceptance, themes related to acceptance by friends, peer groups, and peer group activities also attract teen attention. Hungry for models to imitate in pursuit of acceptance and success, the early teen is also going to pay attention to the behavior and attitudes of popular icons and celebrities portrayed in the media. The teen is also attracted to products perceived to be trendsetting and at the forefront of fashion.

Comprehension

The early teen years mark another milestone in cognitive development—an increased ability to understand, evaluate, distinguish, and select more consciously. With the unmyelinated neuron cleansing that has taken place through the brain's housekeeping and movement into Piaget's "formal operations" stage of thinking, the 13- to 15-year-old is better able to think independently than ever before. While the 8- to 12-year-old stage is a time of comformity, many early teens use their new cognitive "equipment" to challenge the thinking and values prevalent in society, in particular those of their parents and teachers. Characteristics such as individuality, uniqueness, social risk taking, and noncomformity to the wishes of authority come to be both attractive and desirable (whether exhibited personally by the teen or vicariously through the actions of others).

Involvement, Valuing, and Yielding to Wants and Desires

Armed with more aggressive hormones and improved cognitive abilities to think for themselves, teens have greater power to make their desires known and to take a stand for their likes and dislikes. They are quite busy at the task of formulating their own set of values—what they believe to be good or bad, right or wrong, and the hierarchy of importance they assign to ideas, activities, relationships, possessions, entertainment, and so on—during these early adolescent years. The importance of the impact of one's value formation cannot be underestimated.

YES!

Your child's attitudes, values, and resulting behavior are the core components of what is termed *character*. Developing a strong and positive character is critical to becoming a happy and effective member of society and to making healthy product and program choices. For information and practical strategies related to character building, we recommend http://www.charactercounts.org and http://www.characterfirst.com, and for educators, http://www.charactered.net.

Action and Reaction

No longer as dependent on the approval of their parents, 13- to 15-year-olds are making decisions, acting, and reacting much more on their own. They have definite preferences when it comes to products, brands, and programs, along with increased independent buying power. While up to this stage parents made most purchases for them, teens make far more purchase actions for themselves. Teens also are more in control of their "follow-up" activities regarding products and programs as well.

> ## YES!
>
> In today's overconsuming world, many teenagers have an irresponsible relationship with money. Positive attitudes and actions (such as savings and smart spending) can't be "trained-in" too soon. We advise establishing a savings account at birth and full participation of the child in the savings process as he or she develops. For more information, we recommend the Kiplinger Web site (http://www.kiplinger.com/columns/kids/archive.html). There you will find articles on everything from teaching preschoolers about money to obtaining teen jobs.

Communication

Early teens typically do not hesitate to tell others what they think of products and programs they've used or experienced. Early adolescents, as we have established, are very social creatures. They will communicate their likes and dislikes very freely and emphatically with their peer group, and the influence of this communication is substantial.

TYPICALLY POSITIVE PRODUCTS AND PROGRAMS

Healthy products and programs for this age segment include those in categories such as sports equipment, personal hygiene items, school supplies, and traditional board and card games. School, church, club, and sports activities are not to be left out when we consider "programs," for these types of activities assist in the foundation of positive values, attitudes, and behavior. The early teen years are perfect for the kinds of social and emotional learning experiences that are the result of time spent with others camping, hiking, and participating in discussions, healthy games, and the like.

THE NEUTRAL: PRODUCTS AND PROGRAMS IN NEED OF MONITORING

The preceding list of typically positive products and programs is, regrettably, short. Unfortunately, most products and programs need to be monitored for this age group and many must be restricted to provide the early teen with the most healthy journey through this developmental stage.

Toys/Traditional Games

Most traditional toys such as action figures, dolls, and construction sets have long gone by the wayside for the 13- to 15-year-old. Sports equipment and sport "toys" such as Frisbees, high-end bikes, surfboards, and the like are still popular, more with males than females. Traditional board and card games continue to provide opportunities for early teens to have fun socializing, communicating, and interacting with family and friends.

YES!

The early adolescent years are a perfect opportunity for fun family interaction through card and board games. With TV, movies, radio, computers, and video games dominating much of your child's solo time, the need is great for family time together playing fun games such as card games, Monopoly, Clue, Pictionary, Cranium, Scrabble, and so on. Go to http://www.boardgamecentral.com for listings and descriptions of most popular family games.

Some "toys" and games, however, should be carefully monitored or even restricted from use by early teens. Included in this category are board games with questionable content, and guns of any variety, including BB guns, pellet guns, realistic-looking squirt guns, and water cannons. Paintball battles are the rage among many early teens and participation in these battles needs to be monitored as well. Teens who exhibit signs of obsession or perhaps carry violence into life as a result of these mock battles should be encouraged to participate in other, less combative activities. Poker also has become very popular among teens, and is an innocent enough activity for most. Again, however, poker shouldn't become an obsession for any adolescent; too much time spent playing poker could bend susceptible teens toward irresponsible gambling habits.

Technology

Just as for many adults, electronic devices are the "toys" of the 13- to 15-year-old. Depending on the financial resources, many early teens are armed to the teeth with technical devices, including cellular phones, satellite TV, digital cameras, electronic game systems, CD and DVD players, desktop and laptop computers, and handheld computerized address books. Driving the thirst for such electronic machinery is the teen's need to communicate with friends and family and desire for entertainment. The typical cost of too much tech time, however, is (as we have emphasized), increased stress (IIIO) and exposure to negative media content.

YES!

It's way too easy to just accept the domination of technology time in your own life as well as your teen's life. But healthy development and a healthy life require *balance*. The time your early teen spends in tech-oriented activity should be balanced with reading, board games, hiking, sports, music, art, and other creative pursuits. Sit down with your children and create a plan of action that will result in this kind of balance.

Television

What bothers me about TV is that it tends to take our minds off our minds.
Robert Orban

Given the psychosocial dynamics of what is happening during the early teen years—especially the fact that many early teens are separating emotionally from their parents—television has a particular appeal and impact. As teens separate from mom and dad (less time at home, less communication, less hugging, kissing, and loving touching), they look to their peers and to young adult icons for direction, values, ways to think, dress, talk, and behave. During the teen years, young people are busy formulating their worldview—their notions and beliefs about what's good and bad, true and false, right and wrong. TV programs, including sitcoms, dramas, movies, reality TV, and MTV-type musical programming are all filled with potential role models and content messaging.

With TVs and VCRs in most of their bedrooms, and the popularity of TV programming like the *Jerry Springer Show, Howard Stern, South Park, The Osbournes, The Sopranos, Sex in the City, Drawn Together,* and music videos (and let's not forget cable access to the Playboy channel and other sexually explicit programming like HBO's *Real Sex*), there's no shortage of questionable influences available to our children through electronic media.

YES!

Because many teenagers have TVs in their own rooms (as well as VCRs, radios, computers, video-game systems, and DVD players), we recommend that parents establish family TV together time. Sit down with your child and agree on a variety of times or television programs that you'll watch together as a family. Some shows yield important opportunities for communication with your teen, as well, so take the time after viewing to talk over the program with your adolescent and exchange ideas about what you've seen and the messages you've taken away from it.

We are not necessarily against this programming for those over age 18, although we seriously question the trashy values and behavior in some of these and other TV shows (even adults *are* what they pay attention to). In fact, we've occasionally watched one or two of these shows ourselves. But we strongly recommend that parents monitor and manage their children's television viewing, and censor age-inappropriate programming in the home. We understand that by the age of 13 a teen is no longer the child in need of constant supervision that he or she once was, and that many of a teenager's values and the choice making that goes with them are already in place by this age. We encourage parents, however, to stay involved and keep hold of the reins, so they can continuously provide guidance and limits for their children—especially during the early adolescent years.

Bad **A**d **I**nfluence

There also is, of course, the powerful influence of the advertising that accompanies TV programming. On the good side are uplifting messages such as recent ads that leave you with positive, warm, human messages—like the credit card ads that remind readers of the value of spending fun family time together.

Unfortunately, television advertising offers many, many examples of less wholesome advertising, as well. One such example is the ad featuring Hugh Hefner promoting the variety of sandwiches available at Carl's Jr. ". . . because some guys don't like the same thing night after night." The message "take-away" of this ad is that men get bored with the "same ol', same ol'" day after day, clearly undermining the notion of fidelity. Another ad for Las Vegas promises "What happens here, stays here"—an invitation for moral mischief.

Sound innocent enough? Hugh Hefner and hamburgers? Adventures in Vegas? But these messages undermine positive values, so we should think carefully about the cumulative effect of hundreds of such messages pouring into our homes each year.

Films and Film Marketing

Teenagers are quick to say that they can judge the difference between media content that might be OK for them and content that might harm them in some way. We disagree, along with media researcher Joanne Cantor, professor emeritus at the University of Wisconsin and author of *Mommy I'm Scared; How TV and Movies Frighten Our Children and What We Can Do to Protect Them.*[6] Much of the negative impact of film violence occurs below the teenager's radar screen, because of the teen's developmental blind spots. "I fear we are growing a society of alienated, aggressive, untrusting adults," says Cantor. She says neither knowledge nor intelligence can protect a child from the negative emotional impact of images seen in films. "We're talking about an emotional reaction that gets wired into the brain," she says. "Like any other learning you don't feel it happening."

YES!

It's far too easy for parents today to turn a blind eye to the films their young teens are frequenting. Discussion of film ratings and content and strict limits will send a loud and clear values message to your teenager. Check film review sites, such as http://www.filmvalues.com, for details about potentially objectionable content. Also consider family movie times when everyone in the family goes together, ideally followed by discussion.

In 2000, the FTC, after researching the issue of marketing violent entertainment to children, released its findings that applied not only to the film industry but to music and electronic gaming as well.[7] In its report, the commission found that companies in several entertainment industries, including film, music, and electronic games, target children under the age of 17 in marketing products that those very industries have identified as having content that isn't appropriate for children under the age of 17. The report included these findings

Of the 44 movies rated R for violence, the Commission selected for its study, the Commission found that 35, or 80 percent, were targeted to children under 17. Marketing plans for 28 of those 44, or 64 percent, contained express statements that the films' target audience included children under 17.

In addition . . . most retailers make little effort to restrict children's access to products with violent content. Just under half the movie theaters admitted children ages 13 to 16 to R-rated films even when not accompanied by an adult.

Music

As young teenagers look outside of their families for role models, one of the greatest influences on their world outlook is music. We are well aware of the positive effects music can have on teens as well as society as a whole. In a *USA Today* article,[8] Bill Nichols recounts how Andras Simonyi, Hungary's Ambassador to the United States, cited Beatles' music such as *All My Lovin'* as a major factor in the fall of Communism: "The music . . . swept up an entire generation of young people suffering under communist rule and implanted the ideals that would later bring down the Iron Curtain," Nichols reported. Studies have shown that listening to certain kinds of music, including most classical pieces, is healthy for the body and mind.

Music and music videos communicate to teenagers through both lyrics and images, and the messages communicated aren't always healthy or wholesome. Consider these startling facts.

- The Parents Music Resource Center (PMRC) reports that American teenagers listen to an estimated 10,500 hours of rock music between the 7th and 12th grades alone—just 500 hours less than they spend in school during grades 1 through 12.
- *Entertainment Monitor* reported that only 10 of the top 40 popular CDs on sale during the 1995 holiday season were free of profanity, or lyrics dealing with drugs, violence, or sex.
- A recent survey by the Recording Industry Association of America found that many parents do not know what lyrics are contained in the popular music their children listen to.[9]

Sexual content aside, there is no doubt that violent, aggressive lyrics give rise to increases in aggressive thinking and feeling. According to an excerpt from an American Psychological Association 2003 release of findings reported in an issue of the *Journal of Personality and Social Psychology*:[10]

> Songs with violent lyrics increase aggression-related thoughts and emotions and this effect is directly related to the violence in the lyrics, according to a new study published by the American Psychological Association (APA). The findings, appearing in the May issue of the *Journal of Personality and Social Psychology*, contradict popular notions of positive catharsis or venting effects of listening to angry, violent music on violent thoughts and feelings.

Food and Beverages

Early adolescence is a particularly vulnerable time period when it comes to the individual's need for a healthy diet, and his or her ability to make healthy food and beverage choices. Teens' vulnerability increases when pubertal changes are taken into account. A common parental complaint is: "Joey is so lazy. Just getting him out of bed in the morning is a major accomplishment, then he just sits around playing his video games, watching TV, and feeding his face all day."

The laziness of many teens—especially in early adolescence—is no myth. The teen's body is investing a great deal of its energy in rapid physical growth, resulting in an adolescent with less energy for other aspects of daily life.

This laziness is linked also with increases in obesity. The reduced physical activity common in this period often is accompanied by increases in snacking and food consumption. From an APA article, "Getting Children off the Couch and onto the Field," the increase in overweight teens is cited, pointing to a decrease in physical activity as one of the causes. The article refers to a Surgeon General Office's report that "physical activity drops off significantly during childhood and adolescence. From the ages of 6 to 18, boys decrease their activity by at least 24 percent and girls by at least 36 percent."[11]

Many food and beverage manufacturers and marketers are quite aware of early teen "blind spots" and susceptibility to advertising messages. These marketers aggressively pursue adolescents with TV advertising, product placement in film, ads in convenience stores, event promotions, and in-school marketing. With this kind of push power, parents need to do battle to help guide their early teens toward a healthy, balanced diet.

With the pull toward independence and the drive toward increased personal decision making, 13- to 15-year-olds are more in charge of their daily diet than ever before. Parents can't fully control the types and quantities of food and beverages their teens consume; they can, however, offer positive role models by following a healthy diet themselves. Parents also can help their teens by providing healthy food options at home, both for meals and snacks.

YES!

Parents can do four things to prepare and guide their teens in regard to healthy food and beverage choices: (1) Model good choice making themselves in their own consumption; (2) consistently purchase healthy food and beverage alternatives for consumption at home; (3) set rules and limits on types of consumables—especially snacks and treats; and (4) educate their children on the dangers of unhealthy consumption and the benefits of maintaining a healthy diet.

The Internet

Young teens are spending increasing amounts of their time on the Web. Teens are spending nearly 17 hours per week online. That compares to just under 14 hours spent watching television, 12 hours spent listening to music, and nearly 8 hours talking on the phone.[12] Positive use of the Internet definitely consumes part of this time. Teens use the Internet for homework help, research on a wide range of topics of interest, shopping, and communicating with friends. But young people's "relationships" with their computers and the Internet may be cause for concern in itself given how it is becoming a prominent part of their lives.

The World Wide Web holds the potential for possible danger. First among these dangers is the potential for access to your children by sexual deviates and pedophiles. The second greatest concern is your children's possible access to sites with inappropriate content such as pornographic sites, hate sites, and the like. Third, your child's and your home's privacy may be electronically invaded as a result of your teen's Internet activity. Finally, your child may be subject to unwanted Internet advertisements.

Teens as targets for internet marketing. Unlike many societal ills, problems with teen Internet access aren't limited to major metropolitan areas. The Internet travels everywhere, and therefore is of universal concern for parents. Given the number of hours that teens spend on line, marketers are aggressively pursuing them and their dollars. Urging controls on such practices, the American Psychological Association stated:

> Until age seven, children cannot discern the intent of persuasive advertisements. After age seven, children and adolescents are still particularly vulnerable to peer and status appeals. Lengthy exposure to advertising may result in potentially damaging effects on children including increased parent-child conflict, lowered self-perceptions of physical attractiveness, and/or lowered self-esteem, and experimentation with products that may be detrimental such as cigarettes and alcohol.

Protecting young teens from Internet predators. Many parents are worried about how to protect their teens from Internet pornography and potential online predators. Your children's access to the Internet may be an open invitation to purveyors of child pornography. The porn people don't need to lurk around playgrounds or parks anymore—strangers can come into your home via the Internet. The first steps toward protecting yourself and your children from this threat are fundamental: Don't let your children have their own e-mail accounts or Web pages, and don't create family Web pages with pictures of children for distant grandmas and grandpas to view. In addition, make it a point to know where your teens are traveling on the Internet.

YES!

Discuss with your teen the dangers of the Internet, and monitor your child's Internet activity closely. Put in "Parental Controls" wherever possible, and limit in-room computer use. If your child has a computer in his or her room, consider not allowing Internet access from that computer. Many resources offer parents guidelines and suggestions for protecting children from Internet threat. We recommend the FBI's guidelines, posted at http://www.fbi.gov/publications/pguide/pguidee.htm. Tips for your teens can be found at http://www.worldkids.net/school/safety/internet/internet.htm.

Other Categories in Need of Monitoring

In addition to certain toys and games, technology, TV, film, music, food and beverages, and the Internet, other areas parents would be wise to monitor include making sure that their early teens are not privy to publications that have objectionably violent or sexual themes, and that their teens clothing and room decor reflect healthy attitudes and styles.

On the positive side, publications, especially books, are a must for your teen's weekly diet of activity. At their best, reading these materials exercises the muscle of the imagination, stimulates thought, and conveys valuable values-laden messages that impact the reader's personal attitudes and values. From the *Harry Potter* series to titles such as *The Princess and the Pauper; The Earth, My Butt, and Other Big Round Things;* and classics such as *Catcher in the Rye* and *Slaughterhouse 5,* more choices are available for young teens than at any earlier age. Their developing cognitive abilities enable them to tackle important, thought-provoking literature as well as imaginatively entertaining "reads."

Although adolescents should be discouraged from reading dark, violent, or overtly sexual comics, not all comics contain negative content. Very popular among many teens these days are what are referred to as "graphic novels." These positive "comics," including manga (Japanese comics), have far-ranging content including historical themes, science fiction (*Star Wars,* for example), superhero stories, and religious themes. Yes, even the Bible is available in comic form.

YES!

A variety of sources recommend books for young teen readers. Our recommendation is to explore books most preferred by teens themselves as listed and described, for example, at the Young Adult Library Services Association Web site at http://www.ala.org/ala/yalsa/teenread ing/teenstopten/TTTnominations.htm. For guidance regarding graphic novels, our recommendation is http://www.dcn.davis.ca.us/go/webacces/ comics.html.

PRODUCTS THAT ARE INHERENTLY DANGEROUS

While most products and programs targeting early teens are either positive, innocuous, or in need of monitoring and restriction, there are those that are caustically dangerous. These include violence-themed video games, alcohol, tobacco, guns, prescription medications, and illegal drugs. In this section we detail the specific dangers and offer key strategies to assist parents and other youth caretakers for parents are truly the "antidrug."

Age-Inappropriate Electronic Games

Electronic game playing is a perfect "fit" for the early adolescent years. Like it or not, as a perfectly natural evolution toward independence most teens start to separate emotionally and even physically from their parents and their family. While the living room or family room was their place to hang out when they were younger, teens begin to spend more alone time in their rooms, listening to music, chatting on the phone or via the Internet with friends, surfing the Web, or playing computer or home system games.

Estimates vary, but most agree that only 20 percent to 25 percent of electronic game playing is by girls, many of whom don't have systems of their own but use the hardware and software of their family, friends, or male siblings. When you realize that the majority of electronic games are being marketed toward teenage boys, it's easy to see why a good 70 percent to 80 percent of game content is highly aggressive and violent. Electronic games have much to offer the budding teen: competition, challenge, adventure, fantasy, sexy muscular heroes, and scantily clad heroines. With the "juices" of early adolescence flowing, the attraction of strong males and sexy vixens should be no surprise. What may be a surprise to some is that electronic game sales in the United States now have caught up with total sales of toys and traditional games at around $10 billion yearly.

Adaptation levels: upping the violence "ante." Most parents have, by now, heard about the way violence escalates during the play of some electronic games; as the player moves "up" through levels of accomplishment, the violence or sexual content depicted in the game can become more plentiful and much more graphic. As we discussed earlier in regard to the desensitization blind spot, once an individual adapts or gets use to a certain level of stimulation, that level becomes the new standard of expectation. Each new level of increased sensory stimulation (for example, sound levels, visual brightness, rates of speed, quickness of images, numbers of violent acts, degree of violent behavior) establishes a new standard of expectation.

Game makers know this, and so create escalating levels of stimulation—violence, abuse, and sexual content—to ensure that their games remain challenging and compelling.

Proof of this "raising of the violence ante" is demonstrated by the actions of electronic game makers. While some suggest that the mass market is going to want softer-themed, less offensive games as game systems get into more homes, the word in the offices of the game manufacturers is that teen boys want ultra-violent action and more sexy battle vixens, and that's what's going to be delivered. More "give 'em what they want" philosophy in action. The costs of this ever-increasing intensity are steep: desensitization, aggressive attitude and behavior "training," and increases in nervous system response, cortisol release, and stress.

Building better teens—and a better future. Whatever you spend high percentages of time engaged in will result in key learning as well as impact on values, attitudes, and behavior; as we've said before, "You *are* what you pay attention to." It would be an ignorant denial of reality to think that an individual who spends hours and hours with fantastic heroes and villains and with the blood and gore left in their wake isn't in some way negatively influenced. Even worse, imagine the psychological impact that results when "first-person" games require that the player *become* the shooter/perpetrator of the violence. What about the impact on society? If hundreds of thousands of its young people are spending millions of hours with violence and sexual impropriety, isn't it logical to assume some of that negativity is rubbing off? Studies have proven precisely that. Just imagine the positive results if those hours were spent in constructive ways, for example in reading, creative activity, communicating with friends and family, or in service to others.

Industry self-regulation isn't working. There *is* a place for censorship, and electronic games represent a perfect example for that case! We suggest there are essentially four steps parents and youth caretakers need to take to adequately protect their teens from highly objectionable e-game content:

1. Educate yourself about the world of both game system and computer games. Play some of them yourself to experience what their content includes.
2. Familiarize yourself with the games rating system (see "Game Ratings and Advertising," in Chapter 6, "The 'Rule-and-Role' Stage of Development: Ages 8 to 12") but don't rely on it. A "Teen" rating, for example, doesn't mean an electronic game is free of inappropriate or harmful content.
3. As mentioned earlier, consider not allowing your young teen to play electronic games privately or alone in his or her room. Insist your teen play in a place within easy viewing.
4. Consider disallowing electronic game play altogether or strictly limiting game play to the EC- and E-rated games.

Alcohol, Tobacco, and Illicit Drugs

The red flags of danger should be raised high when it comes to both the immediately life-threatening potential of alcohol, tobacco, and drugs and the long-term establishment of habits related to all three of these major vices. The costs to society in medical expenses and productivity are enormous, and the cost to individual lives is nothing short of staggering when you consider years and lives ruined, families destroyed, and quality of life degraded. Even though we all know the dangers and costs, unscrupulous marketers continue to push this stuff on our highly susceptible and vulnerable teenagers, sometimes setting up a lifetime of misery for the teen and his or her family, all to provide profit for company execs and stockholders.

The facts about teen alcohol use. Before launching into an examination of the overt and covert ways that marketers push alcohol consumption to teens, let's look briefly at the facts related to how much and why teens drink in the first place. According to a 2000 survey, alcohol continues to be the most widely abused drug among adolescents in the United States:[13]

Teen alcohol use (2000 survey)

Alcohol Use	8th Grade	10th Grade	12th Grade
Any use	51.7%	71.4%	80.3%
Been drunk	25.1%	49.3%	62.3%

Wendy Hamilton, the national President of Mothers Against Drunk Driving, states:

> Underage alcohol consumption is the nation's number one youth illegal drug problem. . . . Alcohol kills 6.5 times more kids than all other illicit drugs combined and is a major factor in the three leading causes of death of America's teens: motor vehicle crashes, homicides, and suicides. Underage drinking does not just harm the drinker: half of the people who die in traffic crashes involving underage drinking drivers are people other than the drinking drivers. Underage drinking is not harmless fun. There is no such thing as "responsible" underage drinking.[14]

There are many extremely compelling reasons why teen drinking is the alarming and dangerous problem that it is.

- *Drinking and driving.* More than 17,000 people are killed each year in alcohol-related crashes and approximately one-half million are injured. In 2000, 69 percent of youths killed in alcohol-related traffic crashes involved underage drinking drivers. Although young drivers make up a mere 7 percent of the driving population, they constitute 13 percent of the alcohol-involved drivers in fatal crashes.

- *Death from alcohol overdose.* Few people realize that death from alcohol poisoning is as frequent as for other drugs. There are more than 50,000 cases of such poisoning each year and an average of one death each week.
- *Unprotected sex/unwanted pregnancy.* Alcohol impairs judgment. Sexual arousal by itself impairs judgment, then add alcohol, traditional foreplay, and your judgment is almost out the window. You don't think when you use alcohol.[15]
- *Date rape.* Alcohol plays a role in 70 percent of date rape cases.[16]
- *Teen suicide.* Alcohol use and abuse is often a central ingredient in the mix of factors contributing to teen suicide.

Teen alcohol use also, of course, contributes to the potential for other drug experimentation and use as well as contributing clearly to the cumulative and long-term effect of adult alcoholism. And when teens drink alcohol, they also run the risk of brain damage and associated decreases in school performance as well as their ability to function effectively in society. New evidence shows that teens may be more susceptible than adults to brain damage due to drinking, teens needing only half the alcohol consumption to result in the same damage. "Underage drinking makes kids dead," said Dr. Michael Scotti, Jr., a vice president of the American Medical Association. . . . "What we have here is evidence that it makes them dumb, and it may make them dumb permanently."[17]

Marketing alcohol to teens. Adolescents in the United States grow up in a world filled with messages about alcohol. Most of the messages present drinking in a positive light, and most of them show alcohol as a normal part of adult and teen social life. Warnings against underage drinking from parents or in health class may well be drowned out by the barrage of daily messages about alcohol in daily life. From a 2003 report of the National Academies[18]:

Recent content analyses indicate that alcohol use was depicted, typically in a positive light, in more than 70 percent of a sample of episodes in prime time television programming in 1999 . . . , and [alcohol use was also depicted] in more than 90 percent of the 200 most popular movie rentals for 1996–1997. Seventeen percent of the 1,000 most popular songs in 1996–1997 (ranked across five genres of music popular with youth) contained alcohol references, including almost one-half of the rap music recordings.

Research clearly indicates that alcohol advertising and marketing have a significant impact, and that they influence the attitudes of parents and peers and help create an environment that promotes underage drinking.

- A study of 12-year-olds found that children who were more aware of beer advertising held more favorable views on drinking and expressed an intention to drink more often as adults than did children who were less knowledgeable about the ads.
- A federally funded study of 1,000 young people found that exposure to and liking of alcohol advertisements affects whether young people will drink alcohol.
- A 1996 study of children ages 9 to 11 found that children were more familiar with Budweiser's television frogs than with Kellogg's Tony the Tiger, the Mighty Morphin Power Rangers, or Smokey the Bear.
- About $1.9 billion was spent on alcohol advertising in measured media (television, radio, print, outdoor, major newspapers, and Sunday supplements) in 2002. Working from alcohol company documents submitted to them, the FTC estimated in 1999 that the alcohol industry's total expenditures to promote alcohol (including through sponsorship, Internet advertising, point-of-sale materials, product placement, brand-logoed items, and other means) were three or more times its expenditures for measured media advertising. This would mean that the alcohol industry spent a total of $5.7 billion or more on advertising and promotion in 2002.

In the midst of so many "wake-up-and-smell-the-booze" facts, it would be nice if we could point to some efforts to eliminate alcohol marketing to youth; unfortunately, things aren't getting better. And NASCAR, for one, is making things worse. For some time it has limited alcohol sponsorship on and for its racecars to beer and malt liquor companies. Now, however, in an alarming turn for the worse, it is reversing its position and allowing liquor companies in the race as well. How does this mixture of ingredients shake out? The combination of (A) impressionable adolescents who idolize race-car drivers, (B) fast cars, and (C) booze is a sure recipe for disaster.

Just as the video game industry's guideline attempts to self-police have proved unequal to the task of controlling underage access to violent games, the alcohol industry has been ineffective in either setting or conforming to its own standards. They spend about 4.5 billion a year on advertising, and this doesn't include all forms of "unmeasured" marketing such as sponsorship at music and sporting events, logos on clothing, and product placement on TV and in film.

Tobacco marketing.   In Chapter 2, we painted the problem of cigarette marketing to children with broad strokes. The years between ages 13 and 15, however, represent the period when children are most likely to experiment with tobacco.

One of the best sources we found in researching tobacco marketing to young people is Action on Smoking and Health (ASH, http://www .ash.org.uk), a British organization similar to U.S. organizations with the same mission, including Campaign for Tobacco-free Kids (http://www.tobaccofreekids.org) and Patrick Reynolds (grandson of R. J. Reynolds) Foundation for a Smoke-free America (http://www.tobaccofree .org). Here are some key facts about marketing tobacco to children:

- A 1994 article published by the U.S. Department of Health and Human Services in the *Morbidity and Mortality Weekly Report* states, "Approximately three million U.S. adolescents are smokers, and they smoke nearly one billion packs of cigarettes each year. The average age at which smokers try their first cigarette is 14½ years, and approximately 70 percent of smokers become regular smokers by age 18. . . . Of the 1,031 current smokers ages 12 to 18 years interviewed in 1993, 70 percent reported they usually bought their own cigarettes. . . . The three most commonly purchased brands among the adolescent smokers were the three most heavily advertised brands in 1993. In 1993, Marlboro, Camel, and Newport ranked first, second, and third, respectively, in advertising expenditures."[19]

- Cigarette advertising reaches children as young as three years old. In one study, six-year-olds were as familiar with Joe Camel as they were with Mickey Mouse. Other studies found that Joe Camel appeals more to kids than to adults. (Note: We are well aware that using Joe Camel is not permitted anymore in the United States. We continue to cite this example as a reminder of the influence character-based advertising has on children and the need to withdraw character-based ads for unhealthy or dangerous products.)

Documents also show that the tobacco industry and its advertising agencies have:

- Examined children as young as *five years old*—some studies did not even set a lower age limit. As one executive says, "They got lips, we want them."
- Looked at ways of preventing teenagers from quitting.
- Examined the attitudes, aspirations, and lifestyles of the young and how to exploit them. One industry document says the company needs to "Create a Living Laboratory."
- Set out to present cigarettes as part of adulthood initiation—an illicit pleasure, which, like sex, is one of a few initiations into the adult world.
- Equated cigarettes with rebellion, self-expression, self-confidence, independence, freedom, adult identity, and masculinity for boys and femininity for girls.

Publicly, the tobacco companies have always maintained that they do not target youth in their advertising; they claim, instead, that peer pressure is the most important aspect in encouraging a child to begin smoking. But internal documents sharply contradict this by showing that tobacco companies set out to aggressively advertise to youth and even manipulate peer pressure to make people smoke their brand. Consider this statement, taken from a March 15, 1976, document titled "Planned

Assumptions and Forecasts for the Period 1977–1986 for RJ Reynolds Tobacco Company," and stamped "SECRET":[20]

> Evidence is now available to indicate that the 14- to 18-year-old group is an increasing segment of the smoking population. RJR-T must soon establish a successful new brand in this market if our position in the industry is to be maintained over the long term.

The market logic of selling to teenagers is overpowering. The industry knows that people start smoking in the teenage years, and if you can "hook" youngsters early on they could well smoke your brand for life. Indeed, independent surveys show that approximately 60 percent of smokers start by the age of 13 and fully 90 percent before the age of 20. This is the paradox of the cigarette industry: It is both socially and legally unacceptable to advertise to underage teenagers and children, yet it is to this precise age group that the industry has to advertise to in order to survive.

Marketing illegal drugs to teens. Your first reaction to this section's title might be, of course, that no one directly markets illegal drugs in this country. If teens were only exposed to overt efforts at marketing, you would be correct in dismissing this issue. But we must face and take responsibility for a difficult fact: In subtle ways, we as a culture are "marketing" illegal drugs to our young people. First, the hardcore facts from "Findings from the 2002 National Survey on Drug Use and Health."[21]

- *Heroin.* Since the mid-1990s, the prevalence of lifetime heroin use increased for both youths and young adults. From 1995 to 2002, the rate among youths ages 12 to 17 increased from 0.1 percent to 0.4 percent; among young adults ages 18 to 25, the rate rose from 0.8 percent to 1.6 percent.
- *Cocaine.* The percentage of youths ages 12 to 17 who had ever used cocaine increased slightly from 2001 to 2002 (2.3 percent to 2.7 percent). Among young adults ages 18 to 25, the rate increased slightly from 14.9 percent in 2001 to 15.4 percent in 2002.
- *Hallucinogens.* The prevalence of lifetime hallucinogen use among youths ages 12 to 17 was at its highest level in 2001 (6.1 percent)

but declined to 5.7 percent in 2002. Among young adults ages 18 to 25, use increased from 14.3 percent in 1992 to 24.2 percent in 2002. The increase in hallucinogen use in the 1990s appears to have been driven by the use of Ecstasy (i.e., MDMA).

• *Marijuana*. The percentage of youths ages 12 to 17 who had ever used marijuana declined slightly from 2001 to 2002 (21.9 percent to 20.6 percent). Among young adults ages 18 to 25, the rate increased slightly from 53.0 percent in 2001 to 53.8 percent in 2002.

Illicit drug use among teens doesn't stop there. According to the British group ASH, cited earlier, lifetime nonmedical pain relievers are being abused by increasing numbers of teens between the ages of 12 and 17, increasing from just under 10 percent in 2001 to more than 11 percent in 2002. Research also shows that as many as half a million eighth- to tenth-grade students are using steroids.

It's no stretch to see that to "market" something is to promote the purchase and/or use of it. Marshall McLuhan made famous the phrase "the medium is the message." When we ask ourselves as a society how we might be the "medium" that is certainly condoning if not promoting the use of illicit, dangerous drugs such as marijuana, cocaine, heroin, Ecstasy, steroids, and various other drugs and pharmaceuticals, we don't have to look too far. What about the modeling of the use of illicit drugs by many of our so-called sports heroes and entertainment celebrities?

YES!

Tobacco, illicit drug use, and inappropriate use of medications is as great a concern as is alcohol use among early adolescents. Talk with your teen about the dangers of using these substances, and monitor your teen's behavior, attitudes, and friends for warning signs. Establish rules and harsh consequences for infractions. Finally, be a positive role model in your own attitudes and behavior related to tobacco, drugs, and medications.

The problems of early teen drug use and the way society "markets" these drugs must be addressed as early as possible by parents and educators. Elementary school age is not too soon to begin, and by the time your child reaches the age of 13, you certainly need to be concerned and actively involved in monitoring and combating this trend.

Finding Help in the Battle against Harmful Substances

If you had any doubts about the accuracy of this book's title—*Kidnapped How Irresponsible Marketers Are Stealing the Minds of Your Children*—perhaps it seems more logical to you now. Without the awareness of young and old alike, and with full intention, dangerous products are being illegally and irresponsibly sold to our young people. Some of these products are actually "stealing minds" by impairing brain function. Every one of us knows someone in our own families or among our friends who died a premature death due to tobacco, alcohol, or drugs.

We do. I (Dan) watched my mother wheeze her way through the last decade of her life, her oxygen tank trailing behind her as she carefully walked, trying to catch her breath. I was at her bedside as she was dying of emphysema. (My father's alcoholism contributed to *his* demise, and my older brother bled to death two years later at only 55, his organs no longer able to withstand such an onslaught of booze. When confronted he always insisted: "I don't have a problem. I have it under control.") So you see this fight against such early entry into the ominous world of tobacco, alcohol, and illegal drugs is quite personal for us.

Parents and other concerned caretakers can turn to a number of good resources for advice and guidance in battling the influence of these harmful substances and their "marketing" messages on teens. We recommend the following Web sites and resources:

- http://camy.org (The Center on Alcohol Marketing and Youth) and http://madd.com (Mothers Against Drunk Driving)
- http://www.tobaccofreekids.org and http://www.ash.org.uk
- For a description of common drugs: http://www.healthatoz.com /healthatoz/Atoz/dc/caz/suba/tnsa/tnsa_gen_ovw.jsp

- For advice on prevention and intervention: http://www.theanti drug.com and the Web site of the National Institute on Drug Abuse at http://www.nida.nih.gov/Prevention/Prevopen.html

KEY VULNERABILITIES OF 13- TO 15-YEAR-OLDS

As with the previous developmental age segments, let's look at some of the key vulnerabilities of teens in the 13- to 15-year-old age group:

- *Separation.* The fact that the early adolescent is taking the first steps toward independence by separating emotionally and in many cases physically from parents leaves that adolescent often on a tenuous path without the secure emotional anchors of earlier years.
- *Independence.* With independence comes the possibility of formulating different and perhaps contradictory values from one's parents, other authority figures, and mainstream society. While independence is often necessary for the evolution of one's own independent thinking and valuing, with this independent thinking often comes conflict.
- *Peer influence.* As many teens migrate from family to peer groups, they are often more influenced by the thinking, valuing, and behavior of their fellow teens. These teens now quite often seek satisfaction of their need for acceptance from peers as well as, or instead of, their parents and families.
- *Role model influence.* Entertainment icons as well as sports stars and other public figures wield great influence on the early teen. In the teen's desire to be and act "grown-up," there may be many age-inappropriate enticements.
- *Need for control.* The teen's psychological need for control/autonomy increases substantially during adolescence.
- *Experimentation.* Freed up to varying degrees, early teens are much more open to experimentation. They often actively seek or at least are vulnerable to new, often problematic, even dangerous activities involving such things as sex, drugs, and rebellious, even illegal behavior. (Shoplifting incidence goes way up during the teen years.)

- *Sex appeal.* With the onset of puberty and the peer group changes that go along with it, boys and girls are far from "yucky" anymore. The attraction of the opposite sex and the possibility and reality of romance and sex becomes very alluring for teens between the ages of 13 and 15.

A WEEK IN THE LIFE OF A TEEN

Now let's look at a hypothetical week in the life of 13-year-old Sarah and her 15-year-old brother, Dennis:

EXPERIENCE	EMPOWERING	DISEMPOWERING
Parents/ Home Life	Very much aware of the need for their early teens to begin to establish their own independence, Sarah and Dennis's parents maintain solid contact and frequent communication with them while loosening some strings. Their parents, for example, insist on Sara and Dennis's participation with the family in key activities such as evening dinner, get-togethers with friends' families, and attendance at church. They openly discuss issues such as sexuality, drugs, shoplifting temptations, and other threats such as TV and film violence and the Internet. Their parents also monitor very closely what friends Sarah and Dennis have and who they hang out with. Mom and dad have their occasional difficulties but overall are happily married and committed to their family.	"Splintered" describes Sarah and Dennis's household. Everyone pretty much does their own thing. Mom quit her job because of adult ADD and depression and watches TV in her bedroom most days. Dad is either working or is out with his buddies. When he's home, he watches TV in the family room or works with his computer. Sarah and Dennis are gone a lot of the time—at school, over at friends' houses, or just hanging out on the street or at the local park. When they're home, they stay pretty much to themselves in their rooms. When Sarah, Dennis, and their parents *do* communicate, there's often a lot of name-calling and screaming.

EXPERIENCE	EMPOWERING	DISEMPOWERING
Toys/Electronic Games	Sarah and Dennis are no longer interested in most traditional toys. Sarah once in a while will play a card or board game with her friends or with her youth group friends at church. Dennis loves both Monopoly and Yahtzee and a great many electronic games, but is carefully restricted as to which ones he can play by his parents who have taken the time to research game content. Dennis is allowed to play his electronic games only on weekends and then only for two hours maximum.	They've outgrown all traditional toys and most games. Sarah isn't interested in games of any kind. Her life revolves around being with her friends at school or over at their houses, and talking with them on the phone. Dennis, on the other hand, is an electronic game freak. In particular, he plays the bloodiest, hack-'em-up games for hours at a time. A favorite is *The Matrix* game based on the movie. He's even asking for a long, black trench coat, like the one Keanu Reeves wears in the movie, for Christmas.
Room Décor	With mom's guidance, Sarah was encouraged to decorate her own room. She selected some quite adultlike themes from mom's magazines; the result was a very colorful yet stylish outcome. The only vestiges of childhood present are some favorite stuffed animals Sarah displays on a bookshelf. Dennis's room still has a couple of sports hero posters on his walls along with several *Lord of the Rings* posters.	There's hardly any paint visible on Sarah's walls. They're plastered with all kinds of music icons as well as TV and movie stars (mostly female). Madonna and Kelly Osbourne are prominent. Dennis's walls are also plastered with posters—mostly from violent video games and from *The Matrix* movie. His room's typically a disaster zone. On the outside of his door are two signs: "Keep out!" and "No one allowed!" (No one really wants to go in there.)

EXPERIENCE	EMPOWERING	DISEMPOWERING
Television/ Film	Sarah has elected not to have a TV in her room. She loves to read and she's very determined to get straight As in school, so she doesn't watch TV during the week. On the weekends she likes to watch TV movies or rented movies with her girlfriends. She and Dennis both go to family-type movies with their parents and often discuss them afterwards, sharing any personal meaning they extracted from seeing the films. Dennis has a TV in his room, but is only allowed to have it on during the weekends. Dennis loves sci-fi–type movies. R-rated films are out of the question along with PG-13 films that their parents screen carefully, often with the assistance of http://www.filmvalues .com.	There are no limits placed on either Sarah or Dennis. In fact their parents are proud of the fact that "Their kids are mature enough to not be bothered by the so-called violence, gore, and sexuality on TV and in the movies."
The Internet	Dennis and Sarah's parents are very restrictive in how their children use the Internet. They are restricted to e-mail chatting with friends on the weekends only and to using the Internet for study-related purposes. Dennis actually isn't too interested in the Internet— except for research purposes for school.	No restrictions. Both Dennis and Sarah have their own computers in their rooms. Sarah almost got into real trouble when she promised to meet some older guy she met on the Web at the mall but chickened out and told her dad at the last minute. (Her dad went to that rendezvous at the mall, confronted the guy, and scared the crap out of him!)

EXPERIENCE	EMPOWERING	DISEMPOWERING
Food & Beverage	Sarah and Dennis's parents have always modeled healthy eating habits. Meals prepared at home are healthy overall, but order-in fast food like pizza is indulged in on occasion. Their parents drink an occasional glass of wine with meals.	Like almost everything else in Sarah and Dennis's household, everyone's on their own when it comes to almost all meals and snacks. Dennis is 25 pounds overweight and headed for an adulthood of obesity given his bad food and beverage choices. Needless to say, their parents model poor eating and drinking habits. Their mom is an alcoholic and their dad often stays out after work at the local bar.
Music & Radio	Sarah loves music and listens to her CDs of pop and soft rock on weekends mostly. She also plays the piano and lends her singing and playing talents both at school and at church. Dennis isn't into music much; he loves sports and spends as many waking hours as possible playing them. They both have approved music stations on in the background sometimes when studying or hanging out in their rooms.	Dennis listens to all sorts of music. His favorites are rap, hip-hop, and a lot of gangsta rap music with lyrical content that is quite violent and filled with sexuality—content way beyond his years. Sarah, along with most of her friends, is infatuated with female and male music stars and they all try to emulate them in dress and attitude. Sarah's stereo is almost always blasting away and the radio is almost always blaring in Dennis's room.

EXPERIENCE	EMPOWERING	DISEMPOWERING
Apparel	Both Sarah and Dennis wear conventional yet stylish clothing.	Head to skinny toe, Sarah looks for all purposes like one of the music groupies that hang around her music idols. Despite her mom's impotent protests, Sarah wears whatever she likes, including very short skirts. She also has 12 piercings in her ears and a pierced belly button. She has a tattoo on her stomach that her parents don't even know about. Dennis and his friend Guillermo both dress all in black and are considered "outcasts" or loadies by many at school.
Publications/ Books	Dennis reads the Sunday paper and has taken an interest in politics. He also loves sci-fi books and fantasy, and he has read the entire *Lord of the Rings* series. Sarah reads through a couple of her mom's magazines but really prefers other reading, including novels recommended by her English teacher.	Dark comic books, laced with sexuality and violence, are Dennis's preference and he has quite a collection. Sarah's weekly reading consists of the *National Enquirer, Globe,* and *Star* publications, as well as teen and adult-targeted magazines having to do with celebrities, style, and makeup. Neither one reads books.
Telephone	Sarah has a cell phone mostly for safety reasons. She calls her friends occasionally but during the week those calls are restricted to ten minutes. Dennis gets calls and calls others related to sports events mostly.	It seems like Sarah is always on the phone with her friends—so much so she does very little homework and gets mostly Ds and Fs. Dennis talks to his friend Guillermo once in a while on his cell phone but really doesn't use the phone much.

EXPERIENCE	EMPOWERING	DISEMPOWERING
Alcohol, Drugs & Tobacco	Family discussions related to the dangers of alcohol, drugs, and smoking have made a strong impact on both Sarah and Dennis. Their parents also model no tobacco use and only occasional alcohol. Drugs are off-limits, but hardly need to be as both Sarah and Dennis have already made up their own minds to stay away from anything having to do with them.	Dennis and Sarah's parents are poor role models when it comes to alcohol, tobacco, and drugs. Not only do they both overindulge in alcohol, but dad smokes two packs of cigarettes a day. Dennis is sure they both smoke marijuana; he's caught them on several occasions. In fact, his dad now offers Dennis a hit or two and allows him to smoke with him. Dennis already has a problem with alcohol for he and his best friend down a six-pack of beer or two on weekend nights. Sarah smokes marijuana with her friends and has already tried Ecstasy and cocaine. She and her friends have obviously been influenced by the negative modeling of her star icons.

PARENT AND CARETAKER TOOLBOX FOR YOUTH ENRICHMENT STRATEGIES

Here, collected in one spot, are the Youth Enrichment Strategies we've included in this chapter. Use these suggestions to help guide your early teenagers in their consumption of and exposure to products, programs, and advertising.

- We strongly recommend that parents of teenagers not attempt to guide their charges through the challenging stage of adolescence alone. Many resources are available with advice and tips. In addition to numerous books such as *Your Adolescent,* there are magazines such as *Today's Parent, Parents,* and *Your Teen,* and a variety of Web sites including http://www.parents.com, http://www.par

ent-teen.com, and http://www.parenting.ivillage.com (for parents of children of all ages).

- Because teens are not aware of the "use it or lose it" blind spot, it takes strong adult guidance to oversee the development of the core skills necessary for future success. Sit down with your teenager and map out a plan that requires higher order thinking—activities such as reading, discussion groups, writing projects. Even learning to play music has been shown to aid brain growth.

- Your child's attitudes, values, and resultant behavior are the core components of what is termed *character*. Developing a strong and positive character is critical to becoming a happy and effective member of society and to making healthy product and program choices. For information and practical strategies related to character building, we recommend http://www.charactercounts.org and http://www.characterfirst.com, and for educators, http://www.charactered.net.

- In today's overconsuming world, many teenagers have an irresponsible relationship with money. Positive attitudes and actions (such as savings and smart spending) can't be "trained-in" too soon. We advise establishing a savings account at birth and full participation of the child in the savings process as he or she develops. For more information, we recommend the Kiplinger Web site at http://www.kiplinger.com/columns/kids/archive.html. There you will find articles on everything from teaching preschoolers about money to teen jobs.

- The early adolescent years are a perfect opportunity for fun family interaction through card and board games. With TV, movies, radio, computers, and video games dominating much of your child's solo time, the need is great for family time together playing fun games such as card games, Monopoly, Clue, Pictionary, Cranium, Scrabble, and so on. Go to http://www.boardgamecentral.com for listings and descriptions of most popular family games.

- It's way too easy to just accept the domination of technology time in your own life as well as your teen's life. But healthy development and a healthy life require *balance*. The time your early teen spends in tech-oriented activity should be balanced with reading, board games, hiking, sports, music, art, and other creative pursuits. Sit down with your children and create a plan of action that will result in this kind of balance.

- Because many teenagers have TVs in their own rooms (as well as VCRs, radios, computers, videogame systems, and DVD players), we recommend that parents establish family TV together time. Sit down with your child and agree on a variety of times or television programs that you'll watch together as a family. Some shows yield important opportunities for communication with your teen, as well, so take the time after viewing to talk over the program with your adolescent and exchange ideas about what you've seen and the messages you've taken away from it.

- It's far too easy for parents today to turn a blind eye to the films their young teens are frequenting. Discussion of film ratings and content and strict limits will send a loud and clear values message to your teenager. Check film review sites, such as http://www .filmvalues.com, for details about potentially objectionable content. Also consider family movie times when everyone in the family goes together, ideally followed by discussion.

- Parents can do four things to prepare and guide their teens in regard to healthy food and beverage choices: (1) Model good choice making themselves in their own consumption; (2) consistently purchase healthy food and beverage alternatives for consumption at home; (3) set rules and limits on types of consumables—especially snacks and treats; and (4) educate their children on the dangers of unhealthy consumption and the benefits of maintaining a healthy diet.

- Discuss with your teen the dangers of the Internet, and monitor your child's Internet activity closely. Put in "Parental Controls" wherever possible, and limit in-room computer use. If your child has a computer in his or her room, consider not allowing Internet access from that computer. Many resources offer parents guidelines and suggestions for protecting children from Internet threat. We recommend the FBI's guidelines, posted at http:// www.fbi.gov/pub lications/pguide/pguidee.htm. Tips for your teens can be found at http://www.worldkids.net/school/safety/internet/internet .htm.

- A variety of sources recommend books for young teen readers. Our recommendation is to explore books most preferred by teens themselves as listed and described, for example, at the Young Adult Library Services Association Web site at http://www.ala .org/ala/yalsa/teenreading/teenstopten/TTTnominations.htm. For guidance regarding graphic novels, our recommendation is http://www.dcn.davis.ca.us/go/webacces/comics.html.

- Tobacco, illicit drug use, and inappropriate use of medications is as great a concern as is alcohol use among early adolescents. Talk with your teen about the dangers of using these substances, and monitor your teen's behavior, attitudes, and friends for warning signs. Establish rules and harsh consequences for infractions. Finally, be a positive role model in your own attitudes and behavior related to tobacco, drugs, and medications.

MOVING INTO LATE ADOLESCENCE

The early adolescent stage of a child's life is filled with quite formative years. Early teens, though they begin to look more like adults, remain very vulnerable—especially because of the beginnings of emotional and physical separation between kids and their parents and families. Parents need to be aware of the different strategies teen-targeting advertisers employ, so they can talk with their teens about how to think about advertising and the messages it transmits.

Our next chapter on late adolescence will be shorter than this one, for we've already covered a great many of the pitfalls and problems parents face in protecting their teens from the negative impact of potentially harmful products and marketing messages. In the next chapter, we'll focus on special concerns facing parents of teens who have car keys in hand.

You have to hang in there, because two or three years later,
the gremlins will return your child, and he will be wonderful again.
Jill Eikenberry

8

LATE ADOLESCENCE
Ages 16 to 19

*Teenagers travel in droves, packs, swarms. . . . To the librarian, they're a gaggle
of geese. To the cook, they're a scourge of locusts. To department stores, they're
a big beautiful exaltation of larks . . . all lovely and loose and jingly.*

Bernice Fitz-Gibbon, Director of Advertising, Macy's

The late adolescent years of 16 to
19 are marked by three foundational elements. First, the development
of the brain's structure and capacities is largely completed by the end of
adolescence. Second, while still able to be influenced, late teens are rapidly moving beyond direct parental control and are making far more
choices on their own, Third, this age group forms a juicy market for advertisers, so influence is the name of the game. Late teens are going to
be bombarded with advertising and marketing programs designed to
capture their dollars and their minds; parents can't stop the flood or
control their teen's reaction to it; they can only hope that their relationship and influence with their teen, along with the training and guidance
they've offered earlier in the child's development, can withstand the assault, so that the late teen enters adulthood with a healthy set of values,
healthy choice making, and attitudes toward consumerism in place.

In this last of the age segment chapters we explore what makes late
adolescents distinct from previous stages of development and their
unique vulnerabilities to irresponsible marketing.

DIMENSION ONE: THE LATER STAGES OF THE BRAIN'S DEVELOPMENT

In the previous chapter, we discussed the importance of the early teen's use of higher order thinking skills; by exercising these skills, the young teen's brain develops and strengthens the neuron connections within the prefrontal lobe, which, in turn, helps maximize this part of the brain's strength and capabilities. The prefrontal lobe is the *gateway* to the higher thinking skills and critical to long-term success in the adult world, and it will continue to develop and strengthen throughout the late teens and even into the 20s. Many obstacles, however, exist during this later stage of the teenage journey that can make this kind of development even more difficult than at other ages and stages.

Challenges Faced by Teens During This Developmental Stage

The first of these challenges is presented by the continued activity of the hypothalamus. The tiny hypothalamus serves as the "Health Maintenance Organization" of the body, regulating its stable state of equilibrium. The hypothalamus also secretes a number of hormones that are associated with behavior involved in eating, drinking, general arousal, rage, aggression, embarrassment, escape from danger, pleasure, and copulation.[1]

During this late adolescent stage, the rational or logical part of the brain is often overwhelmed by the activity of the hypothalamus, creating a major disconnect between what adults deem "appropriate or reasonable" behavior and what teens call "fun." Even though the prefrontal lobe and its higher thinking skills have the potential to override the activities of the hypothalamus and emotional brain, this doesn't always happen, leaving the teen in the throes of biological and psychological turmoil. While the prefrontal lobe is advising the teen "not to act out" inappropriate behaviors, the hypothalamus is pushing to "go for it," to seek immediate gratification, and to "live for the moment." Particularly active at the onset of puberty in early adolescence, the hypothalamus continues during adolescence in its task of shifting the body toward an adult hormonal and physical state. For some teens, the transition is seamless and not overly emotional. For many, it is a tumultuous roller-coaster ride of ups and downs—particularly in regard to family and peer relationships.

A second challenge for the late teen is related to the hormone oxytocin. Oxytocin is stimulated by the brain during romantic relationships. It is especially prevalent during the "honeymoon" stage of a relationship, causing the hypothalamus to dominate the rational or thinking brain. Most of us have had this "love is blind" experience at one point or another in our lives. When romantic love is in bloom, it is very difficult for rational and logical reasoning to prevail. Teenagers are likely to have their first real romantic experiences during adolescence, and will enjoy the pleasurable and addictive effects of falling in love.

A third challenge, related to reasoning and rational capacities, is something that we call the *observational learning* blind spot. You learn more about this issue in the later section, "Dimension Two: Developmental Blind Spots."

Core Developmental Elements: Key Milestones

If you've played your parenting cards correctly by this time, and if too many negative societal influences or the wrong crowd hasn't diverted your child from a healthy course, your teenager will have reached these milestones.[2]

- *Physical development.* The physical process that began with the onset of puberty becomes fully established at the end of the teen years. Basic physical and physiological changes have taken place. Usually, late adolescents have also developed emotional and intellectual understandings of their maturing physical selves—body image, gender role definition, sexual identity, gender preference, sexual orientation, and even adult sexual patterns may be well established, all within the boundaries of socioeconomic class.
- *Cognitive development.* Most youngsters readily handle abstract ideas and concepts by the end of adolescence. They can make judgments based on more comprehensive and complex thinking. Plus, they can think about thinking—the late teen may frame an argument for discussion or debate and, simultaneously, make an in-

ternal judgment about the strengths and weaknesses of his or her arguments. More than ever before, an older teenager notices and understands how past actions shape and have an impact on the present, and can anticipate consequences of present actions.

YES!

Take every opportunity to include your 16- to 19-year-olds in one-on-one and family discussions on any and all topics, including politics, sexuality, religion, and spirituality. Listen to your teen's views intently, so the teen knows you hear his or her ideas and think they're important.

- *Emotional and social development.* By the end of adolescence, your youngster will react more consistently as an adult. There will probably be a lessening in the intensity and volatility of feelings and in the need for frequent and immediate gratification. The teen's judgment will become realistic and less grandiose; the youngster will show more concern for others. Many teenagers experience the imminent responsibilities of adult choice and independence as an encumbrance. The range of new choices and expectations can be daunting. It is not uncommon for teenagers in late adolescence to feel particularly alienated, vulnerable, and uncertain about their ability to thrive in the adult world.
- *Moral development.* As teenagers consider ways of being and thinking in the world, most evolve a reasonably clear sense of right and wrong. In childhood, their behavior was driven by the fear of punishment and the need to rebel and test limits. Now, their behavior is guided by a true sense of caring about how their actions affect others. While a young teen might feel delighted to get away with something, an older teen is more likely to feel guilty at having violated personal principles.

Prioritization of Needs

The needs for success and for control and autonomy have moved to the top as key priorities of the late teen. Part of their sense of freedom lies in the double-edged sword of the unknown that lies ahead of them. While frightening with all the insecurities of where they are going to live and what they are going to do without so much support from their parents, it is still a time pregnant with possibilities. Marshal Brain in *The Teenager's Guide to the Real World* describes it this way:[3]

Think about that for a minute. The power of these questions lies in the fact that you can choose to become anything you want! Imagine becoming *anything*. Think about the freedom that gives you. The great thing about being a teenager is that you are a blank slate. You can pick almost any answer to the question, "Who do I want to become?" at this point in your life, and you are in a unique position to make it happen.

The age of 16 is also the passage into the world of car keys and all that entails. For many parents this is a troublesome reality, for others it is taken in stride. Whether your teens are going on to college or working or loafing around aimlessly, they are in one way or another preparing for solo flight. There is a great deal of freedom during this period, but at the same time a good deal of trepidation regarding being on one's own.

DIMENSION TWO: DEVELOPMENTAL BLIND SPOTS

Like other developmental blind spots presented throughout the previous chapters, those experienced by late teens represent inabilities to perceive incoming information accurately. It is impossible to limit any single developmental blind spot to a particular age and stage of development. It makes more sense to view the potential threat that these combined "fractures" in our awareness can have over time, especially as these blind spots relate to how marketing and advertising affect our youth. In this section, we look at those blind spots that are of particular concern to children during these years of late adolescence.

The *Unconscious Learning* Blind Spot

Brain research indicates that we are learning even when we are not aware of it. That is, we are gathering information from our surrounding environment through experiences every minute of our waking lives. We accomplish this on *both* a conscious and an unconscious level. What a teen is unaware of can become even more important than what a teen is aware of. The teen's *unconscious learning* blind spot, therefore, is quite important to later development.

Our higher thinking processes, also known as *metacognition,* depend on our ability to take charge of our brain's processing experience and become more and more alert to *what* and *why* things are actually occurring in our personal world. Metacognition is the most important type of thinking for self-management, problem solving, creativity, and critical thinking. Without this thinking skill in place, the teen can in a sense become robotlike, simply *reacting* to both the conscious and unconscious forces that affect learning.

The automatic reaction to imposing forces encourages the teen to fit things into nice little boxes and categories to gain a sense of control and safety and to construct a workable reality. The teen develops a set of invisible or unconscious attitudes and beliefs that keeps him or her locked into tidy little thinking patterns. In a world that floods teens with advertising and marketing messages at an escalating and unprecedented rate, we must ask, what is *actually* being incorporated by these messages into our child's mind map, and how these messages might affect both the teen's short-term behavior and long-term potential.

The *Memory* Blind Spot

When a company is marketing or advertising a product to kids or adults, one of the most important objectives is for the target audience to *remember* the product, and to forget about competitors' products. For business, this translates into designing powerful and innovative strategies to gain the attention of consumers and to have them *retain* the marketing message. The teen's developmental stage during the ages of 16 to 19 can be especially subject to a *memory* blind spot that plays a critical role in how the developing brain retains and retrieves information, and the associated impact of marketing and other images and messages the brain receives.

We often assume that memory is a simple storage-and-retrieval process. For a developing brain, the information with the strongest "attention-getting" potential will have the highest probability to get noticed and therefore processed from sensation and perception into the thinking, feeling, and memory storage areas of the brain. It is no accident, then, that teens today are "blasted" with sensory and celebrity-laden images and sounds, all fighting for selective attention.

How and why your teenager responds emotionally to certain experiences and not others is often beyond her control. But it is not beyond the control of the marketer and the advertiser. The name of the game is to form powerful imprints or impressions in emotional memory. Celebrities, shock, horror, humor, sex, and glitz are all intended to make imprints on the teen consumer's emotional memory. At the adolescent stage of development, the teen, in a struggle for identity and belonging that accompanies the "raging hormones" of radical biological change, is especially vulnerable to marketing designed to appeal to emotional memory.

The *Observational Learning* Blind Spot

Teens will naturally look to outside models, celebrities, and adults to determine "what's hot" and "what's not" in their world. They will observe the current cultural trends and *learn directly* from their observations. This pattern contributes to an *observational learning* blind spot; the teen learns from observation without being aware that the learning is taking place. This blind spot is directly linked to the needs/identification blind spot that we discussed in Chapter 6, which results from the teen's need for acceptance and efforts to identify with images, celebrities, and popular peers to feel like one of the crowd.

Observational learning has five separate stages. The first stage is *attention*. As we have been discussing in our communication model, attention is the prerequisite for observational learning. The model the teen is attending to possesses some unique quality that triggers the "orienting response" and gains attention. The second phase is *identification*. The observer connects or identifies with the quality or characteristic of the model related to what the observer wants or needs. Third, the observer incorporates the model's behavior into his or her *memory*.

Once attention, identification, and memory have occurred, the observer must be capable of *acting out* the model's behavior. This entails a level of skill on the part of the observer that provides a demonstration of the model's behavior in some form. Finally, *motive* determines why the observer demonstrates the model's action. Motive is affected directly by the presence of reinforcement or punishment for the observer or for the model.

It's important to understand that the observer can learn over an extended period, while he or she is developing the ability to actually demonstrate the model's behavior. In this case, the acting-out phase appears to come from nowhere at a later stage in development. For example, the four-year-old girl is introduced to Barbie for the first time. She enjoys the doll's image, hair, colorful clothing, car, house, and other accessories, along with the experience of building a Barbie collection. She has initiated the first three stages of *observational learning* (attention, identification, and memory), but really can't fully demonstrate or act out the adult Barbie's behavior yet. In addition, the motives and the reinforcement for acting out Barbie may be less important at the four-year-old stage of development.

Then as a an early teen, she begins to identify more with Britney, the Olsen twins, Christina Aguilera, and a host of other superstars, and suddenly the implications of acting out Barbie take on new meaning. As a late teen, she becomes an avid fan of the TV drama *Desperate Housewives*, and is attracted to and identifies with some of the adult-oriented sexual situations portrayed in the show.

Finally, as an adult she wonders why she's caught up in so much self-defeating behavior and why her relationships don't work. In this scenario, the observational learning blind spot has been at work for years, with late-stage teen years' final stages of acting out the learned behavior and attitudes coming into their own as the individual reaches adulthood.

DIMENSION THREE:
DYNAMICS OF COMMUNICATION

As has been our approach to examining the implications for marketing for each of the stages of development, we again refer to the communication model you first learned about in Chapter 3's, "Dimension Three: The Dynamics of Communication." The following sections discuss each phase of this model as it applies to late adolescence.

Attention

The 16- to 19-year-old is most likely to pay attention to what he needs most, and as we have established, autonomy is a primary need; the teen needs and wants to gain control over his own life, so he can succeed on his own. Products, programs, and marketing messages that promise and deliver the psychological commodity of autonomy are going to be very attractive.

The late teen also continues to need and want acceptance—especially from his peer group and still from his parents. In the best of scenarios, some of that need for approval is in the process of being displaced by the teen's developing self-acceptance.

Comprehension and Involvement

Except for life experience, all the necessary cognitive tools for understanding even quite complex communications are in place in the late teen's brain. This is not to say, however, that (like most adults) the late teen is immune to the subconscious impact of advertising messages.

While the late adolescent often becomes quite emotionally involved with wanting this or that, the teen's emotionality is tempered with the development of more abstract reasoning skills and with a greater understanding of "the big picture" impact of the fulfillment of needs and wants.

Action, Reaction, and Communication

With more money in her pocket at this stage (many within this age group have part-time jobs), and with greater autonomy regarding what she can purchase on her own, the late adolescent is freer to buy what she wants than ever before. For big-ticket items such as computers, cars, and college, many late teens continue to rely on parental support when possible.

For the purposes of our model, *reaction* is the process of evaluating a purchased product or program after using it to determine one's degree of satisfaction, and to determine whether the item will be used over and over again or repurchased. With all her evaluative capabilities in place, the late teen has all the tools necessary to fully critique purchases and is, therefore, quite a savvy consumer.

As during the previous 13- to 15-year stage, late teens communicate their attitudes about products and programs freely within their peer group. Peer influence remains high, but with the onset of increased independence of thought and action, this influence is less than it was during the tween and early teen years.

THE DEMOGRAPHICS AND PSYCHOGRAPHICS OF MARKETING TO TEENS

Responsible marketers study both their market demographics (the numbers, ages, locations, education levels, and so on of their potential consumers) and psychographics (the attitudes, predispositions, and values of those consumers). As Robert Grede writes in *Naked Marketing: The Bare Essentials*:[4]

> The secret is to know your customer. Segment your target as tightly as possible. Determine exactly who your customers are, both demographically and psychographically. Match your customer with your medium. Choose only those media that reach your potential customers, and no others. Reaching anyone else is waste.

Pushing "Adulthood"

Gathering information about your market isn't unethical, of course, but there is often a fine line between how that information is used—especially when it comes to its use with young people under the age of 18. When marketing programs "push" adult values and behavior on teens, for example, in the search for more sales within the lucrative teen market, the result can be unhealthy for society as a whole. In *Branded: The Buying and Selling of Teenagers,* Alissa Quart writes:[5]

> Some of the latest extremes of marketing to the young involve pushing adult products upon adolescents, things that are jazzed up to appear young and fun. America's distillers spent $350 million in 2002 to sell "alcopops," sweetened, fruity alcohol that is ostensibly aimed at 21-year-olds; but in the drinks' semblance to soda and juice and in their boppy names, such as BoDean's Twisted Tea, the products really target adolescents. Such drinks encourage an early adoption, to use the marketing term, of booze, and perhaps also alcoholism, in teenagers' lives.

Alissa Quart goes on to detail how teen marketers use as many strategies as possible to attract teens, including sexual references that—consciously or unconsciously—promote promiscuity. Quart points to such examples as *Teen Vogue* and *Seventeen,* which have both run ads for Bloussant, an herbal breast enhancement tablet, and ads for muscle and physique-enhancing products and strategies that promote the use of "dubious nutritional supplements" and even steroids. Late-stage teens are also targeted by product placement ads, such as those included in video games or those showing video game heroes eating fast-food burgers and fries.

And candy cigarettes have evolved dangerously. In tobacco companies' search for new ways to entice and involve young people (although they claim they are targeting only adults), they have come up with sweet versions with names like "Sweet Dreams," "Twista Lime," "Mocha Mint," "Caribbean Chill," and "Midnight Berry." These candy flavored cigarettes often come in bright and colorful packages with cartoon-like drawings. Some antitobacco groups worry that the sweet, fruity flavors may make the experience of smoking more pleasant for young, first-time smokers.

Product Placement

Product placement on TV, in films, and in video games is not *necessarily* harmful to young people. Like all of us, older teens need to sort through the massive amounts of marketing stimuli that are flashed in front of them daily and make the choices that will be in their best interest.

At the same time, responsible marketers take special care to avoid strategies that take unfair advantage of the vulnerabilities of older teens. Such strategies include using product placement within films, music videos, and electronic games to promote the use of tobacco, alcohol, drugs, or other dangerous products by exploiting the viewers' vulnerabilities to subconscious modeling or learning.

THE MOST DANGEROUS PRODUCTS, PROGRAMS, AND ADVERTISING MESSAGES

With regard to 16- to 19-year-olds, there is no need to detail individual product and program categories as we have for past stages of development. Most of the dangers associated with product and program content and marketing strategies that were established for the early teen years remain relatively the same for the late teen years.

In fact, the early teen years were more vulnerable years for most individuals. By late adolescence, most of us have laid the foundations of our habits, good and bad. By the age of 18 or 19, teens are making their own choices regarding the TV programming they watch, the food they eat, the clothes they wear, and what technology they use. Late teens also make their own decisions about sexual activity and the use of drugs, alcohol, and tobacco.

Because late teens are beyond most parental control, however, they are not beyond the risks associated with their decisions. Some products, programs, and marketing messages remain inherently dangerous for individuals between the ages of 16 and 19. Here is our list of these threats, in order of severity:

1. Alcohol
2. Illegal drugs, including pharmaceuticals for nonmedical use

3. Tobacco
4. Emotional dysfunction and depression
5. Violence and guns
6. Technology with its related dangers such as IIIO (Invisible and Intangible Information Overload), excessive cortisol release, stress, and obesity
7. Unhealthy diet and insufficient exercise
8. Sexual promiscuity and sexually transmitted disease
9. Manipulative and/or deceptive marketing strategies

KEY VULNERABILITIES OF 16- TO 19-YEAR-OLDS

Especially because of the transition away from so much dependence on family support and toward physical, financial, emotional, and moral independence, the late teen is likely to experience certain vulnerabilities. Although parents, educators, and other caretakers are no longer in control of the late teen's behavior and choices, they continue to provide guidance, advice, and support as the teen moves into adulthood. Your awareness of these vulnerabilities can help you as you attempt to support and guide your own late teen through this period.

YES!

As your late teen transitions from childhood through adolescence toward adulthood, remember the three parental Ps: (1) Parenting: You are still the parent. Continue to enforce agreed-upon rules and expectations. (2) Partner: You are at the same time transitioning toward the role of partner/friend. Listen to him; love him. (3) Patience: Remember, you were a teen yourself once. Exercise a great deal of patience as your late teen deals with new and often daunting challenges.

- *The necessity of learning through mistakes.* The decisions and actions that the 16- to 19-year-old is required to make are bigger and more impactful than the late teen's ever had to deal with before. Driving a car in real life has far more associated dangers and responsibilities than maneuvering a racecar through the curves and challenges of a racing video game. The late teen will make many mistakes. Much of the late teen's learning will occur the hard way.

- *The drive toward experimentation.* More than any other stage of development, the late adolescent stage is the strongest period for experimentation. During the previous stages, parental control was still very much in place and early teens were far more restricted. But with more independence of movement (car keys) and with increased autonomy of choice, the late teen is ready to try a variety of new things he or she was reluctant to or afraid to try before. This is the greatest period for experimentation during all of childhood, and it's global. An article in *El Tiempo,* Bogota, Colombia's leading newspaper, reported surveys showing the ages during which most teens first tried key vices: cigarettes, between 16 and 17; alcohol, 14 to 19; marijuana, around 17; and cocaine, 18.[6]

YES!

Without being paranoid or overly intrusive, keep a close eye on potential problems your teens may be developing with sex, tobacco, alcohol, and other drugs. Also take note if your teen seems preoccupied with violent media or exhibits overaggressive behavior. If you become concerned, have an open discussion with your teen and take appropriate action if necessary—including restrictions and counseling.

- *The powerful attraction of the opposite sex.* For many, flirting and boyfriend-girlfriend fun in the early teen years has now turned into the challenge of learning to manage male-female relationships, complete with all this implies—from sexuality to the compromises and changes in daily living any relationship entails. The allure of the opposite sex and sexuality is definitely on the rise during late adolescence. Far too many marketers prey on this teen vulnerability. Given the late adolescent's burgeoning interest in sex and experimentation, and given those "blind spots," this teen is perhaps more vulnerable now than at any other age segment.

YES!

As a parent you can play an important role in helping your late teen deal with sex and marketing that uses sex to entice. Openly discuss the way advertisers use sex to sell and assure your teenager that he or she doesn't have to "follow the lead" of marketing messages that promote the idea that promiscuity is the norm. Create an atmosphere of openness on issues of sexuality, so that your teen feels free to discuss them with you.

- *The continuing pressures of peer influence.* Even with a relatively healthy family and social environment, peer pressure and influence remains strong during this developmental passage. Association with peers who exhibit negative values and behavior can be especially troublesome at this stage. At the same time, however, there is also a degree of movement toward independent thinking and behavior separate from one's peer group.

YES!

The regulation of your teen's friends is often a sensitive arena, especially if it appears your teen is mixing with the "wrong" crowd—individuals who have questionable, problematic attitudes and behavior. To whatever degree possible, encourage—perhaps even insist upon—your teen's association with healthy, positive friends.

- *The ongoing search for role models.* Because most 16- to 19-year-olds want to be treated like adults, it's only natural that they look to powerful and attractive adult role models. At the same time, these teens have the cognitive ability to evaluate different role models and to determine whether their attributes are real or illusionary. Many superstars fall from grace spectacularly, so most older teens have learned to be cautious when choosing whom to emulate.

A WEEK IN THE LIFE OF TWO TEENAGERS

Now let's look at a hypothetical week in the life of 18-year-old Joyce and her 16-year-old brother, Scott:

EXPERIENCE	EMPOWERING	DISEMPOWERING
Parents/ Home Life	While Joyce and Scott's parents steadily have loosened their control over their teenagers, they have not let go completely. They still set limits and establish rules regarding such things as household chores, expectations, and curfews. They continue to voice their views on the friends Joyce and Scott hang with as well as their activities. They also make it a point to continue traditions such as the evening meal together most nights and everyone's participation in family events, celebrations, and outings.	The only limits set for Joyce are regarding her use of the family car. Otherwise, she's on her own most of the time and doesn't participate in much of anything that is family oriented. She hangs with either her 26-year-old boyfriend or her friends outside the home. She's failing at school and talking about dropping out altogether. Scott mostly hangs out at his friend Doug's house or stays alone in his room with his large screen TV, two video game systems, stereo, and computer.
Toys/Electronic Games	Joyce has no interest in electronic games, but Scott is very much into role-playing, racing, and sports games. Excessively violent games are carefully screened out by his parents. Scott has played some of the ultraviolent games at friends' houses, but he knows his parents' strong cautions regarding them and stays away from them for the most part.	Joyce isn't interested in games of any kind. Scott on the other hand is an electronic game addict in the worst sense of the word and plays the most ultraviolent games he can find for hours on end. His parents were recently called into school because of incidents of his bullying other schoolmates along with two of his buddies.

EXPERIENCE	EMPOWERING	DISEMPOWERING
Room Décor	On her own, Joyce has remodeled her room quite tastefully. In fact, being a decorator is one of the possible careers she is considering. Prominent on her walls are three oil paintings she painted herself. Scott's room hasn't changed much from his early teen years. It's still decorated with sports and superhero themes.	Entering Joyce's room is like entering a black satin–decorated morgue. Curtains, walls, bedspread—all are shiny black. Scott's room is chaos—everything helter-skelter and a mess. It's a wonder he can navigate from one machine and screen to another.
Television/ Film	Both Joyce and Scott now have TVs in their rooms, but have agreed on certain restrictions regarding what and when they watch. Certain cable stations with excessively risqué programming are off-limits. Joyce self-regulates her film choices; her parents trust that she'll avoid violent or excessively sexual films. Scott is not allowed into R-rated films unless one of his parents goes along. Even PG-13 movies with violent and/or sexual content are decided on mutually and discussed.	There are no limits regarding films placed on either Joyce or Scott.

EXPERIENCE	EMPOWERING	DISEMPOWERING
The Internet	There are no restrictions placed on Joyce regarding the Internet. Scott's parents are somewhat restrictive still with his Internet use. His parents have put in as many safeguards and blocks as possible. His "surfing" or other Internet use is limited to weekends only unless he has a school assignment that requires research.	No restrictions. Both Joyce and Scott have computers in their rooms and unrestricted access to the Internet. Their parents incorrectly assume that they are old enough to not be negatively impacted and that they will monitor themselves.
Food & Beverage	Joyce and Scott's parents model healthy eating habits and actively discourage unhealthy food and beverage choices by both Joyce and Scott. For the most part, Scott and Joyce themselves make relatively healthy choices.	Scott is 25 pounds overweight, and his diet consists mostly of fast food and microwavable instant meals. He even has a minirefrigerator in his room. Joyce is moderately overweight and headed for weight trouble as an adult.
Music & Radio	No restrictions. Neither Joyce nor Scott have ever wanted to listen to objectionable music and lyrics—either at home or on the radio in their cars.	No restrictions. Joyce is into the latest hip-hop, rap, or pop songs, and almost always has CD earphones on—even at the dinner table during the occasional times when the family is together in the same room for a meal. Scott likes music that is dark, violent, and misogynistic. He and his friends go to as many concerts as possible and dress like the members of the bands.

EXPERIENCE	EMPOWERING	DISEMPOWERING
Apparel	Joyce makes some of her own clothes for she loves the design aspect. She dresses conservatively and stylishly. Scott isn't into clothes much but does make sure to wear the style of tennis shoes and pants that most of his peers wear.	Joyce's choices in apparel end up having her look like a weird cross between someone who's trying to style herself after Kelly Osbourne and Britney Spears. Scott dresses in black most of the time and has two tattoos his parents don't even know about.
Publications/ Books	Joyce's reading consists primarily of the literature she reads for school. She in particular loves the works of Shakespeare and the poetry of Elizabeth Barrett Browning, Emily Dickinson, and Rumi. Scott's reading consists primarily of his school reading, *National Geographic for Kids* that he still likes, *Sports Illustrated*, and *Golf Magazine*. He loves golf and plays with his dad and two of his buddies at school.	Joyce doesn't read much at all except for the *Soap Opera Digest* and the occasional tabloid. Scott is constantly reading a variety of darkly themed, violent, and sexy comic books and is always adding to his collection. The one magazine he reads is *Guns & Ammo* for he has a fascination with guns. He also pilfers his dad's *Penthouse* magazines and has quite a collection of those stashed under his bed. (His mom found them but said nothing, thinking it's just a part of normal boy stuff in growing up.)
Telephone	Scott doesn't have a cell phone and rarely is interested in being on the phone except for necessary coordination of times together with his friends. Joyce has a cell phone and uses it responsibly for communications with her friends and family.	Scott hardly ever communicates at any length with anyone on the phone. He seldom communicates even in person except for a couple friends. Joyce is always on her cell phone with her friends or her boyfriend.

EXPERIENCE	EMPOWERING	DISEMPOWERING
Alcohol, Drugs & Tobacco	Family discussions related to the dangers of alcohol, drugs, and smoking have made strong impacts on both Joyce and Scott. Their parents don't use tobacco and only occasionally drink alcohol. Drugs are off-limits.	Scott and Joyce's parents both overindulge in alcohol, and dad smokes a pack of cigarettes a day. Their parents know that Joyce and Scott use marijuana; they've found paraphernalia in their rooms. Joyce and Scott both already have a problem with alcohol and Joyce smokes cigarettes. Joyce drinks vodka (it's hard to smell on your breath) and has twice been busted for coming in drunk at 3 AM. Joyce's boyfriend is into occasional cocaine and Ecstasy use and is close to getting Joyce to try them.

PARENT AND CARETAKER TOOLBOX FOR YOUTH ENRICHMENT STRATEGIES

We have reached the end of our journey through the developmental stages leading up to early adulthood. By now, we've outlined the many ways that advertisers and marketers, through commission or omission, can negatively impact young, developing minds. In this chapter as in others, we've presented a number of strategies parents can use to help guide their children through the wilderness of products, programs, and marketing messages they'll encounter in daily life. Here, in summary, are the strategies you learned in this chapter.

- Take every opportunity to include your 16- to 19-year-olds in one-on-one and family discussions on any and all topics, including politics, sexuality, religion, and spirituality. Listen to your teen's views intently, so the teen knows you hear his or her ideas and think they're important.

- As your late teen transitions from childhood through adolescence toward adulthood, remember the three parental Ps: (1) Parenting: You are still the parent. Continue to enforce agreed-upon rules and expectations. (2) Partner: You are at the same time transitioning toward the role of partner/friend. Listen to her; love her. (3) Patience: Remember, you were a teen yourself once. Exercise a great deal of patience as your late teen deals with new and often daunting challenges.
- Without being paranoid or overly intrusive, keep a close eye on potential problems your teens may be developing with sex, tobacco, alcohol, and other drugs. Also take note if your teen seems preoccupied with violent media or exhibits overaggressive behavior. If you become concerned, have an open discussion with your teen and take appropriate action if necessary—including restrictions and counseling.
- As a parent you can play an important role in helping your late teen deal with sex and marketing that uses sex to entice. Openly discuss with him the way advertisers use sex to sell and assure your teenager that he doesn't have to "follow the lead" of marketing messages that promote the idea that promiscuity is the norm. Create an atmosphere of openness on issues of sexuality, so that your teen feels free to discuss them with you.
- The regulation of your teen's friends is often a sensitive arena, especially if it appears your teen is mixing with the "wrong" crowd—individuals who have questionable, problematic attitudes and behavior. To whatever degree possible, encourage—perhaps even insist upon—your teen's association with healthy, positive friends.

MAKING USE OF THE TRIM-TAB EFFECT

Irresponsible marketing not only places dangerous commodities in the hands of your children, it engenders irresponsible attitudes and behavior and promotes antisocial values. In the next and final chapter, we will confront what needs to happen to begin to turn around the irresponsible youth marketing ship before it crashes us all onto the rocks. Changing the ways advertisers target and exploit children won't happen overnight; it will take the concerted and courageous action of many individuals and organizations on many fronts.

Even small shifts in consciousness, attitude, and action will have great effect, however. Inventor and philosopher Buckminster Fuller spoke of this as the "trim-tab effect." The largest ships at sea—huge cargo and tanker ships—he explained, have enormous rudders. These rudders are so large that it would normally take an extremely powerful force to turn them and the ships with so much water force flowing past. So they invented "trim tabs"—small rudders that are inserted inside the huge rudders. It takes only a small amount of force to turn these much smaller trim-tab rudders, but they can begin the process of turning the huge rudders, making the redirection of the great ships much easier. Your individual efforts, as you learn in the final chapter of this book, can serve as the "trim tab" on the rudders of the huge marketing vessels that carry us all through the consumer society we now live in.

> *Courage is contagious. When a brave man takes a stand,*
> *the spines of others are often stiffened.*
> Billy Graham

9

A CALL TO ACTION

*One's philosophy is not best expressed in words; it is expressed
in the choices one makes. In the long run, we shape our lives
and we shape ourselves. The process never ends until we die.
And, the choices we make are ultimately our own responsibility.*

Eleanor Roosevelt

An Ashanti proverb states, "It takes a whole village to raise a child." This proverb emphasizes that children are a product of everything and everyone they come in contact with throughout their development. In today's world, children are raised as much by society as they are by their parents. At the same time, however, communal influence has perhaps never before been so impotent as stated eloquently by Theo Panayides:[1]

What's happened to movie-watching in the 1990s is much the same as what's happened to TV-watching, or to a million other things in our increasingly custom-made, individualized, consumer-oriented world. Quite simply, you can now (increasingly) create your own personalized little world, reflecting your particular tastes; the concept of a communal lifestyle, a shared culture acting as a societal glue, is becoming increasingly obsolete.

Affecting meaningful changes in the products, programs, and marketing messages bombarding our children daily will take concerted and courageous efforts from all who are involved in producing, presenting, and funding them—from the artists who create the video games to the CEOs of entertainment, packaged goods, and media entities to parents, educators, and even the young themselves. Everyone within our society must work to help influence the course of the huge marketing machine that promotes the billions of dollars of goods and media that form the environment in which our children develop. Everyone within our society must work together to help empower its youngest members.

Throughout *Kidnapped* we have offered a number of Youth Enrichment Strategies to give parents, educators, and caretakers sound and simple advice for monitoring and improving their children's environment. As we've emphasized repeatedly in this book, kids today are far too often sitting ducks! Individuals and corporate entities need to confront and create solutions for rising materialism and consumerism, the effects of IIIO (Invisible, Intangible Information Overload), and the horrible potential for damage to individuals and society presented by the unethical marketing of harmful products and programs to our nation's youth and young people all around the world.

In this chapter, we offer some final thoughts on what all of us—parents, educators, manufacturers, advertisers, and so on—can do to help reverse these ugly trends, through individual and group efforts for bringing about meaningful change. We also provide some good news, by offering examples of positive steps taken by individuals and organizations—both private and public—that promote or legislate guidelines for protecting youth from unhealthy or dangerous products, programs, and marketing messages. Finally, we offer a few "big-picture" perspectives and insights into the difficult issues that arise as we seek to protect our young *and* our rights as citizens.

A GAME PLAN FOR PARENTS

Families face a number of challenges in today's world, but perhaps the greatest of these is a fracturing of lives, goals, and family purpose. By working together, parents and children can carve out their own values and practices for living that can help guide them past many of the pitfalls of our modern consumer culture. Here is a summary of the ideas and advice for parents and families that we've offered throughout *Kidnapped.*

- *Pay attention.* Be vigilant and restrictive regarding the toys and games your kids are playing with. Watch what they're eating, and how much time they're spending in active, physical play versus passive screen time and other low-energy pursuits. Observe your children's online activities—no matter how old your kids are or how responsible you believe them to be. Carefully monitor the types of television, film, music, and electronic games your child watches or participates in. Listen to the music your children are listening to—and read the lyrics. If you allow your teenager to watch music videos, sit down and watch some of them yourself, so you know what kinds of messages they're conveying. Be aware of how and to what extent your children are involved in cell phone use. If you have children of varying ages, pay attention to the "secondhand" media, products, and programs your younger children are exposed to through their older siblings. Watch for signs of drug, tobacco, or alcohol use—don't blind yourself to the possibility that your child could become involved with these dangerous substances.

- *Educate yourself about the issues.* If you don't feel knowledgeable about dietary guidelines, use any of the many resources recommended in this book to educate yourself on this issue. Find out what your kids are being served in school, and what kinds of snacks are being offered (and promoted) by in-school vending machines. Insist on knowing what films your kids are viewing, and check out their ratings and reviews with a reliable source. If you use prescription medications, talk with your doctor or pharmacist about their potential for abuse, and then keep these drugs where they can't be accessed by your child or teen. Find out about the events your children want to attend, and exactly which entertainers and sponsors will be present.

- *Talk it over as a family.* Talk to your children about the dangers they face from tobacco, alcohol, and drugs—including the dangers of abusing prescription medications. As your children become old enough to understand the issues of violence and sexuality as portrayed in music, films, and advertising, discuss those issues with them; make sure they know your position and the reasoning behind the guidelines and limitations you've set. Spend time talking with your children about all the media they watch or listen to. In ways appropriate to your child's age and developmental capabilities, discuss advertising and marketing ploys with your children, and help them learn to "read between the lines" of manipulative advertising. Involve your kids in media literacy classes if available in your school district or through the Internet, and use the classes as a springboard to family discussions about the "hidden" agendas and subtle messages that are used today in media.

- *Set and enforce limits.* Create a healthy balance between your children's time with media and electronic games and time they spend with free and creative play. As appropriate, keep media out of your child's room, so you have a better chance of monitoring and controlling your child's exposure. Set realistic limits—both in content and time—for television watching and electronic game play, and then enforce those limits. Set guidelines for the types and amount of food your children are to consume, and provide healthy nutritional options at home; set rules for family mealtimes and adhere to them. Let your children know that you strictly prohibit the use of tobacco, alcohol, and drugs, as well as guns and violent or sexually exploitative games, music, and publications.

- *Model healthy habits for your children.* Model healthy eating and drinking habits; provide healthy food choices at home, and when you eat out, choose restaurants that offer good menu options, as well. Be sound and sensible in your own approach to alcohol consumption, and don't participate in casual drug use in front of your children. Model balance in your life—take time for exercise, reading, relaxing, and family activities. Let your children see that you truly believe in turning off the tube and engaging your mind and body in more physically, emotionally, and intellectually satisfying activities. Also, don't engage in senseless and excessive consumerism; let your children see you making wise purchasing choices, sometimes passing up the "toys" to invest in something more meaningful or rewarding, as well as participating in savings programs.

- *Speak up and lobby for change.* Don't take shoddy product, program, or marketing tactics lying down. Contact your local, state, and national legislators regarding the issues that you feel most need their attention. Join and support groups organized to lobby against inappropriate alcohol and tobacco marketing to youth and for stiffer and more effective penalties for the illegal sale of alcohol and cigarettes to minors. Talk to your school board, too; insist that your children's schools eliminate unhealthy foods and beverages in favor of healthy alternatives, and lobby to establish courses in health, nutrition, and wise consumerism in your school. Let your school board members and local legislators know that those programs are vital and must be funded. Write letters, send e-mail, telephone, and otherwise put pressure on manufacturers to create and market healthier toys, games, foods, films, music, and other products and programs. Register your objections to offensive music lyrics with music producers, retailers, and the performers themselves. Also contact radio and television stations, cable services, and publishers to voice your objections when harmful, inappropriate media of any type invades your home.

Some Right Directions

The Mothers Against Drunk Driving organization—MADD (http://www.madd.com)—is an excellent example of how a group of mothers, led by its founder, Candy Lightner, has led the charge against drunk driving and in support of its victims. MADD has been influential in the enactment of many alcohol- and drunk-driving-related laws.

The nonprofit parent lobbying group Commercial Alert (http://www.commercialalert.org) also provides an outstanding service. Its mission is "to keep the commercial culture within its proper sphere, and to prevent it from exploiting children and subverting the higher values of family, community, environmental integrity, and democracy." The organization accomplishes this mission through four key programs (adult awareness, student and enforcement programs, and diversity issues) that fight against overcommercialism in our culture, our schools, and government, by fighting to restrict advertising of tobacco, alcohol, junk food, and soft drinks, and by working against the proliferation of marketing-related diseases such as obesity, diabetes, and cardiovascular illness.

HOW EDUCATORS CAN MAKE A DIFFERENCE

As secondary caretakers and partners with parents in the nurturance and protection of our young people, teachers, administrators, and school-board members can make a significant contribution, through education and policy making, to improving the environment in which our children develop.

As educators, teachers must do their part to help our young learn of the real dangers present with substances such as alcohol, tobacco, drugs, and unhealthy foods and beverages, and of ways to avoid those dangers. Curricular content in some way must be designed and implemented to address these issues. Media educational curricula should be emphasized as well to assist students in avoiding or minimizing the potential threats present with the Internet and the potential for negative impact of media violence on TV, in film, in music lyrics, and in video games.

Educators need to stand for and be more proactive in the institution of physical education and exercise activity in their schools.

Policy makers, including state educational personnel as well as local school board members and administrators, also need to do their part to ensure healthy school environments. This includes establishing and maintaining policies and procedures related to what foods and beverages are served and are available on campuses as well as policies related to commercialism in the schools, including vending machines, fast-food chains on campus, advertising through Channel One TV in classrooms, product sampling programs, and event sponsorship.

Some Right Directions

Many European countries have outlawed in-school marketing altogether. In the United States, some of the largest school districts have banned or are considering banning the sale of soft drinks on campus (New York, Chicago, Los Angeles, Philadelphia, San Francisco, Las Vegas, Seattle, Scranton, Buffalo, and Boston, are some examples).

PE4Life (http://www.pe4life.com) is a nonprofit organization committed to the existence of effective physical education programs and activities in our schools. The group's mission is to promote active, healthy living by assisting schools and community recreation groups in developing high-quality physical education programs for children. Among other efforts, this organization has partnered with individual "gym teachers" who are revising sports-centered PE programs into fitness/wellness training in junior high and high schools.

ASKING MANUFACTURERS, MARKETERS, PRODUCERS, AND RETAILERS TO STEP UP

From the development of new products and programs through to the endpoint of selling those products and programs to children, teens, and parents, all who participate in marketing must "step up to the plate" and do their part to better nurture and protect our young. Again these efforts are divided into two camps.

First, the content of those products and programs should fall at least within the neutral category established in *Kidnapped*. Products that are inherently dangerous to our young people, such as alcohol, tobacco, drugs, and guns, must be inaccessible to them. Toy and game companies need to eliminate products with excessively violent content. TV and film producers need to look up from the sensation-driven bottom line and focus more on programming with enriching qualities.

Food and beverage companies also must make several changes. First, these companies need to focus on creating healthier products. Furthermore, they need to cut back on the least healthy of their offerings—despite negative bottom-line impact—and reformulate the ingredients of these products to make them healthier choices.

Food and beverage companies and all who assist with their marketing also must stop distributing and advertising unhealthy food to children—especially those under the age of 12. Products heavy in trans fats, for example, and sugar, including soft drinks and candy, and many salty snacks should be removed from schools and replaced with healthier alternatives.

Some Right Directions

A number of groups have formed to provide parents and others will real information about the content of films, music, and other entertainment media. In addition to http://www.filmvalues.com, the National Institute on Media and the Family also has established an informational Web site (http://www.mediafamily.org), where you can find expanded reviews of both movies and video games.

Kraft Foods announced its intent to restrict kid-targeted TV advertising of its least healthy food treats such as Oreos and to create a label-

A Ban on Child-Targeted Advertising?

In the United States, where in large part we have flourished, at least economically, through our philosophy and system of free enterprise and freedom of speech, it's not likely that we will ever go so far as to ban advertising to children on television.

It's very interesting to note, however, that in certain countries in the world this is the case. "Across Europe a number of laws curb television advertising aimed at children. In Sweden and Norway, television advertisements are not permitted on programs directed specifically to children under the age of 12. Holland bans sponsorship of ads between children's programming. Ireland has imposed a ban on ads on late-afternoon television; and the Flemish region of Belgium operates under similar restrictions. Greece does not permit toy advertisements on television. Now that the presidency of the European Union has passed to Sweden, it is thought that Sweden will seek to introduce legislation to ban advertising to children throughout Europe."[2]

Although no current policies in the United States follow the direction of these European countries, let's all keep in mind that if things continue to deteriorate in our culture in part as a result of irresponsible marketing to our youth, we will find ourselves in a situation that makes it necessary to initiate higher levels of protective strategies for our society. While a total banning of kid-targeted TV advertising may not be likely, youth marketers should carefully consider these protective strategies and how they could become law.

ing system on snacks and treats to assist shoppers in identifying which ones (the least healthy) are to be consumed as occasional treats and which are the healthier alternatives.

Frito Lay has removed all trans fats from its snack items and replaced them with healthier ingredients.

McDonald's, Burger King, Wendy's, Hardee's, and other fast-food chains are now offering healthier alternatives including more salad options and fruit drink and fruit snack alternatives for kid's meals. These are small, inadequate steps perhaps, but steps nevertheless.

Finally, Senator Edward Kennedy (D-MA) has introduced proposed legislation that would require that schools receiving federal funds ban vending machines that sell candy, soft drinks, and other junk foods. Entitled the *Prevention of Childhood Obesity Act* (S 2894), this legislation also would give grant preferences to schools that prohibit junk food advertising or marketing on-campus and that provide healthy, nutritional foods and drinks in all food services.

MAKING SMART CHOICES FOR SOCIETY

Some very important, critical issues are on the table today in the United States and, in fact, for every culture and society in the world. On the one hand, we have free enterprise and all the goodies that are its result. On the other hand, we have many young people in this country engaging in the out-of-control consumption of morally questionable and downright dangerous products and programs. Those who would better protect and nurture our young and by that create a more safe and healthy future for all of us need to face the issues squarely and with firm resolve make the choices and take the actions necessary to right the ship. Otherwise, we're headed for jagged and rocky shores.

TO CENSOR OR NOT TO CENSOR

Obviously, many of the recommendations and solutions to today's problems with irresponsible marketing to youth have a great deal to do with censorship in one form or another. The opponents of censorship cite the First Amendment to the Constitution as a guarantee of their right of free self-expression. It reads:

> Congress shall make no law respecting an establishment of religion, or prohibiting the free exercise thereof; or abridging the freedom of speech, or of the press; or the right of the people peaceably to assemble, and to petition the Government for a redress of grievances.

Does this mean anything goes? Not to *abridge* means not to reduce in scope or extent, to shorten or curtail. Taken literally, then, the First Amendment would not allow for the censorship of any number of repulsive and inhumane aberrations that, though certainly highly disturbing and potentially damaging to young viewers, don't break any official state or federal laws.

In our view, given the facts about how children interact with and learn from visual and verbal information, it is actually quite ridiculous and irresponsible to promote the idea that our society should be free of all forms of censorship.

The strict anticensorship proponents argue, however, that no one makes anyone turn on the TV or watch anything, and that viewing broadcast or printed information, therefore, is a matter of individual choice. In a society based on a constitutional mandate of free speech, we can expect groups to form for and against nearly any issue. Censorship is no exception. In fact, it's a good thing that watchdog groups exist to protect our basic freedoms, even as we also attempt to protect our citizens. The National Coalition Against Censorship has stated: "Children, like adults, receive enormous intellectual and other benefits from living in a free society. Children are not harmed by freedom of expression, but by unlawful acts. People who commit those acts, not protected speech, should be the focus of efforts to protect children."[3]

We agree with the benefits of a free society, but we are not in favor of total freedom of expression in all cases. In today's complex society, a society in which TV and all forms of entertainment and informational media are omnipresent, the proponents of this anticensorship argument appear to ignore the potential negative impact some types of media content can exert on children. The fact is that TV and other media saturate the awareness of nearly everyone, and their programs come complete with demonstrations and lessons on the values we should have and how we should all behave and live—far too often in ways that bring harm to ourselves and others.

When commercialism and the quest for the almighty dollar drives companies toward the production and marketing of products and programs that are easily determined to be harmful to our young people, often the only solution is to pass laws and institute regulations and consequences to control such unscrupulous behavior.

Except for the radically anticensorship advocates, few would argue against the idea that well-thought-out limits and censorship have their places when it comes to protecting our young. The sticky question is how to build in censorship in such a way that important basic personal and artistic freedoms remain intact. As we have stated throughout *Kid-*

napped, the way to "unstick" the censorship issue is to rely on basic scientific facts regarding the different types of negative and harmful impact certain media has on our young people. At the end of the day, you as a parent can't afford to wait for others to do the censoring necessary to protect your children. You are the ultimate censor, and ideally we have provided you with enough facts and suggestions to assist in that critical task.

Some Right Directions

In California, Assemblyman Leland Yee (D-San Francisco) recently introduced two bills to restrict the sales of video games that feature graphic violence and criminal behavior. In North Miami, Mayor Josephat Celestin wants retailers of video games to be punished under the city's hate-crime ordinance, and is preparing an ordinance that would ban the sale of any video game that promotes hatred and violence. New Zealand officials have banned the sale of the Manhunt electronic game (manufactured by the company that produced Grand Theft Auto).

A SHIFT IN PARADIGMS

There is a growing need to understand and implement the concept of "enrichment smart choices" for our children today. Put simply, healthier and more growth-producing products and programs need to replace much of what is either questionable or harmful in the marketplace. More individuals and companies that create, produce, and market products and programs for young people need to be more intelligent about how the content and the accompanying interactive processes of those products and programs can empower children's lives and contribute to their positive development.

Dr. Robert Reiher, coauthor of *Kidnapped*, believes that enriching products and programs can be based on a set of integral qualities that he calls the *Inner IQ* (inner integral qualities):

- *Character* or a sense of self and values
- *Competence* or the areas of mastery and self-management, and
- *Communication* or the mastery of interpersonal and intrapersonal communication skills.

Enrichment Marketing and Project DREAM

What if the business community that markets to children was given the opportunity to understand and utilize a new approach to marketing? Enrichment marketing entails learning how to market and advertise products and programs that are specifically designed to appeal to kids but simultaneously offer positive benefits for growth and development. We're convinced children then would begin to enjoy and request more of these positive and healthy products and programs. As consultants we have committed ourselves to enrichment marketing and invite all interested individuals and companies to join us in that commitment. Go to http://www.ymsconsulting.com and http://www.esmartchoice.com for more information.

In addition, after more than 25 years of consulting in the marketing to kids arena, we have created a stable of more than 20 children's enrichment-based concepts. Focusing on each of the age segments as they appear in *Kidnapped*'s chapters, we have developed a variety of concepts and properties from music CDs to full-fledged animation. Many are fully applicable to all forms of licensing and merchandising. In each case, they are based on enrichment principles—meaning they are structured in such a way as to exert maximum impact on the positive development of our young people—especially as they form positive inner qualities such as a sense of self, self-management skills, mastery, positive values, and communication skills. For those interested in learning more about the "PROJECT DREAM" concepts and perhaps participating in their development and marketing, go to http://www.characterlab.com and to the section on proprietary character properties.

The *Inner IQ* provides a broader base for children than does the traditional educational basics or "3 Rs" (reading, 'riting, and 'rithmetic) because times have changed and a new paradigm for success is necessary. We no longer can close our eyes to what is happening in society and assume that the 3Rs alone will provide a strong-enough footing to support children's abilities to deal effectively with the future. The challenge we face as a society is to support the development of enriching products that promote all these developmental areas of mastery.

It's time for action. It's time to get back to some of the fundamental human values that clearly support and protect our youth and our future through them. It's time for character rebuilding to become a national and global priority. It may be our last great chance to change the direction in which we are headed, because as a wise man once said, "If you keep going in the wrong direction long enough, you'll eventually get there."

Your children are not your children. They are sons and daughters of life's longing for itself. They come through you but not from you. And though they are with you, they belong not to you. You may give them your love but not your thoughts, for they have their own thoughts. You may house their bodies but not their souls. For their souls dwell in the house of tomorrow, which you cannot visit, not even in your dreams. You may strive to be like them, but strive not to make them like you. For life goes not backward nor tarries with yesterday.
Kahlil Gibran

Chapter 1

1. Melinda Davis, *The New Culture of Desire: 5 Radical New Strategies That Will Change Your Business and Your Life* (New York: Free Press, 2002).

2. *Kaiser Foundation Report,* February, 2003, http://www.kff.org, Television and the 2003 Report. (Excellent summary of sex and TV.)

3. John Ratey, *A User's Guide to the Brain* (New York: Vintage Books, 2003), 211.

4. *American Academy of Pediatrics Report on Media Violence* 108, no. 5 (November, 2001), http://www.aap.org/advocacy/OKeefemediaviolence .htm.

5. Barbara Meltz, "Legislation Would Target Violence in Video Games," *The Boston Globe,* May 22, 2003.

6. Craig Anderson, Nicholas Carnagey, and Janie Eubanks, "Exposure to Violent Media: The Effects of Songs with Violent Lyrics on Aggressive Thoughts and Feelings," *Journal of Personality and Social Psychology* 84, no. 5 (2003): 960-71.

7. Paul Farhi, "Lieberman vs. Hollywood," *The Washington Post,* December 8, 2003.

8. *National Mental Health Association Fact Sheet,* http://www.nmha .org/infoctr/factsheets/82.cfm.

9. *March of Dimes Fact Sheet,* http://www.marchofdimes.com/search /MsmGo.exe?grab_id=68000070&extra_arg=&page_id=206&host_id= 1&query=teen+pregnancy&hiword=TEEN+PREGNANCY+.

10. See http://www.childabuse.org/.

11. See http://www.obesity.org/subs/childhood/prevalence.shtml and http://www.aap.org/advocacy/archives/mardia.htm.

12. See http://www.health.org/govpubs/rpo995/.

13. *United States Department of Health and Human Services Report,* http://www.os.dhhs.gov/news/press/2001pres/20011004a.html.

14. Michael Medved and Diane Medved, *Saving Childhood: Protecting Our Children from the National Assault on Innocence* (New York: Perennial, 1999).

15. Brian Swimme, Ph.D., *The Hidden Heart of the Cosmos* (Maryknoll, N.Y.: Orbis Books, 1996).

16. Stephen Vincent Benet, *John Brown's Body* (Cutchogue, NY.: Bucaneer Books, 1996). "Troubled Souls," *Newsweek* (September 22, 2003), 68.

Chapter 2

1. "Assortment of dolls give girls variety of messages," Associated Press, *The Sun Newspaper* (Yuma, Ariz.), November 29, 2003.

2. See http://www.lionlamb.org/LL-ToyLists.htm.

3. See http://www.cspinet.org/new/sugar.html.

4. See http://www.cspinet.org/nah/septrans.html (especially see chart at the bottom of this Web site page for a shocking wake-up call about fats and trans fat).

5. See http://print.factmonster.com/ipka/A0779144.html; for the Web site of the Center for Science in the Public Interest's section on kids, see http://www.cspinet.org/nutrition/index.html#kids.

6. See http://www.cspinet.org/new/adhdpr.html.

7. Dana Williams, "Mysogeny in music: Have videos gone wild?" (tolerance.org), http://www.tolerance.org/news/article_tol.jsp?id=911.

8. Howard Gardner, *Frames of Mind: The Theory of Multiple Intelligences* (New York: Basic, 1983).

9. Lorin W. Anderson, *A Taxonomy for Learning, Teaching, and Assessing: A Revision of Bloom's Taxonomy of Educational Objectives,* First Edition (Boston: Addison Wesley, December 29, 2000).

10. Jane Healy, *Failure to Connect: How Computers Affect Our Children's Minds and What We Can Do about It* (New York: Touchstone Books, September, 1999).

11. See http://camy.org/research/mag0902/.

12. See http://www.tobaccofreekids.org/research/factsheets/index.php?CategoryID=3, "Tobacco Use Among Youth Report."

13. See http://tobaccofreekids.org/Script/DisplayPressRelease.php3?D isplay=299.

14. *Journal of the American Medical Association* (September 10, 2003).

15. See http://www.infact.org/youth.html.

16. See Action on Smoking and Health Web site, http://www.ash.org.uk/html/international/html/czechstudy.html.

17. See http://www.futureofchildren.org/usr_doc/tfoc_12-2.pdf.

18. Jonathon Dee, "Playing Mogul," *The New York Times,* December 21, 2003; Chris Sorenson, "Video game lures fanatics," *Toronto Star/Hamilton Spectator* (Ontario, Canada), January 28, 2004.

19. Mick LaSalle, "Tarantino clears it up—'Kill Bill' is great for kids," *San Francisco Chronicle,* October 15, 2003, http://www.sfgate.com/cgi-bin/article.cgi?file=/chronicle/archive/2003/10/15/DD101138.DTL.

20. Jane Healy, *Endangered Minds: Why Children Don't Think and What We Can Do about It* (New York: Touchstone Books, September, 1999).

21. Healy, *Failure to Connect.*

22. Jane Healy, *Your Child's Growing Mind: A Guide to Learning and Brain Development from Birth to Adolescence* Third Edition. (New York: Broadway Books, May 2004).

23. Jane Healy, "Potential Hazards in a Media Culture," *American Academy of Pediatrics News* (May, 1998).

Chapter 3

1. Shelly Wu, Ph.D., http://psychology.about.com/library/weekly/aa041500a.htm.

2. David Perkins, *Outsmarting IQ: The Emerging Science of Learnable Intelligence* (New York: Free Press, 1995).

3. Jean Piaget et al., *The Essential Piaget* (New York: Jason Aronson, 1995).

Chapter 4

1. See http://spfizer.com/brain/etour3.html.

2. Joseph Cqhilton Pearce, *The Biology of Transcendence* (Rochester, Vermont: Park Street Press, 2002).

3. Marian Diamond, *Magic Trees of the Mind* (New York: Penguin Books, 1999).

4. Allan Schore, *Affect Regulation and the Origin of Self: The Neurobiology of Emotional Development* (Hillsdale, N.J.: Lawrence Earlbaum, 1996).

5. Daniel Siegel, *The Developing Mind: How Relationships and the Brain Interact to Shape Who We Are* (New York: Guilford Press, 2001).

6. James U. McNeal, *Kids As Customers: A Handbook of Marketing to Children* (New York: Lexington Books, 1992).

7. Bill Goodwin, "Designing Valued Relationships between Kids and Their Brands," http://www.iirusa.com/businessofbranding/index.cfm/Link=32.

8. Penelope Leach, *Babyhood: Stage by Stage from Birth to Age Two; How Your Baby Develops Physically, Mentally, and Emotionally,* Second Edition (New York: Knopf, June, 1983).

9. Barbara Meltz, "With TV So Loud, No One Is Listening," *The Boston Globe,* November 6, 2003.

10. Kathy Hirsh-Pasek, *Einstein Never Used Flash Cards: How Our Children REALLY Learn* (Emmaus, Pa.: Rodale, October, 2003).

11. Jane Healy, *Failure to Connect: How Computers Affect Our Children's Minds and What We Can Do about It* (Touchstone Books, September, 1999).

Chapter 5

1. Bruno Bettelheim, *The Uses of Enchantment–The Meaning and Importance of Fairy Tales,* Reissued Edition (New York: Vintage Books, April, 1989).

2. See http://www.drjoecarver.com/memory.html.

3. Leonard Maltin et al., *Leonard Maltin's Family Film Guide* (New York: Signet, May, 1999).

4. Michael Wolf, *The Entertainment Economy* (New York: Three Rivers Press, April, 2003).

5. See http://www.lionlamb.org/LL-ToyLists.htm.

Chapter 6

1. Dave Siegel et al., *The Great Tween Buying Machine* (Ithaca, N.Y.: Paramount Market Publishing, June, 2001).

2. Bob Herbert, "An Ugly Game," The *New York Times,* October 17, 2003.

3. See the Web site of the American Dietetic Association, http://www.eatright.org.

4. Naomi Neufeld, *Kidshape, A Practical Prescription for Raising Healthy, Fit Children* (Nashville, TN: Rutledge Hill Press, April 21, 2004).

5. John P. Murray, Hearing before the Senate Subcommittee on Science, Commerce, and Technology, April 10, 2003.

6. Barbara Meltz, "Legislation Would Target Violence in Video Games," *The Boston Globe,* May 22, 2003.

7. *Kaiser Foundation Report,* February, 2003, http://www.kff.org, Television and the 2003 Report. (Excellent summary of sex and TV.)

Chapter 7

1. The Cameron Column, A Free Internet Newsletter, ©W. Bruce Cameron, 1999, http://parents.berkeley.edu/jokes/Telephones.html.

2. Mandy Light, "How Do Cognitive Changes during Adolescence Affect the Parent-Child Relationship?" http://inside.bard.edu/academic/specialproj/darling/adolesce.htm.

3. Dina Castrogiovanni, http://inside.bard.edu/academic/specialproj/ darling/adolesce.htm, "Peer Groups."

4. "Depression in Children and Adolescents," NIH Publication No. 00-4744, September, 2000.

5. See http://pathwayscourses.samhsa.gov/bully/bully_3_pg12.htm and http://www.apa.org/monitor/oct99/cf3.html.

6. Joanne Cantor, Mommy I'm Scared: How TV and Movies Frighten Our Children and What We Can Do to Protect Them (San Diego, CA: Harvest Books, 1998).

7. Federal Trade Commission Report on the Marketing of Violent Entertainment to Children, September 11, 2000. Copies of the report are available from the FTC's Web site at http://www.ftc.gov/.

8. Bill Nichols, "Hungarian Envoy Sings Rock & Roll Praises," USA Today, November 7, 2003, 11A.

9. See http://www.babybag.com/articles/amaviol.htm.

10. "Violent Music Lyrics Increase Aggressive Thoughts and Feelings," Release from the American Psychological Association, 2003. Also see http://www.apa.org/releases/violentsongs.html.

11. "Getting Children off the Couch and onto the Field," American Psychological Association, Help Center, http://helping.apa.org/family/kidsport.html.

12. See http://www.apa.org/monitor/jun04/protecting.html.

13. Center for Science in the Public Interest, http://www.spinet .org/booze, December, 2000.

14. Testimony of Wendy J. Hamilton, Senate Committee Hearing on Underage Drinking, September 30, 2003, http://www.madd.com/activ ism/0,1056,7273,00.html.

15. Teresa Crenshaw, Sex Therapist, with Joe and Terry Graedon, On People's Pharmacy, Public Radio, January, 1997.

16. Ward Dean, M.D., "Will the Real 'Date Rape Drug' Please Stand Up?" Vitamin Research News (June, 2000), J. Analytical Toxicology, 1999.

17. Adam Marcus, "AMA: Alcohol Damages Teens' Brains," Healthday News, December 9, 2003, http://www.healthfinder.gov/news/news-story.asp?docID=510730.

18. "Understanding Youth Drinking," from a report of the National Academies, as it appeared on the CAMY Web site, http://camy.org/fact sheets/index.php?FactsheetID=14.

19. See http://www.ash.org.uk/html/conduct/html/tobexpld3 .html.

20. See http://www.tobaccofreekids.org/research/factsheets/ index.ph p?categoryID=23.

21. See http://www.oas.samhsa.gov/nhsda.htm.

Chapter 8

1. See http://www.geocities.com/hhugs2001/roleofhyp.htm.

2. American Academy of Child and Adolescent Psychiatry, *Your Adolescent* (New York: HarperCollins, 1999), 50–54.

3. Marshal Brain, *The Teenager's Guide to the Real World* (BYG Publishing Inc.: November 1, 1997).

4. Robert Grede, *Naked Marketing: The Bare Essentials* (West Nyack, NY: Prentice Hall Art: April 1, 1997).

5. Alissa Quart, *Branded: The Buying and Selling of Teenagers* (New York: Perseus: 2003), 12.

6. "Drogas, Alcohol y Sexo," *El Tiempo* (de Bogota, Colombia), 15 Noviembre, 2003, 1–11.

Chapter 9

1. See http://www.quotationreference.com/quotefinder.php?byax =1&strt=1&subj=Theo+Panayides.

2. See http://www.commondreams.org/headlines01/0210-02.htm.

3. See http://www.ncac.org/cen_news/cn68cda.html.

Drs. Acuff and Reiher have dedicated themselves to the use of their experience and knowledge garnered over 25 years for the creation, development, and marketing of products and programs that add positively to the healthy growth and development of children, tweens, and teens. *Kidnapped* is intended as the cornerstone of those goals and efforts.

They have served as featured speakers at conferences throughout the world, including the United States, Asia, Europe, Latin America, Canada, and Scandinavia.

DANIEL S. ACUFF, PH.D.

Cofounder and director of Youth Market Systems and the Character Lab, and coauthor of the landmark book, *What Kids Buy and Why: The Psychology of Marketing to Kids*, Dr. Acuff has served as a development, research, and marketing consultant to more than 50 major corporations in the arenas of product and program viability assessment, development, marketing, and advertising. Of particular specialization has been new product ideation, age segmentation analysis, product and program maximization, and character creation and development.

Past and current clients include: Disney, Warner Brothers, Lucas-Spielberg, Microsoft, Paws/Jim Davis, ABC TV, Nestle, M&M Mars, Hershey, Pepsico, Frito-Lay, Quaker Oats, Kellogg's, General Mills, Kraft, Johnson & Johnson, Hallmark Cards, Nickelodeon, Those Characters from Cleveland, Sega, Mattel, Hasbro, Discovery Kids, and the United States Deptartment of Agriculture.

ROBERT H. REIHER PH.D.

Dr. Robert Reiher is President of E-Smart Choice®, a company dedicated to the development and marketing of enriching products and programs. He is also cofounder and director of Youth Market Systems Consulting and the Character Lab. Dr. Reiher is a specialist in the area of media psychology. His integrated expertise ranges from his background in educational and clinical psychology, business, media, and entertainment. He has consulted for more than 65 corporations, including Mattel, Marvel, ABC Entertainment, Hasbro, CBS Television, 20th-Century Fox, United Media, Lucas Film, Disney, Sega, Amblin Entertainment, Saban, Warner Bros., MCA Universal, Microsoft, Broderbund, Davidson, YES Entertainment, Pepsico, Kid Cuisine, Nestle/Carnation, Nike, Johnson & Johnson, Tyco, Nickelodeon, Quaker Oats, and M & M Mars.

Dr. Reiher has served as a featured speaker, including at the Annenberg Public Policy Center. His company, E-Smart Choice®, integrates media research with contemporary psychological principles from the areas of experimental psychology, education, brain research, sociology, learning theory, and human development. Dr. Reiher has developed a wide variety of products and programs using the medium of entertainment to facilitate positive personal and social change at various developmental stages of growth.

Dr. Reiher is currently writing a number of books on enriching product and program development, including *The Enrichment Economy* and *Parental Guidance Required.*

Share the message!

Bulk discounts
Discounts start at only 10 copies and range from 30% to 55% off retail price based on quantity.

Custom publishing
Private label a cover with your organization's name and logo. Or, tailor information to your needs with a custom pamphlet that highlights specific chapters.

Ancillaries
Workshop outlines, videos, and other products are available on select titles.

Dynamic speakers
Engaging authors are available to share their expertise and insight at your event.

Call Dearborn Trade Special Sales at 1-800-621-9621, ext. 4444, or e-mail trade@dearborn.com.

Dearborn™
Trade Publishing
A **Kaplan Professional** Company

DEARBORN TRADE PUBLISHING AND *SCORE!*

SCORE! A Scholarship Sweepstakes

2005 Official Rules

THIS SWEEPSTAKES IS OFFERED ONLY TO LEGAL RESIDENTS OF THE 50 UNITED STATES (EXCEPT RHODE ISLAND) AND D.C. WHO ARE LOCATED IN THE 50 UNITED STATES (EXCEPT RHODE ISLAND) OR D.C. AT THE TIME OF ENTRY.

NO PURCHASE NECESSARY. A PURCHASE DOES NOT INCREASE YOUR CHANCES OF WINNING. VOID WHERE RESTRICTED OR PROHIBITED BY LAW.

1. TO ENTER: Between 12:00:01 AM CST on June 1, 2005 and 11:59:59 PM CST on August 15, 2005 (the "Sweepstakes Period"), send an email to coupons@dearborn.com with the term *"SCORE!"* in the subject line and include in the text of your email your name, complete address and day time telephone number ("entry" or "entries"). No mechanically reproduced entries allowed. Limit one entry per person and/or email address. Entries must be sent electronically during the Sweepstakes Period and received no later than 11:59:59 PM on August 16, 2005.

   Sponsors are not responsible for lost, late, incomplete, illegible, mutilated, or misdirected entries, for address changes of entrants, for technical, hardware or software failures of any kind, for lost or unavailable network connections, or for failed, incomplete, garbled or delayed computer transmissions or any human error which may occur in the receipt or processing of the entries or other problems relating to electronic entries. Entries that are mutilated, incomplete, defective, altered, illegible, forged, or irregular in any way or not in compliance with these Official Rules are void. All entries become property of the Sponsors and will not be returned.

2. ELIGIBILITY: Open to legal residents of the 50 United States (except Rhode Island) and the District of Columbia, age 18 or older who had Internet access on or before May 31, 2005. Dearborn Trade Publishing and *SCORE!* ("Sponsors"), and their parent companies, affiliates, subsidiaries, advertising and promotional agencies and each of their respective officers, directors, employees, and agents ("Sponsor, and their agents") and members of their immediate families and people living in the same household of each are not eligible.

3. DRAWING: Winners will be selected on or about August 18, 2005 in a random drawing from all eligible entries received. The drawing will be conducted by Sponsors or their designee, the judge of the sweepstakes, whose decisions are final and binding on all matters relating to the sweepstakes. Winners will be notified by overnight mail on or about August 22, 2005 and will be required to sign and return an affidavit of eligibility and liability and publicity release (where lawful) which must be received by Sponsors within 14 days of the date on the notification, or the prize will be forfeited and an alternate winner selected. If any prize notification or prize is returned as undeliverable, or the selected winner is ineligible or unable to accept the prize, the winner will be disqualified and an alternate winner may be selected.

4. PRIZE AND ODDS OF WINNING: A six month scholarship for a child age 4-14 to attend classes at a participating local *SCORE!* Educational Center in California; Connecticut; Colorado; Atlanta, Georgia; Illinois; Maryland; New Jersey; New York; Pennsylvania; Texas and Virginia. Approximate retail value: $1,000. Prize must be redeemed by January 31, 2006. Odds of winning depend on the number of eligible entries received. Prize will be awarded. If winner is 18 or older, as required, but minor in his or her state of residence, winner's parent or legal guardian must sign all required releases and consents. No prize substitutions or cash equivalents, except at the sole discretion of the Sponsors if an advertised prize becomes unavailable. Prizes are non-transferable.

5. GENERAL: By entering, entrants agree to: (1) release Sponsors and their agents from all liability, injuries, loss and/or damage of any kind arising from their participation in the Sweepstakes and the acceptance, possession and use/misuse of any prize; (2) be bound by the Official Rules and the decisions of the judge and (3) be contacted by Sponsors by email, mail and/or telephone. By accepting a prize, winner consents to the use of his/her name and likeness for advertising, trade and promotional purposes without additional compensation in all media worldwide (except if winner is a resident of TN or where otherwise prohibited by law). Sweepstakes are subject to all applicable federal, state and local laws and regulations. Winner is responsible for all taxes, including federal, state and local, applicable to the acceptance and use of his/her prize. Sponsors will issue a 1099 tax form for the winner for the approximate retail value of the prize. If for any reason the sweepstakes is not capable of running as planned, including infection due to computer virus, bugs, tampering, unauthorized intervention, fraud, technical failure, human error, terrorism or any other causes beyond the control of Sponsors that corrupt or affect the administration, security, fairness, integrity, or proper conduct of the sweepstakes, Sponsors reserve the right to modify, suspend or terminate the sweepstakes and to select the winner based on the entries received prior to the termination date. Sponsors also reserve the right to disqualify any individual who tampers with the entry process. In the event of a dispute regarding the identity of the person submitting an entry, the entry will be deemed to be submitted by the person in whose name the email account is registered. This sweepstakes is governed by the laws of Illinois, with venue in Cook County, Illinois and all claims must be resolved in the state or federal courts of Cook County, Illinois.

6. REMOVAL FROM FUTURE MAILINGS: To have your name and address removed from Sponsors' future mailings regarding sweepstakes, hand print your name, address, and a statement saying, "Remove me from all future mailing lists" on a piece of paper and mail it to: Dearborn Trade Publishing and *SCORE!*, Removal Notification, 30 S. Wacker Dr., Ste. 2500, Box LB, Chicago, IL 60606 or email your name, address and removal request to coupons@dearborn.com. Sponsors will process your request within 60 days.

7. WINNER'S NAME: For the name of the winner, send a stamped, self-addressed envelope to be postmarked by August 15, 2005 and received by August 22, 2005, to: Winner's Name, Dearborn Trade Publishing, 30 S. Wacker Dr., Ste. 2500, Box LB, Chicago IL 60606.

8. SPONSORS: Dearborn Trade Publishing, 30 S. Wacker Dr., Ste 2500, Chicago IL 60606 and *SCORE!*, 10 S. Wacker Drive, Suite 3425, Chicago, IL 60606.

SCORE! A Scholarship Sweepstakes

Enter to Win a 6-Month Scholarship to SCORE! ($1,000 value)

Dearborn Trade and *SCORE!* are working together to offer a chance to win a 6-month scholarship for your child at your local *SCORE!* Educational Center.

SCORE! helps children of all learning levels, ages 4-14, make academic progress and develop a love of learning. From reading and writing to math and science, *SCORE!* offers a customized curriculum that lets children learn at their own pace and in their own way.

SCORE!'s highly trained Instructors work directly with each child to provide the confidence and motivation necessary for catching up, keeping up, and getting ahead. What's more, *SCORE!* offers an environment that's positive, encouraging, and most of all, fun – because that's how children learn best.

To learn more about *SCORE!*, and find a center near you, please visit **www.escore.com or call 1-800-49SCORE.**

See preceeding page for complete list of rules.

How to enter: Send an e-mail to coupons@dearborn.com with the term *"SCORE!"* in the subject line and include in the text of your e-mail your name, complete address, and day time telephone number. No mechanically reproduced entries allowed. Limit one entry per person and/or e-mail address. Entries must be sent electronically between June 1, 2005, and August 15, 2005.

NO PURCHASE NECESSARY. A PURCHASE DOES NOT INCREASE YOUR CHANCES OF WINNING. VOID WHERE RESTRICTED OR PROHIBITED BY LAW.

Dearborn
Trade Publishing
A **Kaplan Professional** Company
www.dearborntrade.com

SCORE!
EDUCATIONAL CENTERS